THE

Symbols of Government

THURMAN W. ARNOLD

NEW HAVEN

Yale University Press

LONDON · HUMPHREY MILFORD · OXFORD UNIVERSITY PRESS

Preface

IN the preface of this book it may be well to explain the title. What is meant by the *symbols of government?* This can be made clear by using an analogy.

Every individual, for reasons lying deep in the mystery of personality, constructs for himself a succession of little dramas in which he is the principal character. No one escapes the constant necessity of dressing himself in a series of different uniforms or silk hats, and watching himself go by. In primitive conditions, man may get along with only a few principal rôles. As life becomes more complex, the number of plays which he must write for himself increases. Those who are unable to construct a worth-while character for themselves in any particular situation lose morale; they become discouraged, ineffective, confused.

When an individual has created for himself an acceptable rôle, he is compelled to believe that his conduct conforms to that rôle. Sometimes the realization of inconsistencies rises to the level of his consciousness. From such inconsistencies he must necessarily escape. This escape is sometimes made through such an overelaboration of the rôle he is playing that he can forget the inconsistencies in a maze of words or ceremonies. Sometimes it is effected through the assumption of a different and inconsistent rôle. Such conflicts make up the story of each individual life.

Thus it is that most of man's behavior is symbolic of the various characters which he assumes. This is true not only of his behavior as a warrior or a priest, but extends even to such practical concerns as eating and drinking, with their little rituals of highly decorated tables and service. The words, ceremonies, theories, and principles and other symbols which man uses make him believe in the reality of his dreams and thus give purpose to his life.

As with individuals, so it is with the institutions which cement groups of individuals together in such a way that they achieve a sort of separate personality. Institutions—whether courts, commercial banks, or government bureaus—develop institutional habits, entirely separable from the personal habits of those who spend their working hours in their service. They build for themselves little dramas, and play varied rôles. They are confronted with conflicts which they resolve by constructing complicated theories, or by splitting themselves up into different institutions through which the same men play inconsistent rôles. And it is this process which makes up the story of government.

By the symbols of government we mean both the ceremonies and the theories of social institutions. Ordinarily, these ceremonies and theories are collected and studied, not as symbols, but as the fundamental principles of the separate sciences of law, economics, political theory, ethics, and theology. In this book we propose to examine law and economics, not as collections of truths, but as symbolic thinking and conduct which condition the behavior of men in groups. A single phrase is needed to describe all of these sciences and to indicate that they are all part of a common folklore and for that purpose the term "Symbols of Government" has been chosen.

The history of the symbols of government is a succession of romantic but unnecessary sacrifices of human life or comfort in their honor. Sometimes men die for their ideals of things as they ought to be rather than tarnish those ideals by practical compromise with things as they are. More often they are content to permit other people to suffer for them. Such romance and faith are among our greatest realities. They give purpose, beauty, and symmetry to the drab business of living. Yet important as they are in their place, they are not the tools by which discoveries are made. When men observe human conduct in the light of principles which they consider sacred or fundamental, they develop priests but not scientists. Egypt was thought to be the medical center of the ancient world, because it was the fountainhead of the fundamental principles of medicine to which all men turned. Yet, as Victor Robinson has pointed out in *The Story of Medicine,* Egyptians who opened up the human body in the light of their accepted principles were unable to observe what was before their eyes. "Century after century millions of dead Egyptians were eviscerated by the embalmers—and the living Egyptians learned no pathology. . . . The priest-physician was a hybrid that could not survive; the priest conquered the physician and medicine succumbed in the enfolding arms of magic."

This was once true of medicine. It is still true of the science of government. As Edward S. Robinson points out in his book, *Law and the Lawyers,* "The world is not divided into scientific people and unscientific people, but rather into groups of problems for which our general culture provides us with a scientific or an unscientific approach."

Must the problems of government continue to be studied in the light of faiths and symbols rather than by scientific observation? To a discussion of this question, this book is directed.

My principal indebtedness is to Edward S. Robinson, a professor of psychology at Yale. Four years ago Mr. Robinson began a joint seminar with me at the Yale Law School. It is principally as a result of this collaboration that this book has been written. Professor Robinson's own book, *Law and the Lawyers,* is in a sense a companion volume to this, since it came from the same joint enterprise.

For suggestions leading to changes in the manuscript I wish to thank Leon Green, Karl Llewellyn, Eugene Davidson, Roger Foster, Frederick Steinhardt, Max Lerner, William O. Douglas, and Walter Nelles. A less concrete, though nevertheless real, obligation is to Jerome Frank, Felix Frankfurter, Reed Powell, Harold Laswell, Abraham Chronbach, Underhill Moore, Fred Nunbaum, Walton Hamilton, Frank Coker, Wesley Sturges, and Hessel Yntema, from whose writings some of the ideas in this book have been taken. To enumerate the further indebtedness to the many legal and economic scholars who are writing to-day from the same point of view would accomplish no purpose other than to support the hope that we are experiencing a revolution in our attitude toward social organizations.

Some of the materials in this book are revisions of articles heretofore published. Chapter VIII appeared in more extended form as "Trial by Combat and the New Deal" in 47 *Harvard Law Review* 913. Portions of Chapter IX are included in "The Role of Substantive Law and Procedure," 45 *Harvard Law Review* 617. Chapter IV is an elaboration of "Theories of Economic Theory," *The Annals of the American Academy of Political and Social Sciences* (March, 1934). Chapter IX is a revision of "Law Enforcement," 42 *Yale Law Journal* 1.

T. W. A.

New Haven,
  September, 1935.

CONTENTS

PREFACE   iii

I. THE SOCIAL SCIENCES ARE STATIONARY   1

II. THEORIES ABOUT LEGAL THEORY   31

III. THE MYSTERY OF JURISPRUDENCE   46

IV. ECONOMICS AND THE LAW   72

V. SPIRITUAL VS. TEMPORAL GOVERNMENT   105

VI. THE CRIMINAL TRIAL   128

VII. LAW ENFORCEMENT   149

VIII. TRIAL BY COMBAT   172

IX. COURTS VS. BUREAUCRACY   199

X. A PHILOSOPHY FOR POLITICIANS   229

INDEX   273

CHAPTER I

The Social Sciences Are Stationary

THE principles of Washington's farewell address are still sources of wisdom when cures for social ills are sought. The methods of Washington's physician, however, are no longer studied. Political and legal science only look to the past. Other sciences are concerned with the present, and filled with hope and expectation for the future. In medicine the most authoritative pronouncement is almost always the latest. In law or economics we are accustomed to go back to our forefathers. The distant past is no longer relevant to the inventor, the surgeon, or the engineer. Yet it is the very lifeblood of the sociologist, the economist, and the lawyer. These men study the lessons they learn from history. The scientist studies the lessons he learns from observation and from experiment.

The contrast in these two attitudes toward the past is accompanied by startling contrast in the development of governmental as opposed to a scientific technique. The advance of technical achievement during the past century has, of course, been bewildering. Ordinary persons today are trained in methods and scientific skills which would have been beyond the powers of the greatest experts of the past. In comparison the science of government has been stationary. Nations are believed to be capable of "learning" from experience (as if a sick man could learn the complicated techniques of modern medicine through a succession of illnesses). The result in the development of governmental science is what might be expected. There are no recognized technicians in this art nor any recognized methods of political training. Indeed, ignorant and even psychopathic personalities seem more skilful in moving great masses of people to their will than persons of learning and humanity. Nor is there any sign of progress. Our forefathers were fully as proficient at affairs of state as their successors of today.

Government itself has not been quite as stationary as thinking about government has been. Humanitarian notions such as those concerning the care of the aged and the sick, public health, and even of relief by government action have crept in. Yet principles and rational ideas of government, instead of making easier the introduction of new techniques in sanitation or housing have only served to make it harder. Principles have been obstacles, and not aids. Governmental theory has been the chief support of social abuses. It continues to offer fundamental reasons why any humanitarian or practical movement is unsound, and such measures succeed only after a prolonged battle over the fundamental principles of government. In the complicated thinking necessary to conduct this battle most of the force of the original humanitarian impulse is lost.

These emotional reactions by the man on the street are important factors in studying the nature and effect of social theory. Nevertheless, when we observe students of government thinking about the problem in the same terms as the man on the street, and intent only on formulating theories and counter theories, we begin to realize that there is a fundamental difference between the social and physical sciences which makes the latter capable of discovery and advancement while the former are only capable of restatement, logical arrangement, and the preaching of ideals.

This struggle to formulate ideals and principles which are sound, systematic, and consistent leads only to the building of utopias on the part of reformers and the defense of abuses on the part of conservatives. This is as true in small affairs as in large ones. The struggle for procedural reform in law offers us an example of the slowness of change in an institution whose critics and reformers refuse to think objectively. Courts flounder without practical guidance while experts battle about what really are the correct fundamental theories of procedure. The situation becomes so complicated that real help can come only from laymen uncontaminated by respect for legal theory and thus able to treat it as an obstacle, rather than as an aid. The political or legal theorist usually solves the problem by blaming some unidentified group in society. The reformers blame the conservatives for blocking the reform. The conservatives blame the reformers for introducing it on the theory that present abuses are always better than utopian idealism. The laymen blame the bar for making legal procedure so complicated, and the bar blame the laymen for not understanding that procedure must be complicated. You can read the entire literature of one of these conflicts between experts over procedural reform without finding any intelligible explanation either of the habits of the judicial institution, or of how to change them.

Rational and Moral Explanation of Social Problems

CERTAIN questions today confront every social thinker, unanswerable in the terms of the separate sciences of law or economics: Why do we starve in the midst of plenty? Why do we refuse to utilize to their utmost the great sources of productive energy made available by a power age? Why do we fear bureaucracy? What is this thing called "bureaucracy" which we fear? Why do great idealistic schemes for governmental control crash on the rocks of conservative prejudice, or radical intolerance? Why when new types of social organization are attempted do we find them attacked by both liberals and conservatives? How does it happen that Clarence Darrow, the radical lawyer, suddenly finds himself fighting on the same side as the *New York Herald-*

Tribune against the N.R.A.? How does it happen that a realistic conservative like Tugwell suddenly becomes classed as a radical? How does it happen that primitive societies whose premises are not to our mind rational produce law which can be explained on rational grounds? On the other hand, how does it happen that rational societies achieve more irrational results in trying to follow their reason than when they act on impulse?

It is curious that today there should be no better answers to such questions than there were in the time of the eighteenth-century philosophers. Stuart Chase in a current book[1] points out certain imperatives which society must recognize and follow in the recently arrived "Economy of Abundance." His critics call him impractical because he does not show us how to do it. Yet neither he nor anyone else can point to any organized body of learning which is devoted to the task of finding methods by which society can be induced to recognize and follow its best interests. If there has been any advance in creating such a body of learning since Aristotle it is scarcely perceptible. We are, therefore, compelled to turn to the principles of the past because they at least are hallowed with age, and because we can observe nothing very different or more efficient in the present.

Why have the social sciences developed no technique comparable with that of the physical sciences? Is it because there is something inherently static about such knowledge, or is there something wrong with our methods of seeking it? The engineer is able to give an adequate explanation of what is wrong with a bridge which falls without blaming the girders that collapsed because they did not have the moral stamina to stand the strain. The scholar in government cannot answer the similar questions about social organization without blaming something which he calls "human nature." It might, therefore, be well to consider what obstacles this kind of thinking puts in the path of discovery.

1. *The Economy of Abundance* (1934).

The chief obstacle may be stated simply. Rational thinking compels us to seek complete and rounded systems of doctrines and principles. The intellectual who makes one of these systems necessarily believes that it represents the "truth." Desirable social results achieved by contradicting the system must be bad. If the results are so obviously desirable that they cannot be attacked on practical grounds, the intellectual must then insist that they can only be temporary. Desirable results achieved without principle through immorality, dishonesty, or irrationality are necessarily specious, or accidental. Even those who advocate immediate and vast expenditures for public works as an economic necessity, often prefer to hold up the program in order to avoid the appearance of graft. In the same way a court of law which achieves a desirable result by an inexact use of legal conceptions arouses more criticism from legal scholars than one which achieves an undesirable result in a learned way.

Actual observation of human society, however, indicates that great constructive achievements in human organization have been accomplished by unscrupulous men who violated most of the principles which we cherish. There was nothing either temporary or specious about the Union Pacific Railroad after it was built, in spite of scandals in the building of it. Thrifty, moral communities have a tendency to remain in the backwoods while a city like Chicago astonishes us with both its civic improvements and its political corruption. The industrial development of this country was accomplished by the same conspicuous display of unethical conduct on the part of the industrial robber barons which always accompanies the seizure and exercise of great power everywhere. Even religious groups which try to be "sincere," and cease to be politically sagacious, disappear. Principles, once formulated into a logical system, and accepted, seem to paralyze action in the actual arena of human affairs. Therefore the man who completely masters any set of fundamental legal or economic principles usually retires to the cloister of some institution of learning while politicians run the government and trial lawyers like Max Steuer or Clarence Darrow get practical results out of courts.

Legal and economic thinkers can therefore never discover new techniques in government, because they cannot look at the world as it is without a shudder. A physician who maintains an attitude of horror and disapproval every time he enters a sick room would soon be compelled to retreat to some quiet place where he could philosophize on illness in the abstract. It is only natural that our governmental scholars should go back to the learning of the past. The confusing events of their own day constantly contradict their most fundamental assumptions. The road to discovery is thus closed to all who refuse to accept the world as it is.

REALISM VS. REALITY

Acceptance of the world as it is, however, does not imply a belief that because our accepted scheme of principles is not "true" or "good," therefore it must be "untrue" or "bad." Disillusionment is a frame of mind as inimical to a scientific approach as the most fanatical idealism. "Realism," effective as it is as a method of political attack, or as a way of making people question ideas which they had formerly considered as established truths, ordinarily winds up by merely making the world look unpleasant. Since, for most people at least, the world is actually not an unpleasant place, the realist remains in the sun only a short time.

The realist is ordinarily a man who is emotionally conscious of the discrepancy between the behavior of the world and the way it talks about that behavior. He is not, however, conscious of the fact that talking and writing is just as much a form of behavior as eating. The fact that a man dresses differently when he is making a speech at a formal gathering and when he bosses a gang of laborers, does not bother the intellectual. However, the fact that the man talks and thinks differently on these separate occasions fills the realist with dismay. He does not refuse to recognize the obvious fact before his eyes, nor does the fundamentalist, but he cannot help feeling indignant and disillusioned about it.

Thus "realists" insist that the principles upon which society thinks it operates are a species of hokum. They cry out at the foolishness of a society which thus "deceives itself." The fact that rational or moral principles do not lead to rational or moral conduct is taken as proof that they have no effect on conduct, or else that they have a "bad" effect on conduct. The human race appears under this attack as a group of "unconscious hypocrites," or "dupes." Adults are described as children. Businessmen are thought of as knaves and thieves. Such realists sit on pillars and laugh or weep (according to their temperaments) at the human race because it is what it is, instead of something which it isn't. They are in the same intellectual position as a naturalist who insists on writing on the foolishness of animals or as a beekeeper who discourses on the "empty and meaningless" buzz of a bee. The probability of such a point of view producing competent biologists is small.

It is not the purpose of these observations either to attack or discourage those who, under the name of realism, seek to debunk human institutions. Human institutions inevitably gather around themselves burning idealists seeking to attack unprincipled practices, even when they are producing humanitarian results; dignified conservatives willing to defend the worst social abuses because even human suffering is preferable to the adoption of unsound principles; stern realists intent on showing that society is a sham; and devoted scholars busy painting a rational, logical, and moral paradise for the comfort of those struggling in an irrational world. These groups exist because of an emotional need for the dramatization of conflicting ideals to which all of us respond. Thus the search for the right principles of government, economics, or law and the denouncing of fraudulent principles must go on continuously in the climate of opinion in which we live, if people are to believe in their institutions.

Important as this search is, it is nevertheless also important to point out that the people who are engaged in it in answer to this need are significant rather as actors in a great human drama, than as observers. They are not really treating attitudes and theories as anthropological data. Their ways of thinking, whether called "realism" or not, are not in essence the methods of the detached scientist who observes, records, and experiments. Indeed, because of their point of view, these students of law and economics generally fail to see those obviously significant social facts which interfere with their assumption of what society ought to be.

For a long time the fact that an individual was psychologically a whole cast of characters incapable of acting consistently with any conceivable set of moral or rational principles escaped the rational thinker. He was compelled to invent a devil and a conception of "sin" to account for what was happening before his eyes. This enabled him to go on preaching instead of observing, on the theory that, while preaching did not necessarily abolish the devil, it did at least annoy him. Therapeutic techniques in the treatment of psychopathic personalities had to await the time when the conception both of "sin" and of the "devil" disappeared, at least from the laboratory.

In social thinking, however, we are still reluctant to accept even in our laboratories the fact that no human institution can possibly follow any consistent or systematic set of principles. We are still using the concept of sin. We blame "politics" or "ignorance" or "human nature" for the failure of our institutions to be rational and moral. We insist that the only way out is to keep trying to make human institutions more rational and consistent by holding up to them a set of impossible ideals. A sudden realization by confirmed believers that their gods have feet of clay, can cause a loss of morale which may have unfortunate social consequences, regardless of the "truth" or "falsity" of the beliefs which are attacked. The loss of morale will be proportionate to the fervor with which the beliefs were held. But it will depend neither upon their content nor upon their logic.

The significant facts which might be gleaned from the foregoing by anyone with a detached point of view may be stated as follows:

1. Human institutions, in an environment which worships reason, fail in influence and prestige unless they appear to be firmly founded on reason and fundamental principle. They are apt to go to pieces out of sheer lack of self-confidence if their philosophical assumptions are attacked, just as a devout individual may suffer intensely if he loses faith in his religion. The "truth" or "falsity," or even the content of the fundamental principles to which the institution clings for moral support is completely immaterial.

2. While it is of the utmost importance that the principles of an institution appear to be logically consistent, it is of equal importance that they be loose enough to allow for the dramatization of all sorts of mutually inconsistent ideals. The various advocates of social and economic plans, of procedural reforms, of better ways of handling criminals, of more humanitarian treatment of workers, and all the other various sensible reforms which are so constantly advocated never realize this. They suffer agonies of futile rage against society because it is so slow to accept the most obvious schemes for improvement. The trouble with their

schemes is that they violate currently important symbolism. Therefore even if the reform is accomplished it is apt to find itself twisted and warped by the contradictory ideas which are still in the background in spite of the reform. A people will never accept an institution which does not symbolize for them the simultaneously inconsistent notions to which they are at various times emotionally responsive.

3. Human institutions cling to their varied fundamental principles with a tenacity which is born of the instinct of self-preservation, but they cling to so many of them and they are mutually so conflicting, that no systematic set of doctrines can ever be used as either explanations or predictions concerning the habits of an institution.

All this is somewhat paradoxical and troubling from a rational point of view. From the viewpoint of the detached observer, however, it is both interesting and instructive. He begins to see that this situation will not be altered by wishing it were otherwise. He realizes that rational or moral principles are useless as explanations, or bases for prediction, but that they are of the utmost utility in moving groups of people, and that a symbol which is a fundamental philosophy, as religion, or an eternal truth in the mind of one man, may be a very useful tool in the hands of another, who wishes to exercise social control.

EXAMPLES OF CONFLICTING RATIONAL IDEALS IN OPERATION

To make clearer how conflicting rational and moral principles condition the behavior of civilized institutions, just as taboos condition the behavior of savage institutions, it may be useful to present some instances to show how rational thinking may lead us in opposite directions at the same time, and how the more elaborately rational institutions, such as our modern courts, can produce completely irrational results.

Over ten years ago a criminal was convicted of murder in the State of New York. Shortly before he was to hang he got into that state of mind which is commonly called insanity, scientifically described as a psychosis, and legally defined as the inability to determine right from wrong. It was clear that this made it morally, logically, and legally impossible to hang him because he could not know what he was being hanged for. Thus, it could not be a lesson to him. It would be as illogical as hanging an animal—as inhumanitarian as punishing a sick person, a step back to the dark ages when people were punished because they were insane—it would be immoral and contrary to principle. Superficial principles of efficiency might indicate hanging him to get rid of him, but second thought indicates that efficiency which does not promote morality is not really efficient, since morality is always the best policy. Therefore he must not hang.

What is to be done with him? Reason, morals, and mercy all agree. We have classified him among the sick. Sickness rationally demands curative treatment. Therefore he goes to a hospital, and incidentally is treated much better than if he were merely unemployed.

He is kept in the hospital for ten years. Thousands of dollars are spent on him. Finally by a miracle of psychiatric skill he is pronounced cured. Obviously we must now hang him. He is a murderer. If he is turned loose there will be no respect for law. It is logical to hang him because logically we cannot refuse to hang murderers simply because they have been ill.[2]

Nevertheless, there was something wrong with the picture and Governor Lehman commuted the sentence to life imprisonment. It would be hard to explain legally, eco-

2. The case of Paul LoGiudiece, reported in the *New York Times,* October 26, 1933. On November 24, 1933, Governor Lehman commuted the sentence to life imprisonment.

nomically, or rationally just why this man should be saved when cold reason demanded his execution. Yet somehow the expenditure of all this money and skill for the purpose of getting him in a frame of mind so that he could realize why he was being hanged appeared somewhat ridiculous. Therefore, quickly and without public debate, the show was called off. Had there been public argument, perhaps devotion to principle would have required hanging. Since there was not, it was well to forget it. Therefore the man was not executed.

Recently in Indiana a man about to die attempted suicide by cutting an artery with glass. To keep him alive until he could be hanged a blood transfusion was necessary. Ironically, the blood was taken from the guards.[3] No pardon was even thought of because not sufficient time had elapsed or enough money been spent on his cure to make his execution ludicrous. We will not pause to outline in detail the numerous attitudes, symbols, or principles illustrated by the contradictory performance of curing a sick man in order to kill him. A moment's reflection will indicate that they go to the very roots of our social and economic structure; that though each is completely rational in itself, each nevertheless contradicts the other.

The symbolic values of this process, belonging to that part of the government which we call the judicial system, are many and varied. We have here dramatically illustrated first, the whole theory of criminal responsibility; second, the principle of proper treatment of the sick; third, the doctrine of separation of powers giving to a practical executive the right to supplement without entrenching upon a logical and blind justice; fourth, the whole vague ideal of law enforcement; fifth, the whole hazy ideal of penology; finally, the

3. Associated Press dispatch, March 1, 1934. For a discussion by a psychologist of the uncompensated conflicts represented by these cases see Edward S. Robinson, *Law and Lawyers,* chap. 13, pp. 291, 292.

necessity for the stern acceptance of the consequences of principles, since a court acts publicly, as contrasted with the tacit approval of ignoring the same principles in private. Each step in the process except the final pardon is logically unescapable. Yet, put together, these logical steps appear to reach an irrational result.

In a recent case in New York[4] the plaintiff in a suit for damages alleged that he had attempted to steal a ride on a freight train. He testified that just as his head appeared over the top of the box car a burly brakeman kicked him in the face. He was thrown under the train, his leg was cut off. The law has been working at situations like this for a century. Its principles are as follows: As a matter of law hoboes are undeserving characters who ride at their own risk. However, the law does not tolerate inhuman conduct on the part of railroads. The risks hoboes assume are only those incident to traveling in a dangerous way, and they have a right to expect as kindly treatment on the part of brakemen as such a situation will permit. Therefore the railroad must pay for the damage to the hobo caused by unnecessary roughness. The certainty of this liability is supposed to compel railroad companies to hire only humane brakemen.

In this particular case, however, it is not likely that the plaintiff's story is true. This brakeman is perhaps a kindly individual, and such conduct on his part may be completely outside the normal pattern of his life up to date. However, there is no way we can determine this. Therefore, the law calls it a question of fact and summons a jury. The jury symbolizes the common sense of the ordinary man. If we get an acceptable result out of a jury we feel that our entire democratic institutions, depending as they do upon the

4. *Kurzer* vs. *N.Y., Chicago & St. Louis R.R. Co.*, 243 *App. Div.* 696 (1935). (A memorandum opinion omitting the facts and giving only the grounds for reversal.)

judgment of the ordinary man, are justified. If on the other hand we get an unacceptable result out of them we are free to criticize this jury without in any way appearing to attack the judicial system itself. Every system which owes its prestige to deep-seated ideals must have an irresponsible body somewhere on whom the blame may be put when the ideals go wrong. Otherwise the system itself would have to absorb it, and one of the essentials of any of our fundamental institutions is that they be exempt from criticism as institutions. Thus the jury offers us an opportunity to be indignant at the actual result, but satisfied with the fundamental principles of law under which the result was reached.

A jury is therefore impaneled which awards the hobo the sum of $40,000. Realistically, we suspect that this verdict might be due to the jury's desire to help a poor man who sues a rich corporation. Symbolically, we prove this is not so by giving both parties a chance to challenge any juror who is suspected of prejudice. We make the attorneys officers of the court, to prove that in theory at least they will be more interested in the integrity of the judicial process than in the result of the case. We bolster up this theory by constantly advocating that juries be removed from political influence, that shysters be not admitted to the bar, that courses in legal ethics be given in all of our reputable law schools, and, in general, that through our public schools, our homes, and our churches there should be instilled into the American people that respect for everything respectable without which democracy must fail. If even after all this talk we still suspect that juries are irrational, we comfort ourselves by stating as a matter of principle that the cure for the evils of democracy is more democracy—a doctrine on which the whole rational theory of democracy is irrationally based.

The defendant appeals. On the printed transcript of the record of appeal it appears that certain hearsay evidence was carelessly admitted over objection because at the time the Court was not sure it was hearsay. (In fact nobody could be sure that it was hearsay until the court of appeals had passed upon it.) The case is therefore reversed, and instead of getting $40,000 the plaintiff gets nothing whatever. This refusal introduces a new symbol. It dramatizes the ideal of an appellate court carefully insisting on rules which preserve a calm and unprejudiced attitude on the part of juries.

The realist raises the question, "Why not disregard all these symbols and consider the actual problem." A moment's reflection shows the impossibility of this. Under the rules of the game the Court has only the power to affirm a verdict of $40,000 or give the man nothing.[5] Either alternative is equally absurd as a solution of the actual problem. We do not wish to have the hobo begging on the streets. Yet the sensible alternative does not consist in giving him a small fortune which he is undoubtedly unfitted to invest. Some sort of an annuity would seem to be a common-sense solution. But the Court has no notion of how such an annuity could be provided by the present social structure. The very idea seems to verge on some sort of socialism.

We, therefore, recoil back to our comforting symbols. The result as it stands at least shows that the law in principle compels railroads to be humane to trespassers, and requires trials to be impartial investigations, through the application of rules of evidence. So long as those benevolent principles are established by the case, the actual result is of minor significance.

We are not as yet willing to face the problem of the best way to care for injured hoboes. Neither are we willing to

5. This statement is accurate enough for the purposes of the illustration in spite of a certain limited power of the appellate courts to reduce the amount of damages.

refuse to hoboes their day in court. Therefore the trial of this case becomes the dramatization of a set of ideals which are totally irrelevant to the practical situation, but which are very important to us as representatives of justice in the abstract.

Let us take an example from the field of government. The Tennessee Valley Authority is conducting a great experiment in the utilization of power by government for the benefit of a large number of poverty-stricken people. The direct way would be to furnish the power to these people and to give them the equipment with which to make it useful. In effect this is what is being attempted, but it must be accompanied by the most elaborate make-believe. The Government acting as one corporation must deal with the Government acting as another corporation, and loan money to itself, issue bonds, take promissory notes from the inhabitants on the security of which the Government's loans to itself are based. The net effects of all this complicated bookkeeping may be that power and electrical equipment will be distributed and the benefits of capacity production over a large area will be realized. Yet the complicated make-believe by which this is accomplished is, curiously enough, not for the benefit of the purchasers who are unable to understand it (coming as they do from a group uneducated in such mysteries), but for the moral comfort of others who would regard as unsound any system of distribution which does not follow the forms to which they are accustomed. Without such formal gestures toward the familiar practices of the past, it is doubtful if even those in control would know how to act. Yet the formal gestures begin to be a bit transparent. For example, one of the objects of the Tennessee Valley Authority is to provide a standard for private rates based on what the Government is able to charge and still make a fictitious profit, after deducting the same charges that the private utility would be forced to make. The Government threatens to enter into competition with any private company which does not meet this standard of rates. In this way the public utilities will have their values fixed without benefit of public-service commissions, under the symbolism of competition. Great alarm is felt because, while it looks like unfair competition, we are not so sure that it really is competition at all.

Out of all this conflicting symbolism arises the very interesting fact that of all the people in the United States those who least desire cheap power and electrical equipment are the only ones to whom we can give it without upsetting our ideological and economic structure. These mountain farmers in the Tennessee Valley do not want to be improved. They refuse to buy electrical equipment on their own motion. Therefore it is forced on them. The writer, living in civilized and advanced Connecticut, being already a user of electrical equipment, cannot get it on such favorable terms because the process of decreasing prices in an already established market would be entirely too destructive of existing values and purchasing power. By helping only those who least appreciate it, we do not interfere with existing markets, therefore these people are the only ones we can help.

Turn wherever you will, to any form of social activity, and you will find the contradictions illustrated in these few examples repeated. Almost all human conduct is symbolic. Almost all institutional habits are symbolic. The symbols are everywhere inconsistent. Society is generally more interested in standing on the side lines and watching itself go by in a whole series of different uniforms than it is in practical objectives. The chief interest of the intellectual is to prove that such irrational conduct is inherently rational—or else the product of some form of group sinning.

The Attempt To Reason Away the Inconsistencies of Institutions

LOOKED at with any logical set of rational values, social institutions seem unsatisfactory indeed. Therefore, if we are to be happy at all in a climate of opinion where reason purports to be king, we cannot rest until we have discovered the thread of a rational principle running through the apparent confusion. We succeed in doing this by failing to observe the irrational elements of institutions, or, where such factors cannot be ignored, by refusing them a place in our system. To accomplish this task of keeping alive the faith that institutions are somehow rational the study of government is divided into three separate sciences in order to conceal the fact that the symbols found in situations like those which we have just analyzed are contradictory. Law proves that good government is achieved by constantly refining and restating rules. Economics convinces us that everything will work out all right if we only leave it alone. Sociology, a loose and cloudy way of thinking, provides us a shelf on which we may put the humanitarian ideals which run counter to the eternal rule-making of the law and the eternal automatism of economics. This makes the intellectuals happy because they can toss facts inconvenient to one science over to another science for cataloguing and classification. Unthinking people are comforted by the belief that somewhere in books which they never get time to read there is absolute proof of the rationality of their symbols.

Thus arranged, all goes well until something happens to make the unthinking lose faith in their philosophers. Such a thing can happen, not through propaganda, but through incidents like the following. The writer sat in a conference in which a scheme for the control of the citrus-fruit industry was being discussed by members of that industry and the Government. It was conceded that the production would have to be curtailed. The suggestion was advanced that a control committee allot to the various growers their quota of a total limited crop. The problem of what to do with the surplus then arose. Most of those present thought that the only feasible thing was to dump it in the Gulf, otherwise it would be bootlegged on the market and destroy the effect of the agreement. Suddenly one of the fruit growers remarked: "I suppose that if we shipped the surplus to Russia we would never collect for it. Yet the Russians would pay us more than the Gulf. And isn't the only difference the fact that we would get sore at the Russians when they did not pay, and would not get sore at the Gulf?"

With startling suddenness this conservative farmer had seen all the inherent contradictions of the notion of value which had suddenly appeared on the surface—the absurdity of the situation, the utter impossibility of doing anything rational so long as men insisted in clinging to rational beliefs, the complete lack of knowledge of any technique which could change these beliefs—the final paradox that rational systems of law and economics compelled irrational action. This farmer had no solution of his problem, but his faith in current rational creeds was irreparably damaged.

The Politician Functions While the Scholar Preaches

IF the farmer in the above case puts his problem before an economist he will get a solution which either involves a complete overhauling of the economic structure (if the economist happens to be a radical), or else recommends letting the farmer suffer for the good of the existing economic structure (if the economist happens to be a conservative). In either case, economic theory will start out with a general world plan, and treat the farmer's case as a mere incident, or illustration. If he asks a legal scholar there will be much talk about the doctrine of due process or the separation of powers in a scheme for the compulsory destruction of citrus fruits. Both the economist and the legal scholar will lose interest in what happens to the farmer because of the primary importance of the principle involved. Great impatience will be expressed at mere temporary solutions, because they are beneath the notice of those engaged in searching for permanent solutions and long-run policies.

The expert on the ground, however, faced with the task of doing something for the citrus-fruit industry, will find himself in a world where the present is more important than the future. He will first have to decide whether the farmers have sufficient political power to compel compromises otherwise undesirable. The form which his plan for relief takes will necessarily be molded by that important consideration. He will then have to persuade the farmers to accept his plan. In formulating the plan, however, he must not only have the farmer in mind, but also the influential economist who will write articles about it which ignore all political considerations as unworthy. The plan must, therefore, appear to conform to all the best economic symbols in order to forestall attack from that direction. The plan must also keep the conservative lawyer in mind and be dressed in the conventional legal symbols which surround the literature of due process. It may be well to start out by calling the plan a contract, even though its provisions are to end by being in effect compulsory regulations. However, this plunges the expert into a maze of doctrines, which range from technical formulas to general moral aphorisms, running through the ideals of separation of powers, delegation of legislative and judicial powers, judicial review, adequate hearings, freedom from searches and seizures, the sanctity of the home, bureaucracy, and the protection of our cherished liberties against the forces of tyranny. Every time the plan steps on any of these legal or economic symbols (which increases in number as the preparation of the written documents proceeds), it encounters danger.

It is quite apparent to the expert by this time that economic and legal theories are methods of preaching rather than of practical advice. These sciences are talking about communism, capitalism, fascism, socialism, bureaucracy, and individualism as separate and identifiable things. They are testing any plan to meet a particular situation by identifying it as belonging to one of these classifications.

As a result knowledge of the anatomy of governmental institutions has fallen behind almost every other field of thought. We have failed to develop a competent governing class—that is, a group gifted with the necessary techniques for social cures. Everywhere one looks one sees nothing but planners for a better society among the reformers, and persons who cling to the present as the best possible of all societies among the conservatives. We are still informed by the scientists most learned in both law and economics that governmental institutions are not to be experimented with. That method which in affairs of science was the only road to new knowledge is closed to the student of government.

In such a situation it is inevitable that the only persons who understand the techniques of government are a group called politicians. They lack social values, their aims are imperfect, but society clings to them rather than to the occasional reformer who does not understand its emotional needs, and tries to fit it into some procrustean bed made in the world of his own dreams.

Thus, because of their ways of thinking, the disinterested type of men we would like to see in government fail to acquire skill at the techniques of the trade. They are effective only for the purpose of throwing the politicians out for brief periods as a curb on their rapacity. They understand too little the manipulation of groups of people to stay in power. Their only place is in colleges, or on lecture platforms. They usually bungle their brief opportunities in power because they are too much in love with an ideal society to treat the one actually before them with skill and understanding. Their constant and futile cry is reiterated through the ages: "Let us educate the people so that they can understand and appreciate us." It never occurs to them to stop preaching and to begin observing. This would require abandonment of separate sciences of law, political theory, and economics for the study of the moving stream of humanity before their eyes in which law, political science, and economics are so inextricably mingled that there can be neither truth nor wisdom in their separation. They constantly adopt the rôle of missionaries to the heathen, instead of playing the part of anthropologists in a society so filled with complicated and contradictory taboos as to make the average savage seem comparatively wanting in superstition. When they do recognize a taboo, they condemn it, instead of realizing that of such is the stuff which binds society together and makes it orderly and comfortable in its spirit. And when they find that their reforms do not reform, and their plans do not develop as plans, they end with a discouraged skepticism.

Out of persons with such attitudes a competent governing class cannot be made. If society is to be freed from the domination of high-class psychopaths, in whom the sense of dramatic popular appeal is peculiarly developed, or from the more tolerant rule of kindly but uneducated Irishmen whose human sympathies give them an instinctive understanding of what people like, it will be because we have developed among those who ought to govern a few skills like those acquired by the physician when he deserted his unreal anatomy and accepted the discovery of the circulation of the blood.

Are We Developing a Competent Governing Class?

MUST the slow, detailed methods of objective science always remain alien to cures for group ills, however pertinent they may become for the cure of individual afflictions? Are we never to make great discoveries in the technique of human organization similar to medical and psychological discoveries about the individual organization? Is there no process by which social institutions may be objectively directed?

It is interesting to present by way of analogy an attitude on the part of medical scholars which delayed the discovery of the circulation of the blood until the beginning of the seventeenth century. Galen formulated his fundamental principles of anatomy before human dissection had become respectable. When dissection began, the ideal structure, in which each supposed organ of the human body had its divine purpose, was so generally accepted that no one dreamed of questioning its basic principles (except perhaps a few dissenters who had another set of principles). This attitude toward dissection is illustrated by an old print picturing a lecture on anatomy at Padua in the fifteenth century. We see the master, seated on a sort of throne at some distance from the cadaver, with Galen's book open before him. Below, a robed assistant with a pointer indicated those portions of the human body which are relevant to illustrate the text. The actual dissection is being done by a menial who is not permitted to wear the robes of learning. Students stand around, but do not dissect. It is not surprising that such methods always proved the text of Galen, which contained an anatomy composed of the jumbled portions of all sorts of animals. Differences could be explained by pointing out that the human constitution had degenerated since the days of the constitutional fathers, or else that they were those inevitable minor details and border-line cases which always conflict with any body of learning. Generally, however, differences would not be noticed. Anatomy was a learned pursuit and therefore, true to its type, it had to ignore, or else to explain away as immaterial, matters which created disorder in its organized ideas. It seems to be the eternal paradox of the human mind that principles and faiths which are so essential to its comfort and to the orderly organization and transmission of ideas should at the same time always stand as the greatest obstacle to discovery.

It is not difficult to make a comparison between this ancient print and the methods of social and legal studies of our own day. It is as applicable to the realist who thinks rules are unimportant as to the fundamentalist who accepts them. Both ignore the structure of the institution before them except as it illustrates their theories. The dissection of social phenomena such as the election of Ma Ferguson in Texas, the power of Huey Long in Louisiana, and the bonus army in Washington are beyond their sphere, except in so far as it becomes necessary to point out that they are all bad things which deserve no sympathy or tolerance. They are thought of as examples of social decay which can be cured by educating the people to the dangers of demagogues, the evils of politics, and the folly of communistic ideas. The political or economic scholar does not attempt to dissect because it would destroy his learning as a separate science.

The legal scholar, compelled to study only one institution, the courts, does resort to dissecting methods, but his dissection is that of the followers of Galen, designed to illustrate and prove various ideal legal anatomies. The bar and courts in general are shown to be what they are supposed to be. Departure in conduct from the ideal is always caused by degeneration as typified by the shyster, the politician, or the ignoramus. If the speeches before bar associations are wordy and platitudinous, the scholar insists on looking forward to the better-educated bar of tomorrow. If corpus juris is too often cited by courts in place of more careful legal effusions, we resolve either to wean the lawyers away from it by the American Law Institute, or to push them in a different direction by showing the hollowness of all legal formulas. What we are most concerned with is not the imperfections of the present but the probable effect of better ideas on the better judges who will appear when politics are finally taken out of politics. The content of present popularly conceived legal and social ideas, good, bad, and indifferent, and their effect upon governmental institutions—the way they give life to, and mold the growth of, the bench and bar, as we now have them—are seldom considered.

This is of course to be expected, and it is neither to be deplored nor applauded. It is simply one of the phenomena of human organization. The preaching technique, perhaps one of the most powerful of social factors, is always the first to be mastered, perhaps because it is the most essential to an orderly society (or possibly because it is the easiest). Poetry always appears before science, and certainly no one would claim that poetry is an unworthy occupation for legal scholars. Nor is the fact that preaching must contend against the disorganizing influence of new ideas and new methods to be considered other than as one of the objective phenomena incident to all human organization. This fact is an integral part of the anatomy of any institution, and to deprecate it is like deploring the handicap which child-bearing puts on women. Preachers who preach against preaching are still preachers.

If we are to escape from Galen's anatomy in one form or another, we must consider institutions and the mass psychology surrounding them as living organisms, not dissimilar to human personalities, molded by habit, shaken by emotional conflicts, turned this way and that by words, constantly making good resolutions which affect them but not in the way that the terminology of the resolutions might indicate, and never quite understanding themselves or the part they are actually playing because of the necessary illusions with which they must surround themselves to preserve their prestige and self-respect. This attitude is not common to either the law or the social sciences, yet it must be the attitude of one who is making an objective dissection.

We may illustrate by pointing out that the late John Mc-Cooey, political boss of Brooklyn, had a certain verbal or emotional magic by which he was able to exercise an astonishing control over his borough. It is difficult to say that he did not have a very penetrating knowledge, or at least a successful technique which should concern the science of government. However, his admission to the faculty of any respectable hall of learning was unthinkable; his information fitted into no established classification. It was unorganized. He had no "field." Clarence Darrow appears not to believe in any legal principles, yet few are more successful in their chosen type of cases in getting results with the legal principles which he so distrusts. Yet persons like Clarence Darrow are not seriously regarded as legal scholars because their variegated experience with the legal system has prevented them from having the time or perhaps even the inclination to make any close and careful study of the "*law*." What trial lawyers know is unorganized and therefore unteachable. That such techniques are kept out of organized learning as long as possible is certainly something the social anatomist should expect as a matter of course and recognize without any particular feeling of indignation. However, perhaps the barriers may be broken when some accident offers a chance.

We may illustrate with another medical analogy. At the

time of Louis XIV some of the most important discoveries and most useful medical techniques, the most important of which was surgery, were the property of the barber surgeons of the day—a group who were related to the physicians of that time in much the same way that the Tammany politician is related to the statesman and to the scholar in government today. Not only was their social standing none too good, but their approach and ideas were upsetting to the logical structure approved by the University of Paris and adopted by all right-thinking doctors. What they knew was also unorganized and therefore unteachable. Louis XIV had the misfortune to develop an uncomfortable carbuncle which required an operation. Obviously, no commoner could touch the divine person of His Majesty, so a barber surgeon had to be elevated to the nobility. An epidemic of boils on the persons of the nobility followed. More barber surgeons were elevated. The physicians held a parade in protest, but it was too late.[6] The technique of surgery was already on its way to respectability. Knowledge of surgery was soon to be indispensable to the physician.

Today there unquestionably exist developed techniques in the operation of governmental institutions, but such techniques are never admitted to the realm of the student of government because the people who practice them are not respectable or because their inclusion would disorganize an ancient ideology. The only realistic test of a political speech is its vote-getting effect. This is recognized by the tradesmen of politics but denied by political scholars and high-minded persons generally. Such persons judge politi-

6. The incident is related by Victor Robinson, *The Story of Medicine* (1931), p. 319: "The story of the Paris Faculty, arrayed in wrath and their red robes, brandishing a skeleton and parading the streets in protest, defied by the surgeons and teased by the mob without any cringing at the sight of their actions, the dignity of the doctors finally disappearing in a snowstorm which seemed made to order, constitutes a surgical melodrama."

cal utterances by standards of sincerity and economic analysis. The idea of using words and prejudices as tools to push people into desired courses of conduct, without any particular anxiety as to the absolute truth of these ideas or prejudices, is one of those "bad things" which a sufficient amount of preaching is supposed to cure. The preconceived or ideal anatomy of society is constantly substituted for the real. Appeals to emotional impulses are not looked upon impersonally as forces which, regardless of their truth, mold institutions in various ways. Instead, we adopt the ancient medical assumption that society is possessed of a devil who must be driven out with incantations. The net result is, not that political speeches become more sincere, but that scholars are notable failures in understanding political institutions.

When we turn to legal institutions we find the same situation. Ideas are pursued for their own sake—not examined to determine their force or effect in the sphere within which they operate. Legal principles are discussed as things which govern a society which has never studied them, or else as meaningless ritual which has no effect, even upon the courts which use them. A word like "estoppel" or "trust," the utterance of which in properly solemn tones at the right moment may cause a court to step aside suddenly and let some established doctrine go whizzing harmlessly by, is treated as if it must be made to have some definite meaning or else dropped. The writer recalls the emphasis with which a great law teacher used to say, "The loose use of the term estoppel is an infallible sign of a weak intellect." On the other hand, if the discovery is made that no legal formulas can long retain any definite meaning, the assumption is that their pronouncement should not affect judicial conduct, and therefore something else should be substituted. The failure of the New York code to get rid of the distinction between law and equity is treated either as showing that these legal distinctions are fundamental to correct thought, or else as a proof of judicial stupidity, instead of as an example of reformers' lack of understanding of the mass psychology of the judicial institution from which not even judges can escape. The distinction between courts, bureaus, and commissions becomes a matter of elaborate definition, instead of a recognition of the fact that the differences between a judge sitting as a court, and one sitting as a bureau, is simply the difference of our attitude toward him, reflected in his attitude toward himself. Finally, the failure of our definitional schemes to work is generally laid to the lack of those "better judges" who will finally appear when astute politicians are unable to obtain lucrative offices.

May we not subject governmental institutions to something resembling the process of dissection in order to find out the stimuli to which they respond, without judging as to whether those stimuli are moral or sincere according to the precepts of some preconceived social anatomy? Perhaps in this way we might learn why so many high-minded schemes fail, and so many low-minded schemes succeed, without recourse to the naïve idea that the institution is possessed of a devil which can be exhorted away.

This book will attempt the dissection of social ideals and attitudes. In so far as the program and premises for that sort of undertaking can be stated, they might be summarized as follows:

1. Rational thinking will neither be attacked nor defended, but regarded as one of the inescapable habits of the human mind.

2. Doctrines and principles derived from rational thinking will be examined to find out their effect on institutions. They will be regarded neither as "true" nor "false."

3. The place of philosophers in a system of governmental technique will be examined without preconceived assump-

tions either that philosophers make good kings, or that theories of government are mere shams.

4. The theory that the most important factor in human government is the way people think about it will be discussed.

5. This method of examining governmental institutions should be without any assumption that because this is a good way for those engaged in conducting governmental institutions to think, it is necessarily a good way for everyone to think. The eye of the artist or poet looking at the human body is different from the eye of the physician looking for pathological symptoms. Neither one has the "true" nor the "false" view of the body. The physician, however, is the better person when therapy rather than decoration is demanded.

6. The essence of this point of view is that one should not expect a logically formulated set of principles to develop from it. It is the system under examination which can no more help producing principles than a hen can keep from laying eggs. The detached observer should produce instead of a system, however, a series of observations, mostly concerning details. The complete anatomy of the human organization may be made up from such details but it should come far in the future, and only after all the details have been examined and synthesized.

This technique is as old as the parables of the New Testament. It is only its dialectic formulation that is modern. It is difficult to state in logical sequence because it represents the paradox of a logical statement of an alogical system—a formulated theory against all formulated theories. If this point of view must have a name we prefer to call it an anthropological approach toward social ideals.

CHAPTER II

Theories about Legal Theory

FAR older than economics as a way of thinking about society, stands the "Law." It is perhaps the most mysterious and most occult of all branches of learning, because both the student and the layman are constantly warned that there is so much more here than meets the eye—something above and beyond any particular set of books or institutional habits. A man from Mars, looking over the operation of our judicial system, might conclude that here existed the easiest of all the branches of learning. True, it consists of an infinite variety of small rules and exceptions, which, if they were to be carried in one's head, might constitute a body of required information even more formidable than that which the Chinese scholar is supposed to commit to memory. However, such a feat is not required, or even expected. Accommodating publishers have arranged the material with such excellent indexes and digests that a person of reasonable intelligence can learn to find his way about in a short time. Most other sciences require unusual manual skill, or specialized knowledge, before the tricks of the trade can be practiced with any proficiency. In the law, however, almost anyone with a persuasive literary style and an ability to handle indexes well may write a competent brief. This has been proved often enough by the fact that many of our greatest jurists, including the illustrious John Marshall himself, were men with very little specialized preliminary training. Nations other than America seem to regard a general education with emphasis on legal terminology as sufficient preparation to enter the practice. A large proportion of the much-admired English judges do not have the equivalent of an American legal education, and seem none the worse for it.

We find, of course, among practicing lawyers experts in various fields of commercial activity whose skill and judgment are not simple or easy things to acquire. Yet such expertness is not part of the study of the "law" as we conceive it. Indeed, such techniques are not studied at all. Those principles of the law which are subjects of examination in our schools have little to do with any particular form of business activity. A student may be well grounded in the law without knowing anything about them. The chances are ten to one that his professor is as ignorant of the specialized knowledge employed by practicing lawyers in the actual conduct of their clients' affairs as is the practicing lawyer about the general principles of jurisprudence. Further than that, in spite of the fact that he is a professor of law, he is not even interested in such specialized knowledge. Only recently one of our greatest law schools was approached with the idea of giving a combined course with a school of business administration. The idea was rejected, because the curriculum of the business school was considered as irrelevant to the proper study of the law.

We also find among practicing lawyers experts in the art of the presentation of evidence in a dramatic way so that verdicts and court decrees are obtained largely through the use of an efficient dramatic technique. Yet such skills are not part of the study of the law. Indeed, legal scholars charge such a writer as Jerome Frank, who attempts to show how the literature of the law actually works in such situations, with superficiality and lack of understanding of the real "law" which is apart from litigation. In spite of all the irrefutable logic of the realists, men insist upon believing that there are fundamental principles of law which exist apart from any particular case, or any particular human activity; that these principles must be sought with a reverent attitude; that they are being improved constantly; and that our sacrifices of efficiency and humanitarianism in their honor are leading us to a better government. The truth of such a philosophy cannot be demonstrated or proved. It exists only because we seem unable to find comfort without it.

The thing which we reverently call "Law" when we are talking about government generally, and not predicting the results of particular lawsuits, can only be properly described as an attitude or a way of thinking about government. It is a way of writing about human institutions in terms of ideals, rather than observed facts. It meets a deep-seated popular demand that government institutions symbolize a beautiful dream within the confines of which principles operate, independently of individuals.

The fact that today as a necessary gesture toward a new habit of thought the "Law" is dressed up to look like a "science" does not change it as a way of thought. It means only that the earliest conception that the law came from God and the later conception that it arose from logic and reason have both been worn thin. However, the new word "science" has not given the law a different point of view. It has merely set up a new line of defenses against the attacks of those detached observers who insist upon recording what they see.

Of course, there are countless rules, institutional habits, and various kinds of social compulsions in every society. These are often called law. It is not with these that we are dealing when we study "law" in Western civilization. The fundamental principles of law do not represent what we do, but what we ought to do. The science of the law is not the method which judges actually use, but the method which they ought to use. It is a sort of Heaven which man has created for himself on earth. It is a characteristic of all paradises that they should be different from what we actually experience in everyday affairs. Otherwise there would be no object in creating them. Therefore no one should be surprised because there is so little similarity between the ideals of the law and what the courts actually do. It is part of the function of "Law" to give recognition to ideals representing the exact opposite of established conduct. Most of its complications arise from the necessity of pretending to do one thing, while actually doing another. It develops the structure of an elaborate dream world where logic creates justice. It permits us to look at the drab cruelties of business practices through rose-colored spectacles.

The principles of law are supposed to control society, because such an assumption is necessary to the logic of the dream. Yet the observer should constantly keep in mind that the function of law is not so much to guide society, as to comfort it. Belief in fundamental principles of law does not necessarily lead to an orderly society. Such a belief is as often at the back of revolt or disorder. Respect for fundamental principles of law performs the same function in stiffening the morale of those who are in revolt against established institutions as it does in holding in line those who defend these institutions. Everyone should respect and obey the law in this country even if he does not like it. But no one should be hindered or prevented from relying on his constitutional rights, and if this involves disobeying mere statutes, the act of disobedience intended for this purpose is most praiseworthy. Thus the law at the same time contains both the contradictory philosophies of obedience and revolt.

"Law" is primarily a great reservoir of emotionally important social symbols. It develops, as language develops, in spite of, and not because of, the grammarians. Though the notion of a "rule of Law" may be the moral background of revolt, it ordinarily operates to induce acceptance of things as they are. It does this by creating a realm somewhere within the mystical haze beyond the courts, where all our dreams of justice in an unjust world come true. Thus in the realm of the law the least favored members of society are comforted by the fact that the poor are equal to the rich and the strong have no advantage over the weak. The more fortunately situated are reassured by the fact that the wise are treated better than the foolish, that careless people are punished for their mistakes. The trader takes heart by learning that the law ignores the more profitable forms of dishonesty in deference to the principle of individual freedom from governmental restraint. The preacher, however, is glad to learn that all forms of dishonesty which can be curbed without interfering with freedom or with economic law are being curbed. The dissatisfied minority is cheered by the fact that the law is elastic and growing. The conservative is convinced that it is becoming more and more certain. The industrial serf is told that no man, not even his great employer, is above the law. His employer, however, feels secure in the fact that his property is put above ordinary legislative law by the Constitution, which is the highest form of law there is. It protects us on the one hand from regulation, on the other hand from arbitrary power exercised without regulations. It saves us from the mob, and also from the dictator. It prevents capitalism from turning into communism, democracy from becoming the rule of an unthinking people. It gives all people an equal chance for success, and at the same time protects those who have been born in more favored positions of privilege and power.

From a practical point of view it is the greatest instrument of social stability because it recognizes every one of the yearnings of the underprivileged, and gives them a forum in which those yearnings can achieve official approval without involving any particular action which might joggle the existing pyramid of power. It permits the use of an argumentative technique by which powerful institutions can be defended on the ground that taking away privileges from them would take away freedom from the poor.

For example, there is very little resemblance between the Russian Government's agricultural policy and the recent currency legislation of the present administration. Yet a great lawyer, the late Senator Reed of Missouri, moving into the analogies of the law was able to declare with great sincerity as follows:

The Bolshevist government declares that any person owning more than three cows is a capitalist and must surrender his cows to the state. If he does not, the government takes them by force.

The Administration declares that if you have more than $100.00 in gold and do not surrender it, you will be sent to the penitentiary.

The injustice in each case is the same. The charge of grosser cruelty rests upon our government.[1]

These remarks are made in the course of a speech on the Constitution of the United States. They would be impossible in a talk about the practical results of the two policies. They are, however, most effective in the symbolic atmosphere of the "Law" where tendencies, rather than actual effects, are the tools of discourse, because we are moving in the world of symbols.

Obviously, "law" can never be defined. With equal obviousness, however, it should be said that the adherents of the legal institution must never give up the struggle to define law, because it is an essential part of the ideal that it is rational and capable of definition, rather than a psychological adjustment to conflicting emotional needs. Hence the verbal expenditure necessary to the upkeep of the ideal

1. From "The Constitution of the United States," an address delivered at the World's Fair in Chicago on September 17, 1934, by Senator James A. Reed of Missouri (*Vital Speeches*, I, 6).

of "law" is colossal and never ending. The legal scientist is compelled by the climate of opinion in which he finds himself to prove that an essentially irrational world is constantly approaching rationality; that a cruel world is constantly approaching kindliness, and that a changing world is really stable and enduring.

The "Law" must pretend that legislatures have a composite intent, and a group free will, and find means of discovering that intent, in spite of the troublesome inner conviction of everyone that such an enterprise is nonsense. It must pretend, in spite of modern psychological research, that criminals may be divided into persons having free will and those not having it. It must always pretend that its own institutional ways are the best ways of accomplishing practical objectives, even in the face of overwhelming evidence to the contrary.

The impact of modern ideas upon this institution which has been compelled to give lip service to the validity of the scientific or objective approach has been a source of great confusion and unrest among the ranks of the initiates. It has resulted in great defensive institutions, such as the three-year graduate law school in America, devoted to the task of absorbing these ideas without changing the fundamental idealistic and dramatic character of the institution. It has resulted in the philosophy of the law becoming so unbelievably complicated that not even lawyers can understand it. But it has not affected the emotional importance of the symbol.

So far as the public is concerned, the struggle of the so-called school of realism against the tenets of an older group of devoted priests has created more emphasis on the emotional necessity of a belief in fundamental principles, but it has not impaired their emotional importance. Realists prove incontrovertibly that there can be no objective reality behind the law as a brooding omnipresence in the skies—

only to find their own writings swallowed up and becoming a part of that brooding omnipresence which they are insistently denying. The brooding omnipresence defends itself simply by including realism as one of its principles existing along with all of its other principles. "In the house of jurisprudence there are many mansions."[2] The theory that no homogeneous body of principles can exist apart from specific cases ends up as only one of the principles of that homogeneous body of principles which exists apart from cases. As Emerson has put it:

> They reckon ill who leave me out
> When me they fly, I am their wings,
> I am the doubter and the doubt
> And I the song the Brahmin sings.[3]

To put the matter in prose, this means that one cannot deny the existence of ghosts without creating and putting special emphasis on the ghosts which one denies. In saying that ghosts do not exist, a very concrete conception of what a ghost would be if it did exist is essential. This concrete conception in the unbeliever's mind is, of course, a ghost and we may, therefore, go on talking about and defining its characteristics as we did before. Indeed, the realist by denying ghosts only focuses public attention on them so long as they remain a part of the common conception of society as it ought to exist. Among nations today which are touched with occidental rather than oriental culture, the dream of an impersonal justice dramatized by the settlement of disputes by a governmental agency, seems to be so fundamental that attempts to be realistic about it are instinctively brushed aside.

To illustrate this we may step into the clear, cold realism

2. Roscoe Pound in "The Call for a Realist Jurisprudence," 44 *Harv. L.R.* 711.

3. Brahma.

of the Russian revolution and observe its effects on the Russian judicial system. The Russian revolutionists, immediately on coming to power, discovered that the entire structure of Western law was simply designed to protect propertied classes. They felt the need of no elaborate make-believe—indeed, their principal ideal was the destruction of make-believe. Therefore, they argued that the proper way of accomplishing their object, the protection of the working class, was to design courts frankly dedicated to this task, without mystical folderol. Thus the entire existing system of substantive law or procedure was abolished in 1917. The Congress of the Communist party stated their ideal in 1919 with these triumphant words:

The soviet government has replaced the former endless series of courts of justice with their various grades by a very simplified uniform system of people's courts accessible to the people and devoid of useless delay.[4]

It was only a short time after this that a new system of courts appeared called Revolutionary Courts, professing dedication to a splendid ideal called the Revolutionary conscience. No one could say exactly the limits of this ideal, but certainly it included more than mere practical objectives. In many respects it came to resemble what the Supreme Court of the United States has called "due process." The Revolutionary Courts attempted to dramatize this ideal and to give it content. A law review appeared dedicated to its philosophy, in a country which had spurned the notion of "substantive law," lawyers, and legal philosophy.

Two effects of these Revolutionary Courts may be noted. In the first place they gained in prestige over the more practical people's courts, and their jurisdiction was con-

4. Judah Zelitch, *Soviet Administration of Criminal Law* (1931), p. 27. This book is an excellent discussion of the Russian judicial system as of 1931.

stantly extended. In the second place they made of the revolutionary conscience something which began to resemble a "law" above even the Russian dictatorship. When Lenin, in 1921, announced his new economic policy, commonly called the "Nep," these courts set themselves against such a radical innovation with the zeal and fervor of judicial institutions everywhere, when confronted with new things. They referred to it in terms which in Russia were the equivalent of what 100 per cent Americans mean by the word communistic. The only Russian legal periodical of the time ran true to form by filling its pages with grave warnings of the "risk of being drowned by the petty bourgeois wave" and admonishing the courts to "carry through their class encroachment and preserve their own proletarian essence."[5] Just as a ship gathers barnacles or an oyster secretes pearls (the choice of the figure depending on one's attitude), so does a judicial institution accumulate great defensive fundamental principles. Constitutional law has a habit of appearing even where there is no constitution.

The reaction of the Russian Government showed a remarkable understanding of popular psychology. Instead of engaging in involved arguments as to whether the N.E.P. actually did conflict with the Revolutionary conscience—an argument as incapable of immediate decision as the argument whether the New Deal really is constitutional in America—the Government proceeded to completely reorganize the entire judiciary in 1922. The new judicial system bore little resemblance to the simple and realistic people's courts. It consisted of a three-story appellate court structure in each separate Soviet Republic with a supreme court of the United Socialist Soviet Republics at the top. But strangest of all, in this country which had forsworn legal theory in favor of swift practical results, ten schools of jurisprudence were established,[6] dedicated to the development of a

5. Zelitch, *Soviet Administration of Criminal Law* (1931), p. 50.
6. *Idem*, p. 51.

legal philosophy which would make the Russian system of values seem logically and philosophically impregnable. Since the establishment of this judicial system in 1922, the appellate structure has been increased to four stages in many of the Soviet republics. Appeals are made easy. The Russian trial has been deliberately made to become a miracle play in which governmental ideals are exemplified. Indeed, in some instances, the court proceedings have been broadcast where the setting was such that the state appeared to be engaged in a contest with its enemies.

And what, one may ask, has become of the people's courts, which originally were to be the whole structure? They seem to have gone the way of practical everyday courts everywhere. They are to be found at the very bottom of the judicial hierarchy, manned by judges with a minimum of prestige, and they are a constant source of worry because they are no better than they should be.

A series of investigations in the magistrates' courts in New York City illustrates the similar nature of the judicial process in Western countries. It is pointed out with tiresome reiteration that it is with the lower magistrates' courts that most of the public come in contact. The prestige of the judicial system must necessarily rest with these courts because they are the only courts which most of the people know. Therefore we must have higher paid, better, less political, and more dignified magistrates. Nevertheless, after the wave of every reform has died down, we may go back to the magistrates' courts of New York and find them much the same as they have always been—careless, slovenly, politically minded, and undignified. The fact is that they are in too close touch with everyday reality to serve as the dramatic symbol of that government of laws which is not a government of men. "Law" in that sense must reside in higher and more empyrean realms.

That we are able to find in Russia, which deliberately

started out to avoid our legalistic structure, a development
so similar to ours is a startling illustration of the function
which the ideal of law plays in dramatizing the various conflicting ideals. It is also an interesting proof that the emotional cement which binds governments together, which
gives them prestige and power, is not furnished by the realist, or by the scientist but by priestly literature and ceremony.

Another interesting observation which may be made on
the Russian legal development is the effect which the vague
ideal of the Revolutionary conscience had upon the actual
conduct of the judiciary. Certainly there was no content in
this ideal at the beginning sufficiently definite to constitute
a direction as to any particular judicial action. Almost anything could have been done and justified under the magic
of the phrase. Yet because the judges appear to have approached it with reverence, because they desired to make a
beautiful and admired thing out of it, we see that even in
the heat of the Russian revolution the Revolutionary Courts
accorded far more lenient treatment to political offenders
than can be found elsewhere. The effect of a parade of sonorous phrases upon human conduct has never been adequately studied. Nevertheless it appears to have the poten-
tiality of making different characters out of those who
conduct it. It seems to be the attempt to create "law" rather
than the content of the law itself which is important in preserving the values to which any given society is emotionally
committed. At any rate, it is certain that when the Russian
Government desired to commit one of its revolutionary out-
rages, it could be done better through some non-phrasemak-
ing body like the Cheka than through its Revolutionary
Courts.

No realist or skeptic ever quite escapes the influences of
the symbols of his time, because most of his own conduct
and the conditions under which he maintains his own

prestige are based on those symbols. The more disorderly countries south of the United States can scarcely be accused of an undue respect for a law above men, yet the following incident, which is set out here on the authority of one of those most concerned, is most illuminating.

Certain students were implicated in a bomb explosion which had killed some government officials.[7] They were haled before a court-martial. Prominent attorneys were induced to undertake their defense. Their first move was to attack the jurisdiction of the court-martial, in order to remove the case to the civil courts. Before the motion was argued they were informed by the President that the Government had no objection to allowing the fullest defense, but unless the motion attacking the jurisdiction of the court-martial was withdrawn, serious consequences to the attorneys might ensue. The attorneys, knowing that their gesture was futile so far as the safety of their clients was concerned, refused to withdraw their motion out of respect to a principle which could never be realistically justified. Thereafter one of them was assassinated in the street. The other escaped with great difficulty and finally reached the United States.

Here a lawless executive preferred to commit murder rather than involve himself in something which his lawyers advised him might be a legal contradiction. It is doubtful if he had any clear idea of the intricacies of the concept "jurisdiction," or of the extraordinary results which might be obtained by the skilful use of analogy. He controlled the courts, yet he could not help believing that he did not control the law. His only course therefore seemed to be to prevent the motion from being made. He did not hesitate to use his power to violate the law, but even his dictatorship did not make him feel safe in denying the

7. The writer omits the time and place of the incident for obvious reasons of protection to his informant.

existence of something which theoretically controlled his own actions. Like the Chinese, he felt entitled to cheat the gods with imitation money, but he did not dare to ignore them. Unconsciously he had the feeling that here was the cement which bound even his dictatorship together. The fact that nothing whatever would have happened had he directed his judges to overrule the motion and refrained from assassinating the attorney could never be known to him, because this was the one thing which he did not dare to try.

Thus we see that "Law" represents the belief that there must be something behind and above government without which it cannot have permanence or respect. Even a dictator cannot escape this psychology of his time. He does not quite believe in his own government unless he is able to make gestures toward this prevailing ideal. It is child's play for the realist to show that law is not what it pretends to be and that its theories are sonorous, rather than sound; that its definitions run in circles; that applied by skilful attorneys in the forum of the courts it can only be an argumentative technique; that it constantly seeks escape from reality through alternate reliance on ceremony and verbal confusion. Yet the legal realist falls into grave error when he believes this to be a defect in the law. From any objective point of view the escape of the law from reality constitutes not its weakness but its greatest strength. Legal institutions must constantly reconcile ideological conflicts, just as individuals reconcile them by shoving inconsistencies back into a sort of institutional subconscious mind. If judicial institutions become too "sincere," too self-analytical, they suffer the fate of ineffectiveness which is the lot of all self-analytical people. They lose themselves in words, and fail in action. They lack that sincere fanaticism out of which great governmental forces are welded.

The abstract ideals of the law require for their public acceptance symbolic conduct of a very definite pattern by a definite institution which can be heard and seen. In this way only can they achieve the dramatic presentation necessary to make them moving forces in society. Any abstract ideal which is not tied up with a definite institution or memorialized by particular ceremonies, becomes relegated to the limbo of metaphysics and has little social consequence. The institutions which throw about the law that atmosphere of reality and concreteness so necessary for its acceptance are the court and the law school. The one produces the ceremonial ritualistic trial; the other produces a theoretical literature which defends the ideal from attack by absorbing and weaving into its mystical pattern all the ideas of all of the critics. In other words, trials today are the product of courts; books the product of law schools.

It is important to remember that in this chapter we are not dealing with "law" as an argumentative technique which wins or loses cases. The art of using the varied concepts to get results for clients is not ordinarily regarded as "law" at all. Legal scholars and judges are not supposed to be concerned with it except so far as they need to be careful that they are not misled. Our law schools and courts refuse to admit publicly that legal doctrine is simply a method of argument and classification of cases. Their function is rather to keep an ideal alive.

The "Law" as a body of principles and ideals which is above men, lives in a vast metaphysical literature, and in a succession of ceremonial trials. The function of these two and their effects are different. Both are necessary to create faiths and loyalties concerning governing forces. However, they play their parts in different ways, and therefore must be treated separately. Since the ordinary approach to any institution is first through its literature, we will examine the literature of the law in the next chapter, leaving the ceremonial trial for later treatment.

CHAPTER III

The Mystery of Jurisprudence

IT may seem odd to the reader that in a book which purports to select for analysis the more important symbols of government, a chapter should be given to jurisprudence. Here is a subject which not even lawyers read. Its content is vague; its literature abstruse and difficult. Nevertheless there is a general feeling that under this title are hidden the most sacred mysteries of the law. Even in popular nomenclature, ordinary men at law are called by the commonplace name of attorneys, or lawyers, and great names at the bar bear the title of "Jurists." It is considered undesirable to teach law efficiently as a trade, and socially important to omit the tricks of the trial lawyer in order to teach it as a philosophy.

Jurisprudence is the holy of holies of government, the science of that great symmetrical body of principles which is supposed to constitute the law, the description of its deepest sources, and the unifying element of the law throughout history. Without a science of jurisprudence, law might be considered a collection of man-made rules for practical situations. With it the Law becomes the cornerstone of government. Therefore the literature of jurisprudence is a most important symbol of our rational moral attitude toward human institutions. By analyzing it we may begin to understand how similar the effects of that moral rational attitude are whether they appear in other great literatures such as economics, or in minor literatures such as common-law pleading.

The way of thinking that we are describing here as moral and rational must be distinguished from another way of thinking which may be described as practical, or benevolent, which produces entirely different social results. Where we take the latter attitude we do not philosophize at all. No complicated rational sciences arise out of conduct which we take as a matter of course, and which we do not seek to fit into a logical and symmetrical scheme. The difference between these two attitudes is difficult to define, but it is easy to illustrate. For example, there is no great logical structure of moral principles involved in the treatment of an insane man who has committed murder. We do not hang him, even though society might be better off if he were out of the way. We preserve him in an institution where he is better treated than he would be in a penitentiary. No logical reason can be given for so preserving him. We simply do not argue about the matter, and let it rest on general sentimental or humanitarian grounds. There is no jurisprudence concerning the proper treatment of insane criminals. Jurisprudence steps in only when we try to draw a logical line between the sane and the insane. Once we designate a man as "sick," whether mentally or physically, we proceed to cure him, and are shocked at any discussion as to whether he morally or logically deserves to be cured.

The difference between the two attitudes is well illustrated by an incident which was reported in the *New York Times,* during the early years of the depression, when governmental relief was still regarded as the ruin of national character. On a cold winter day a shanty colony was being removed from a vacant lot in New York City to make way for the erection of a building. The newspaper report of poor hungry people driven from makeshift dwellings was pathetic. Yet nothing could be done about it. To give them a dole would establish a dangerous precedent and be contrary to the rational and moral ideals of rugged individualism. The eviction of these unfortunates was therefore a symbol of a faith that economic competence can only be developed by refusing to protect incompetence.

After the work of demolition began two unconscious men were found under one of the improvised dwellings. Immediately a whole new set of attitudes and symbols rose as if by magic. Rational moral government ended and pure benevolence took charge. The idea that it was wrong to protect men from the results of their incompetence vanished. Twenty thousand dollars' worth of ambulances, consuming an inordinate number of gallons of gasoline to the mile, clanged their way through crowded streets, manned by the most expensive nurses and internes that money could buy. The men were transferred to surroundings which in sanitation and equipment were beyond the reach of even the millionaire of fifty years ago. If a logically minded individual had asked why so much money should be expended on individuals who would never be anything but a burden on society, and who would have to be turned out to suffer again after their stay in the hospital, he would have been simply brushed aside. Humanitarian ideals are not defined by logic. It was the duty of the ambulance to get the men to the hospital, not to discuss jurisprudence.

Thus a practical or humanitarian attitude develops techniques, and not logical arguments. A rational moral attitude develops philosophies and priests, rather than technicians. The institution which is at the head of the hierarchy representing the rational moral attitude today is the law. A hundred years ago its place was shared by the church.

The treatment of jurisprudence as a symbol of government makes it unnecessary to go into the refinements of the various theories associated under that name. For the purposes of the social effectiveness of the symbol, such details are unimportant. It is significant here only to describe the way of thinking which has resulted in this voluminous and unread literature.

The reader is asked therefore to consider this chapter, not

as a chapter on jurisprudence as a separate science, but as a chapter on the kind of literature which all rational thinking about government in general, or its details, inevitably produces. Considered as such he will find that the subject is not complicated, but simple, and that the ideas are simply the vague notions of the man on the street done into a great arabesque of words.

The Practical Function of Abstract Jurisprudence

As we have shown, the law consists of a large number of mutually contradictory symbols and ideals. Such contradictions are apparent to any man on the street who becomes involved in the judicial process. He must therefore believe, if he is to keep his faith that government is symmetrical and rational, that there exists somewhere, available to him if he only could get time to study it, a unified philosophy of science of law.

Therefore he believes that there exists a science of jurisprudence, and gives a place in the social scheme to a priesthood whose duty it is to expound that science, unmoved by the irrelevancies of practical day-to-day governmental action.

An official admission by a judicial institution that it was moving in all directions at once in order to satisfy the conflicting emotional values of the people which it served would be unthinkable. It would have the same effect as if an actor interrupted the most moving scene of a play in order to explain to the audience that his real name was John Jones. The success of the play requires that an idea be made real to the audience. The success of the law as a unifying force depends on making emotionally significant the idea of a government of law which is rational and scientific.

The unifying principles which are behind all of the various activities of admittedly legal institutions are the concern of jurisprudence. Its task is to prove that such principles exist, and to define them in general terms sufficiently broad so that all the little contradictory ideals appearing in the unending procession of particular cases will appear to be part of one great set of ideals. Functionally the primary purpose of the science of the law is to be a sounding board of both the prevalent hopes and the prevalent worries of those who believe in a government of law and not of men; to reconcile these hopes and worries somewhere in the mists of scholarship and learning; and never to admit that this is what it is doing.

Jurisprudence must necessarily be different for different times and for different people living in the same age. Its task is much simpler for an age which is willing to accept on faith that truth is revealed to judges from some mystical source beyond and above the light of reason. Perhaps, in some future time which accepts "Experimentation" as the source of knowledge and is willing to trust in the personal expertness of judges, as today we trust in the expertness of physicians, jurisprudence may again be simple. Yet neither faith in the notion that truth is revealed to judges, nor trust in the personal expertness of any individuals sitting as judges, is congenial to our ways of thinking today. We still think as Newton thought, as Blackstone thought, that our governmental institutions must be rational.

This way of thinking has its discomforts in a world which also reverences science. It compels us to assume that there is a separate faculty of the human mind called "reason," and another separate faculty called "will." This so-called "faculty theory" of psychology is no longer held by scientists. They, indeed, have a tendency to regard thought as only another form of behavior. Hence the rise of realists in juristic debate just as they used to rise in theological debate, equipped with arguments unanswerable and at the same time emotionally unacceptable because we have no formula to reconcile the attitude of the scientist with that of the theologian.

The scientific attitude is useful in order to study the folkways of the people and to determine what kind of formulas most appeal to them. However, this way of thinking violates the great idea that jurists must be "sincere." They must not be politicians, and they should not be permitted to advance theories for a purely practical purpose. Hence jurisprudence has been forced to supply the deficiencies of the rational process by applying more reason. Such conflicts always have the effect of producing an enormous amount of argumentative literature.

A practical result of this conflict, and one which affects even the most ignorant layman, is the fact that twenty-five thousand cases pour from our appellate courts every year. This great literature follows from the idea that the inconsistencies of the reasoning process can always be cured by applying more reason. If the law gets complicated, the only way to simplify it is to add more law to it. Therefore the American Law Institute spent millions in producing a restatement of the fundamental principles of this mass of cases. However, this restatement was not intended to be a substitute for the cases but only to clarify them. It therefore becomes only an additional source of argument.

Out of the confusion, elasticity is undeniably obtained, and at the same time the appearance of certainty, symmetry and order. This order is not observable in practice, and those who come in contact with the courts are constantly complaining about the lag between the law and social justice, or the law and efficiency. In answer to their complaints they are informed that great law schools are working day and night to eliminate these minor inconsistencies as fast as "politics" and "human nature" will permit. The better judges of the future are expected to come out of these law schools, equipped with the training to reconcile the contradictory behavior of the various legal institutions into a rational unity, and to weave into a syllogistic design of pure intellectual beauty all the contradictory ideas which people have about law and government.

Thus the law school has come to symbolize the unifying principles necessary to make the judicial institution with all its complexity appear to be a government of abstract law. It is a guaranty to the public that somewhere, professors, separated from the confusing irrelevancies of a moving world, are working out a rational system which the world may someday follow. The public of course does not read the works of the professors. If it did, doubts might arise as to the efficiency of their efforts. It is enough for the public to have faith in institutions of legal learning as guaranties that principles, forgotten in the wickedness of a political world, are being constantly refined and made more useful for the world of tomorrow.

Social Pressure for an Abstract Science of Law

SINCE the rôle of the law school is to justify faith in an abstract science of law, it is natural that when this rôle is abandoned social pressure appears which compels a return to it. Therefore law schools are for the most part conservative and conceptual in their thinking. There is of course much revolt. The ideas of objective science are constantly appearing in law-school faculties and causing disquiet among believers. One of the vexed problems of legal science has been to absorb these ideas without changing the logical character of the science. The most frequent solution is to admit that these ideas are all true, but to deny that they have any part in the study of "law." In this the conservatives are aided by the temper of students who expect to find law to be something which they can take down in notebooks, and who do not wish to be confronted with the confused picture of what is actually going on. They do not object to new and realistic theories of law, as long as these can be formalized so that they can be taken into notebooks. They dread only the position of looking at the world before them without the aid of someone's theories. Hence "realism" in law schools tends to become only the same old jurisprudence with a new terminology. Professor Williston of Harvard remarked to the writer that the newer philosophy had resulted only in the same old courses with new names. This is probably true, and with the rôle assigned to the law school in the present climate of opinion it is difficult to see how it can be otherwise, since principles are so insistently demanded.

Thus men without a flair for spinning theory do not find a congenial atmosphere in our schools of law. And where professors rush out to take part in the government which they are studying, social pressure is exerted to make them feel that the art of understanding government is destroyed by taking an active part in it. For example a prominent Yale alumnus voiced the sentiment of most of his brethren when he spoke as follows:

Many unfortunate incidents would have been avoided during the past year and a half if professors had not gone to Washington heralded as representing this or that university, whereas they were really representing a minority of one. There is no reason why Yale should let one of these fellows go down there with the public assuming that he embodies all the learning at this University.

It is not in the interests of our universities to have them running down to Washington *for they will never again be able to judge these problems in an unprejudiced light.*[1]

1. Speech of Dean Acheson before Davenport College, Yale University. *New Haven Register,* November 28, 1934.

The pressure is also felt by the heads of the universities who must represent the institution to the public as fulfilling the function which our climate of opinion demands. President Hutchins of Chicago has always been one of our leaders in bringing to the law a scientific approach. Yet when he is put at the head of the University of Chicago he begins to realize the symbolic part which the law school of today must play. In a brilliant speech he reviews his former attempts to be scientific and realistic at the Yale Law School and comes to the following conclusions:

We must, then, devote ourselves to legal research. But if the law is what the courts will do and we are going to be scientific we must get the cases, and the facts outside the cases, and the data of the social sciences. But when we get this material it is useless because we don't know what to do with it. It is a hopeless job anyway, because there is so much material that we can't possibly accumulate it all, and we have no basis for selection and discrimination.

Now I put it to you that these dilemmas are the inevitable consequence of our notion of law and our conception of sciences. I do not deny that our definition of law and our conception of science are possible. I do assert that they are not complete and not fruitful for the study of law.

.   .   .   .

Now I suggest that if we are to understand the law we shall have to get another definition of it. I suggest that the law is a body of principles and rules developed in the light of the rational sciences of Ethics and Politics. The aim of Ethics and Politics is the good life. The aim of the Law is the same. Decisions of courts may be tested by their conformity to the rules of law. The rules may be tested by their conformity to legal principles. The principles may be tested by their consistency with one another and with the principles of Ethics and Politics.[2]

2. *Handbook of the Association of American Law Schools* (1933), pp. 90, 92. Note the startling similarity in the article quoted above and an article written in the seventeenth century to show the futility of the scientific meth-

If President Hutchins had been referring to a medical school he would not have paraphrased his remarks on the law like this:

We must then devote ourselves to medical research. But if medicine is a study of the reactions of individuals to germs and psychopathic states and we are going to be scientific we must get the cases, and the facts outside the cases, and even the data of the man's environment from the social sciences. But when we get this material it is useless because we don't know what to do with it. It is a hopeless job anyway because there is so much material that we can't possibly accumulate it all and we have no basis for selection and discrimination.

Such was indeed the attitude of the medical man at the time that the barber surgeon had the techniques and the physician the theory.[3] Today we find that those who hopelessly delved into the complex material that no one knew what to do with did perform a service. We have abandoned our notion of a "jurisprudence" of medicine. We no longer talk about the divine purpose of the various organs of the human body in an attempt to make it a logical and rational piece of construction.

We have paraphrased President Hutchins' remarks to

ods of Malpighi. "Of what use is the knowledge of the structure of the lung and stream of blood through it? Everyone knows that animals breathe, but no one knows why, and it may be said that even in this modern 17th Century, with all this new knowledge at our command, we are not even quite as successful in curing pneumonia as were the fathers of old. Everyone thought, until the work of Wirsung, that the pancreas was just a cushion to support the stomach. What better off are we to know that it is a duct? Above all, of what use to cut up plants and study the hatching of eggs? Can we cure the troubles of women, knowing how the hatching of eggs goes on?" (Victor Robinson, *The Story of Medicine* [1931], p. 302).

3. "The Paris Faculty was consistent in refusing to recognize any discovery or to permit experimentation. The Paris Faculty believed in interminable discussions and not in demonstrations, and when the candidate—after infinite mental torture—finally received the cap and accolade, he was a full fledged doctor, but had never seen a patient. Under its auspices, medicine marched backward to the dark ages" (Victor Robinson, *op. cit.*, p. 294).

bring into relief that the difference between law and medicine today simply consists in our different ways of thinking about them. The same difference applies to all our thinking about social institutions. This way of thinking about law puts certain limitations on legal and social education and makes it difficult for us admittedly to handle unrelated material and cases in the way of a medical scientist. It compels the search for a unifying principle in our schools and the discarding of whatever data cannot be reconciled with it. Whether we like it or not, law schools are maintained and endowed as centers of abstract thought. If they refuse to accept that rôle, they are in an awkward political situation. If, however, they accept the medieval rôle which they are expected to play, much work of an entirely different character may be done within their walls. The jurisprudence of today does not explain the judicial system, but it is imperative that this be not asserted in public. So long as the ways of thought of Blackstone are required to give morale to our governmental institutions, an open avowal of a different approach by the head of a university may cause so much public disquietude as to endanger both the training of students and the public esteem of the university itself.

A Definition of Jurisprudence

WE may describe jurisprudence or the science of the law in our present day as the effort to construct a logical heaven behind the courts, wherein contradictory ideals are made to seem consistent. Naturally the contradictions are reconciled in the only way logical contradictions can ever be reconciled, by giving each a separate sphere to work in, and pushing the inconsistencies back into the obscurity of great piles of books which are taken on faith and seldom read.

Since jurisprudence must necessarily include as its most vital part something lurking in the ultimate recesses of things, it follows that it is different for different classes of people. For the layman, the entire body of legal literature represents jurisprudence, because it is here that he thinks that the fundamental principles of the law have all been worked out to be revealed to him piecemeal in the occasional decision which comes to his attention. For the lawyer, jurisprudence is that part of the law which he never gets time to read—the part adorned with learned names like Austin, Jhering, Pound, which is separate from, and above, the legal arguments which he uses in court. He assumes that in jurisprudence is found the bridge from one legal subject to another, the philosophy that law is a seamless web, that it is based on logical theories which are sound, that it governs society, that it is the product of ages of conscious thought consciously synthesized into a uniform system. The lawyer's attitude toward this voluminous literature is a mixture of condescension and respect. In private he is condescending and advises his son to stay away from courses labeled jurisprudence, because such intricacies form no part of a busy and successful life devoted to the law. Publicly he acknowledges the great need for more of such courses to give a broader viewpoint. He therefore sends his son to a law school which offers courses on jurisprudence on the theory that such courses have a good effect on the professors, and therefore in a general way make the school better. His attitude is like the attitude of the nonchurchgoer toward the church, or like the attitude of the tired business man toward the opera.

For the educator, jurisprudence is one of the things which makes the law learned, and thus distinguishes the law school from a mere trade school.

For the jurist, involved in the enormous literature of his subject, the vital part of jurisprudence is removed farther into something which has not yet been written. He cannot deny the relevancy of ideals which are inconsistent with a rational explanation or theory of the law. Yet he has the very sound instinctive feeling that such realism is destructive of the moral sanction of the institution itself. He therefore regards the real jurisprudence as the work of men yet to appear upon the stage, who will synthesize the fundamental principle of a somewhat confused present. No one has better expressed this idea than Dean Pound.

In many ways the present state of the legal order throughout the world suggests the sixteenth and seventeenth centuries. There is the same groping for new ideas and ideals. There is the same failure of authority with nothing as yet discovered to take its place. There is the same resort to personal justice, administrative tribunals, and sometimes crude individualized methods. There is the same chafing, on the one hand, at rule and form and, on the other hand, at a loose and unlimited judicial process.

As the strict law gave us rule and form as a means to certainty and uniformity in the granting and applying of legal remedies, as equity and natural law gave us the idea of making conduct certain by insistence on reason and good faith, the nineteenth century gave us the system of individual legal rights as a means toward security, an end toward which the other means had been reaching. Thus each stage in the development of the modern legal order has left some permanent contribution, to which we have added others without losing them. *What the stage on which we seem to have entered will bring forth, it would be useless to conjecture. But we need not doubt that it will build on these achievements of the past.*[4]

We may finally define jurisprudence as the shining but unfulfilled dream of a world governed by reason. For some it lies buried in a system, the details of which they do not know. For some, familiar with the details of the system, it lies in the depth of an unread literature. For

4. Roscoe Pound, "Law and the Science of Law in Recent Theories," 43 *Yale L.J.* 535, 536.

others, familiar with this literature, it lies in the hope of a future enlightenment. For all, it is just around the corner.

An Analogy between Law and Theology

THEOLOGY and jurisprudence are compelled to face the same logical contradiction. Just as jurisprudence today is the ultimate justification of the ideal of a rule of law above men, so the theology of yesterday was the ultimate justification of a rule of a moral and logical god above men and even above governments. If an omnipotent God really rules the world in a rational and moral way, how are we to account for so much disobedience of his mandates? If the law really directs society, how are we to account for its failure to direct in the practical world and in the ordinary lawsuit? Of course it can be done by a mystical act of faith. But just as the Protestant Church abandoned the mystical basis of religion and sought a rational basis for its creed, so the common law repudiated the notion that there was a divine right behind its decrees. In a remark which echoed down the ages and became a slogan for modern constitutional government, Coke informed King James that there was a law above the king, based on a special kind of reasoning which was different from ordinary reasoning. The attitude expressed in this famous saying is at the foundation of both jurisprudence and theology as rational bases for a moral and logical world. Both are the results of a craving for a moral order, logically supported, which we have described as rational moral thinking.

A comparison of the law of today and theology of yesterday brings into startling relief the fact that once we take a rational and moral attitude toward any human institution our thinking runs along the same grooves and is complicated by the same logical and moral conflicts. These conflicts are reconciled by the same logical devices in both law and theology. The names may be different, the style of writing dissimilar, but the literature which is produced bears the same pattern. Where institutions are based on mystical faith they are dramatized by ceremonies which bear a marked similarity all over the world, from primitive to modern times, marked by reverence, color, peculiar dress, and parades. When mystical ceremony is abandoned for a rational basis of governmental institutions there is even less variety because more permutations and combinations are possible in color, design, and parade formation than in ideas. Thus the rationalizing of institutions throughout the ages is a constant repetition of the same naïve concepts appearing under different names.

The fundamental ideal of moral government is that the good should be rewarded and the wicked punished. Sometimes it is the wise or shrewd who are supposed to be rewarded and the negligent or foolish who are to be punished if the ideal operates in a commercial field, but the central logical scheme is the same. Bishop Butler, the great logician of protestant theology, writing in the eighteenth century, expressed this underlying notion of our moral and rational attitude in a chapter on the moral government of God. He said:

Moral government consists not barely in rewarding and punishing men for their actions, which the most tyrannical person may do; but in rewarding the righteous and punishing the wicked; in rendering to men according to their actions considered as good or evil. And the perfection of moral government consists in doing this with regard to all intelligent creatures in exact proportion to their merits and demerits.[5]

Such is the central ideal. What are its conflicts? The first logical struggle is with those notions of benevolence, com-

5. Joseph Butler, *The Analogy of Religion, Natural and Revealed, to the Constitution and Course of Nature* (20th ed., 1864).

mon sense, and compromise, which no one can escape except in his more solemn moments. Butler is aware of the difficulty. He points out that it is of course possible to conceive of the government of God as one dedicated to the benevolent notion of providing for everyone the greatest possible happiness, regardless of his deserts. Yet, answers Butler conclusively, this cannot be a right conception of the government of God because it would be immoral to imagine God not moved by moral considerations and illogical to conceive him not following logic. It is the same answer which is used to quiet those who advocate pure benevolence in the law today. It is illogical to conceive of the law as illogical. The ancient maxim "hard cases make bad law" is simply a way of saying that if judges are permitted to use their common sense and follow their benevolent impulses, law would not be moral and logical.

Even with this defense, benevolent and practical considerations continue their constant interference with orderly logic. A new argument is required. Therefore much of the vast literature both of law and theology is devoted to showing that more benevolent results in the long run are achieved by refusing to consider benevolent principles in particular cases. The argument is repeated over and over again as different problems arise. In the early days of the dole it was conclusively proved that fewer people would go hungry in the long run if we refused to feed the unemployed. The development of character in the unemployed through hardship and competition would automatically care for more of them in the long run than would the dole. Most people implicitly believe in this form of argument. A worry about the ruin of the human race because it is gradually getting into a position where more people can be comfortable with less work has been the constant obsession of the moral men of this generation.

In this way, in both law and theology, we prove that

moral and logical principles are the only moral and logical solution, and that in the long run they produce more kindly results than actual day-to-day kindness could ever accomplish. However, since the whole idea is psychological, since there is no truth in the notion that man develops anything other than cruelty and rapacity by being constantly forced to fight his fellow men for an existence, the humanitarian ideas still keep rising up to trouble the calm serenity of moral and logical law or theology. It finally becomes necessary to give these benevolent and practical ideas representation in the system. The only way to do this is to isolate them in separate institutions where benevolent and common-sense ideas can be dramatized without interfering with the stern and inevitable logic of the law, or of the logical government of God. In theology a separate personality known as the Redeemer appeared to represent benevolence, and thus enabled God to escape from the logic of punishment for sin. Law has in a like manner set up a series of separate institutions to represent common sense and benevolence. There were first the courts of equity, which did not interfere with the law, but enjoined the litigant from enforcing it if it were unjust or impractical. Later came the administrative tribunals and governmental bureaus, which are an affront to the stern morals of the law but nevertheless a useful method of getting things done unhampered by its complications. The existence of these separate institutions is justified by a complicated literature which explains why a merciful father had to sacrifice his son in order to be merciful, and why a court of law had to be checked and enjoined by a court of equity. Such a literature continues to grow and expand so long as men require a moral and logical ideal to satisfy their sense of symmetry, and a humanitarian and practical ideal to satisfy their impulses toward mercy and common sense.

A mystical person who took the whole idea of supremacy

of the law on faith might combine both of these ideals into one institution. The logical person must go through a more complicated process. First he must separate them so that they do not obviously conflict. Then he must put them together again to prove the law is a unit. This tendency to separate the two ideals and then to combine them produces most complicated results. We find, for example, the Lord and the Redeemer separated, and then combined and then separated again in different creeds. We find separate courts of law and equity, faced with the bombardment of enraged rationalists who thunder the query, "How is it possible that a court of law needs to be supplemented by a court of justice?" Since we cannot conveniently answer this query the Code reform appears, and the distinction between courts of law and courts of equity is abolished. Yet the emotional need for a government which is moral and rational on the one hand, and benevolent and merciful on the other, still persists. Therefore the distinction is no sooner abolished than there arise those who say with profound conviction and eloquence that the distinction between law and equity can never be abolished because it exists back in the nature of things, and truth crushed to earth must necessarily rise again. As a matter of procedure, these people point out these two separate things may now be administered by one court but their separateness must be maintained by all judges who desire to preserve the sanctity of the law.

The confusion which has arisen is not the result of the stupidity of judges, as many contend, but the result of attempting to combine two conflicting symbols into one institution in a climate of opinion which demanded their separation. It is not difficult to tell the difference between law and equity when they are housed in separate buildings because they can be defined by describing the building. When they issue from the same desk, the only way of establishing the distinction is by the rational process. But the distinction is inherently irrational. It neither arose, nor did it persist, because of the deliberate reasoning of thinking men. Thus, for example, the task of keeping these two emotional attitudes apart in New York has led to a code of civil procedure which is the most peculiarly involved and incomprehensible body of supposedly logical doctrine that the literature of the law has yet produced. A never-ending conflict of arguments keeps going on because of the never-ending conflict between the ideals of a moral and benevolent government.

The only way to end this argument is to stop thinking and talking about it, as has indeed occurred in the field of religion. There are signs today that this is happening in the case of law and equity. Nevertheless the same conflict of ideas appears on another battleground. Law and equity have been joined together and we have become used to the notion. But the idea of law as a logical, certain, and moral body of rules still persists. Therefore when we wish to become practical we must create a separate tribunal. The court of equity is gone, but with its disappearance arises the administrative or quasi-judicial court endowed with the freedom of action which the old court of equity had. Huge treatises are now appearing showing the compatibility of administrative justice with the law. Just as theology was not able to exist without a Redeemer, so the "law" must have its equity or its administrative law in order to save mankind from the consequences of its logical systems.

Thus the great dialectic struggle to separate morals and reason from benevolence and practicality and then to bind them together rationally goes on. Both in law and theology we explain it in the same way. Equity or its equivalent must aid the law, not because "law" is imperfect but because the human mind, with its unfortunate capacity for sin, perverts the true logic so that some sort of intervention is necessary to set it back on its proper course. Though this has been reiterated over and over again by both jurists and theologians in their separate spheres, no better explanation has been given than is found in Butler's *Analogy,* written in the very midst of the age of reason, the eighteenth century, and representing the same method of thought which is the basis of the science of jurisprudence.

But the dialectical troubles of theology or jurisprudence are not over when they have set up separate institutions to represent logical and humanitarian ideals. The problem of reconciling those institutions immediately confronts the priest. It becomes obvious to the ordinary man that something is wrong. In an age of pure faith he may be told that the ways of Providence are beyond human understanding, and therefore he should drown his doubt in simple reverence. But in an age of reason a rational explanation must appear from somewhere. And it is at this point that the most curious phenomenon of rational thought occurs. Thinking men, unable to reason the thing out, simply throw up their hands and pretend that it has been reasoned out by someone else. This requires an act of faith which is more complicated than a belief in the mysterious acts of Providence. The attitude is that of the executive who does not pretend to know certain aspects of his business, but has them all collected by experts ready for consultation in his files if he ever needs them. He does not know the rational explanation of certain problems, but he knows where it can be found if he ever has time to give it sufficient study.

Here we find jurisprudence, in its higher and more rarefied form, as the unifying element in the apparently inconsistent institutions of the law. When it is examined carefully it explains nothing. It is found to be a compendium of all of the generally accepted ideas of the man on the street, woven together in such a way that it is almost impossible to read. This unintelligibility is the element that makes it work. The mass of verbiage is so impossible to read that a mere reference to it is sufficient to confound the superficial person who questions the underlying unity of the law. It therefore continues as a unifying force until the institution no longer needs it.

This final end of all attempts to explain the world on moral and rational grounds is the same in every religion, and in every judicial system which rests on reason instead of ceremony. Faith in reason compels reasoning man ultimately to pin his faith on a mass of literature so complicated that he cannot see its contradictions. The unifying element of the inconsistent institutions which rise out of the attempt to make the world logical and symmetrical must therefore be completely unintelligible. In theology this element was for some the Holy Ghost, an idea which no one ever quite grasped. For others it was the mere existence of the vast theological literature which filled the shelves of the eminent divines. The conception of the Holy Ghost and the intricacies of the general literature took the place for theology which the science of jurisprudence takes today for the law.

Thus the great literature of the theology of yesterday is astonishingly like the great literature of the law today, both in style and content. There are almost one hundred law reviews in the United States today filled with unpaid for and unread articles. In the same way in the last century the presses of the day were flooded with books of sermons and theological reasoning, like the modern law reviews devoted to the patient exploration of argumentative possibilities. The ordinary practicing preacher who read these tracts was almost as unknown as is the lawyer today who reads the law reviews. However, the tracts were handy for the writing of sermons, just as the law review today may be handy for the writing of briefs. Today these tracts are completely forgotten. Most of them are not even preserved in libraries. Yet if anyone takes the trouble to peruse them he will be astonished to find how similar is their tone and content to that of the modern law review.

The very names of the treatises sound like modern legal textbooks. For example, *Bush on the Resurrection;*[6] Noble's *Plenary Inspiration;*[7] Perkens, *Cases on Conscience;*[8] McCosh, *Method of the Divine Government;*[9] Wits, *Economy of the Covenants.*[10] If one opens these works, he finds them divided like a brief into headings and subheadings, with proper footnotes and citations of authorities. And even more interesting is the fact that there is scarcely a dialectic problem which is discussed in the modern law school of which one does not find at least a hint in the argumentative technique of the theology of the last century. The recurrent idea in most Western systems of jurisprudence that there is a constitution above the ordinary law is matched by the very definite idea that there is a law or set of principles even above God. For not even God himself could change the law which required man to be punished for his sins. Therefore the forgiveness of sins must be accomplished by a very elaborate indirection, by setting up an illogical institution alongside of a logical one, and reconciling the two logically. There is a constitution, and a plan above God, which is the only plan God could have made, since it is the best plan, and God is capable of following only the best plan, even though he has infinite free will. It is the best plan which was ever struck off by any religion, just as our Constitution is the greatest document ever struck off by the mind or pen of man.

The writer has elsewhere[11] set out the similarities, even

6. New York, Wiley & Putnam, 1845.

7. Cincinnati, The Book Committee of the Western Convention (of the Episcopal Church), 1839.

8. London, Legatt, 1639.

9. New York, R. Carter & Bros., 1880.

10. New York, Forman, 1798.

11. Thurman W. Arnold, "Apologia for Jurisprudence," 44 *Yale L.J.* 729.

with respect to minor doctrine, between law and jurisprudence in much more detail than is possible here. Suffice it to say that the same rational moral attitude toward the details of procedure produced the same results as it did in the explanation of broad generalities. Even the conception of pleading of our present judicial system was duplicated in the church of fifty years ago. Today there is a struggle between those who favor informal pleadings in litigation and those who are sticklers for correct technical form. The same struggle raged between the Episcopalians with their liturgy and the Presbyterians with their informal prayer. Tracts were written about the correct way to present petitions to the Deity which contain most of the *legalisms* of the lawbooks of today on the correct form of petitions to a court. The eternal question as to whether or not a defect in a pleading is "jurisdictional" (that is, such a defect as makes the paper no pleading at all) was argued in discussing whether defects in prayers were mere matters of form, or whether they eliminated some element so vital that they were not prayers at all.

Rational theology has become one of the forgotten arts. The questions which eager seekers after the truth used to ask of the ecclesiastical pedagogues have not been answered, but they are no longer asked. The vast literature which formed such an imposing rational façade to the Protestant faith is falling into ruins through neglect and disuse. More purely humanitarian and benevolent attitudes seem to prevail. Preachers are rated according to the ability to organize and to exhort, rather than on the closeness of their reasoning. A separate science of theology in the most modern seminaries has not the importance which it once had.

The science of jurisprudence today is going through somewhat the same struggle which the church experienced when it was shaken by the realism of the modernists. In the church that controversy was never decided. Men simply ceased to worry about it. It may be that men will simply cease to worry about jurisprudence. However, one desiring to indulge in prediction along this line should not forget that the heat of dialectic argument in the church did not die down until the church had lost most of its importance as a governing force. Before the American Revolution the church was also the repository of the law, and its power over local government was always felt. Later it had in its peculiar charge that most important institution, the college. Losing this, it still was preëminent in the field of charity. Today it occupies a rather precarious place in our social life. Interest in its theology has died down as the activities of the institution itself have become narrowed.

A similar result in law, however, seems unlikely unless the judicial system is to lose its prestige, or unless the faculty of "reason" is to take a less important place in the hierarchy of ideals. So long as our belief in rational moral government depends upon the law, it must continue to balance logically the contradictory ideals which that government must express. In a climate of opinion where the ultimate appeal is to reason, the constant succession of ideological contradictions developed by reason when applied to practical problems can only be settled by the application of a higher reason. The result is jurisprudence.

In the science of jurisprudence all of the various ideals which are significant to the man on the street must be given a place. It must prove that the law is certain and at the same time elastic; that it is just, yet benevolent; economically sound, yet morally logical. It must show that the law can be dignified and solemn, and at the same time efficient, universal and fundamental, and a set of particular directions. Jurisprudence must give a place to all of the economic, and also the ethical, notions of important competing groups within our society, no matter how far apart these notions may be. In its method it must make gestures of recognition to the techniques of each separate branch of learning which claims to have any relation with the conduct of individuals, no matter how different these techniques may be.

Such a task can only be accomplished by ceremony, and hence the writings of jurisprudence should be considered as ceremonial observances rather than as scientific observations. This is shown by the fact that the literature of jurisprudence performs its social task most effectively for those who encourage it, praise it, but do not read it. For those who study it today it is nothing but a troubling mass of conflicting ideas. However, it is not generally read, so that its troubles are known only to the few people who read it for the purpose of writing more of it. For most of those who reverence the law the knowledge that there is a constant search going on for logical principles is sufficient.

The observations in this chapter on the function and effect of the mystical science of jurisprudence have an application which goes beyond present-day legal institutions. They are important as an example of the way rational thought is always compelled to retire into an unintelligible and abstract literature in order to reconcile finally the conflicting ideals which it must represent. The reasoning process is a very limited one. There are only a few avenues which it can take, and they are astonishingly similar. And when man seeks to establish a moral government on this earth by rational means, the literature which he builds up in the attempt, whether it be ecclesiastical, metaphysical, ethical, or legal, always comes out in the same pattern, and with the same concepts. There is comfort in such a literature, but there is no progress and no discovery.[12]

12. "Hippocrates left medicine free, but Galen fettered it with hypotheses. Hippocrates related his failures, and used to say, 'I do not know,' but Galen always imitated an oracle. 'Science and Faith,' said Hippocrates, 'are two things: the first begets knowledge, the second ignorance'; but Galen sought to mix the observations of Hippocrates with the metaphysics of Plato. Galen

Such ideas complicate beyond belief the institutions to which they are attached. Yet there seems to be no escape from them for an incurably romantic human race. The student of government needs to understand that while the presence of the ideal element in law is a confusing factor, its omission leads to a spiritually unstable institution, backed by the harsh exercise of power, lacking that permanence and strength which come from unquestioning public acceptance.

abhorred doubt; his mind craved for finalities. Galen admired Euclid's method of proving things, and he tried to make medicine as exact a science as geometry; it is difficult to decide which was the greater—the absurdity or the audacity of the attempt. In his system everything was explained; everything was catalogued and tabulated. He answered all questions, he solved all problems. There seemed nothing left for others to do except to say, Amen. And so it was. Galen was the last of the Greeks and when he spoke no more, the voice of the ancient world was hushed. Galen was the final star that shone in the twilight of antiquity, and when his effulgence was extinguished, there settled over Europe a darkness that was not lifted for many centuries" (Victor Robinson, *op. cit.,* p. 133).

CHAPTER IV

Economics and the Law

ECONOMICS represents an attitude toward social conduct which is like jurisprudence in that it strives to be logical and orderly and to reconcile inconsistent institutions and conflicting ideals. Like jurisprudence, it furnishes faiths and slogans most effectively to those who never thoughtfully read its literature, while it raises only doubts and confusion for those who do. Karl Marx and Adam Smith both give a feeling of scientific certainty to different groups who know them only as names. In the various daily conflicts about governmental policy—whether it be protection vs. free trade, sound money vs. inflation, budget-balancing vs. governmental spending in a depression—editorial writers and financial preachers, generally, could not talk on both sides with the positiveness of an engineer who is dealing with blueprints were it not for their belief that economics is a body of scientific fact. Without that belief the present type of political speeches and editorials would be impossible. The entire flavor of political campaigns would change.

Economics is unlike jurisprudence, however, in that it attempts to exclude the moral element. Here is a science which is above Morality, where ethical good may even be an economic evil. Economics assumes fundamental rules of cause and effect which are physical limitations on the power of man-made law to achieve social justice. It makes that philosophy palatable by proving that the maximum social justice can only arise out of the unfettered operation of human selfishness. These is complete agreement that man cannot change the economic laws of nature together with complete disagreement as to what particular things cannot be changed. However, by and large, it is assumed that since most established practices must be the result of economic cause and effect, therefore most established practices cannot be changed. Economics, therefore, becomes the philosophical justification of the temporal world of affairs as distinguished from the spiritual world of law and morals.

In the Middle Ages the temporal world needed no dialectic explanation. It was the unfortunate result of man's first disobedience, and was trivial compared with the eternity of a future life which lay beyond. The commercial conduct of the temporal world occupied a place not unlike the place which politics occupies today. Everyone was vaguely aware that it was a necessary pursuit, but it was not one in which the highest type of man would care to indulge. Hence the Jew came to be representative of the merchant and moneylender, performing his function under the constant attack of the better elements of society. Laws were passed against lending money at interest, just as laws are passed today to eliminate the very necessary functions of the political machine. And like the political machine, the moneylending went on as before, but under the handicap of social disapproval, and without justifying symbols or creeds.

The science of economics rose with a merchant class which demanded its place in the sun. As the comforts of the present world increased, the future life became less important and the church, the chief custodian of the blessings of that life, lost its influence. Reason displaced mysticism and the law became the great repository of the symbols of government. Yet the law did not entirely explain the competitive struggle of commercial interests. Its ideals were too high. A large part of its reasoning was devoted to proving that it should not interfere with the details of commercial competition. Hence a philosophy was needed to justify the disorderly struggle of a commercial class which insisted on respectability and prestige. This philosophy was required to justify a selfish struggle for money and power by a class which refused to submit to regulation in terms of ethical ideals. Therefore the philosophy of economics was created to show how unhampered selfishness, on the part of competing groups, was productive of the greatest good in the long run. The fundamental laws of economics were invented to prove that the greatest good to the world comes from the unimpeded competitive activities of enlightened greed. A man who would work only for profit was postulated as the typical human being, and a complicated theory showing how this selfishness was the real cause of all our temporal blessings was painstakingly built up. That theory today supplements the law as one of our most important symbols of government.

The place given to the activities of the business world in our philosophy and thinking about government is different from the place given to politics. Business is not considered a necessary evil, but a source of the highest good. Therefore it must appear to be orderly and rational in order to maintain its prestige. However, when we look at actual business control it ceases to appear orderly and rational. From the point of view even of conventional legal and economic ideals it often resembles a sort of anarchy. The examination of almost any field of industrial activity leads to uncomfortable conclusions. For example, we quote from Walton Hamilton, writing about the coal industry in 1925, long before the depression brought to light similar situations in almost all lines of industrial endeavor.

So the Man from Neptune seems to catch a vision of the great confusion in which the industry is caught. He sees a clash of vested interests in which operators, mine-workers, and consumers alike refuse to surrender current advantages for the greater promises of a nebulous afterwhile. He sees an array of vested rights compelling individuals to do as they will with their own even though their blind doings return to plague their authors.

He sees the chance of action by all concerned with coal pent in by the laws of the land which make a unified direction of the industry impossible. He sees a bewildering ignorance of the larger situation and a confusing abundance of fearless and ill-informed advice. He sees an inertia which rejects the new for the reason that it is the new, and clings blindly to the old because it is the customary. And, permeating it all, as the creator and the created of all the rest, he discovers the strange notions, the obsolete thoughts, the confused ideas which thwart vision, promote disorder, and hold a chaotic industry as in a vise. He wonders if it can be that vested chaos, like established order, creates in men's minds a defensive scheme of thought which makes its overthrow impossible.[1]

Such situations have to be rationally and scientifically explained. If the disorder can be attributed to persons whom we are accustomed to call politicians, we can resolve the mental conflict simply by preaching against politicians. If, however, the responsibility for the disorder is on persons called business leaders, we are faced with the necessity of showing that what appears to be anarchy is really the most efficient way of obtaining order in the long run. The "law" as a system of control is therefore conceived to be limited by fundamental principles which are above even the law, called economic principles. Economic theories prove that what appears to be anarchy is not really anarchy at all, but a system of control by natural forces which the law may guide and drive, but must not distort. People who produce ethically irrefutable arguments that the law should do more than it does in controlling human activities can thus be told that their ideas, while in accord with the general aims of the law to promote social justice, are nevertheless economically unsound.

The truthful and practical answer to the reformer usually is that his particular reform, because of the existence of cer-

1. Walton Hamilton, *The Case of Bituminous Coal* (1925), p. 255.

tain vested interests and sentimental ideals, is politically impossible. Such an answer, however, satisfies neither the reformer nor the defenders of the system. For the reformer, it is only an incentive to further activity. For the defender of the system, it offers no formula which allows him to live at peace with his conscience. It makes him look like a politician, and not like a public benefactor. Hence arises the necessity for an abstract science of economics in order to explain the practical limitations of another abstract science called law. These two sciences are absolutely essential to each other. Without the one, the other would not exist as a separate branch of learning. The law could not dramatize great moral and humanitarian ideals unless there were an explanation in the background, based on something higher than mere political or practical reasons, as to why these moral and humanitarian ideals cannot be followed.

General ethical and humane ideals with which most people agree but which happen to be politically impossible because of the conflict which the operation of those ideals would have upon vested interests and accepted symbols, are usually called socialism. It is the business of economics to prove that these ideals would be opposed to the general good, *even if they were politically feasible,* because the political obstacles are not temporary things, but fundamental in human organization. It is further the business of economics to explain the refusal of the law to enforce its ideals in business affairs.

Thus the separate sciences of law and economics have been essential in a rational society to preserve the faiths which we have had in our forms of social organization. Much talk there used to be about the union of law and economics, by persons who had discovered that these sciences dealt with the same phenomena. Yet this union was always sterile in times when affairs were running well, and faith in government ran high. Today, when economic symbols are distrusted, and when the great principles of the law do not appear to be the guide they once were, law and economics are getting inextricably tangled up. The result of this union of legal and social sciences, curiously enough, is to create a lack of faith in either, and thus to make government meaningless and without an orderly philosophy. The reasons for this lie back in a series of mental pictures in the mind of the ordinary man on the street which must be examined in order to understand either law or economics.

The Abstract Man behind Theory

LEGAL and economic theories maintain their consistency by relating themselves, not to actual men, but to an abstract man, who represents men as they ought to be. These theories are tested not by comparison with reality but by checking them up with the abstract man behind them. Every *separate* science which deals with human beings must have a generalized conception of what the average human being is like, in order to keep its identity and separation from other sciences dealing with the same subject matter. Even medicine has had to base itself on the conception of a body as mechanically constructed as an automobile in order to justify a system of therapeutics which ascribes all disease to a physical cause. Psychiatry on the other hand introduced the idea of an abstract man with a subconscious mind. In the same way, law, since it was a moral and logical science, had to be based on an abstract man who needed to be preached to in order to save him from sin. He is capable of being trained by judicial parables and statutory exhortation. The economic man on the other hand, since he is invented to explain why moral and humanitarian ideas cannot be pushed too far, is an automatic fellow. All he needs is intelligent selfishness, and under the great economic principles, his sins will all cancel each other, and everything will work out for the best. He doesn't need to be preached to. He doesn't even need to understand the economic principles, since he can't help following them. All that he needs to do is to follow his self-interest intelligently. If he does not do so, it makes no difference whether the reason is temporary greed, or lofty humanitarianism—the result is the same. Economic law is violated, and disaster results. In broad general outline, the economic man is an automaton, who needs only to be wound up and set going. The legal man is a sinner who must constantly be exhorted, and subjected to the influence of ideals hung just in front of his nose.

The institutional effects of this conception of the abstract sinner behind the law are most important. It shows itself in the ponderous preaching technique so characteristic of all judicial utterance. Preaching consists of an elaboration of ideas usually accepted as obvious, a consistent repetition of simple texts. For example, when the Supreme Court of the United States wants to decide whether tomatoes are a fruit or a vegetable they must be solemn and pontifical, and not shrewd and practical. Note the atmosphere of the following opinion:

Mr. Justice Gray, after stating the case, delivered the opinion of the court.

The single question in this case is whether tomatoes, considered as provisions, are to be classed as "vegetables" or as "fruit," within the meaning of the Tariff Act of 1883.

The only witnesses called at the trial testified that neither "vegetables" nor "fruit" had any special meaning in trade or commerce, different from that given in the dictionaries; and that they had the same meaning in trade to-day that they had in March, 1883.

The passages cited from the dictionaries define the word "fruit" as the seed of plants, or that part of plants which contains the seed, and especially the juicy, pulpy products of certain plants, covering and containing the seed. These definitions have no tendency to show that tomatoes are "fruit," as distinguished from "vegetables," in common speech, or within the meaning of the Tariff Act.

There being no evidence that the words "fruit" and "vegetables" have acquired any special meaning in trade or commerce, they must receive their ordinary meaning. Of that meaning the court is bound to take judicial notice, as it does in regard to all words in our own tongue; and upon such a question dictionaries are admitted, not as evidence, but only as aids to the memory and understanding of the court. Brown v. Piper, 91 U.S. 37, 42; Jones v. United States, 137 U.S. 202, 216; Nelson v. Cushing, 2 Cush. 519, 532, 533; Page v. Fawcet, 1 Leon. 242; Taylor on Evidence, (8th ed.) secs. 16, 21.

Botanically speaking, tomatoes are the fruit of a vine, just as are cucumbers, squashes, beans and peas. But in the common language of the people, whether sellers or consumers of provisions, all these are vegetables, which are grown in kitchen gardens, and which, whether eaten cooked or raw, are, like potatoes, carrots, parsnips, turnips, beets, cauliflower, cabbage, celery and lettuce, usually served at dinner in, with or after the soup, fish or meats which constitute the principal part of the repast, and not, like fruits generally, as dessert.

The attempt to class tomatoes with fruit is not unlike a recent attempt to class beans as seeds, of which Mr. Justice Bradley, speaking for this court, said: "We do not see why they should be classified as seeds, any more than walnuts should be so classified. Both are seeds in the language of botany or natural history, but not in commerce nor in common parlance. On the other hand, in speaking generally of provisions, beans may well be included under the term 'vegetables.' As an article of food on our tables, whether baked or boiled, or forming the basis of soup, they are used as a vegetable, as well when ripe as when green. This is the principal use to which they are put. Beyond the common knowledge which we have on this subject, very little evidence is necessary, or can be produced." Robertson v. Salomon, 130 U.S. 412, 414.

Judgment affirmed.[2]

2. *Nix* vs. *Heddon*, 149 U.S. 304, 13 *Sup. Ct.* 881 (1893).

The case is old but to show that the attitude is still with us we quote a footnote to the case appearing in the most recent case book on evidence in use in our law schools.[3]

1. Commonwealth v. Marzynski, 149 Mass. 68, 72, 21 N.E. 228 (1889): "Cigars are manufactured articles familiar to everybody. The materials of which they are composed are carefully prepared and put into form, until they lose their original character as mere materials, and become articles of commerce, known by a new name and adapted to a particular use. We are of the opinion that cigars sold by a tobacconist in the ordinary way are not drugs or medicines, within the meaning of these words as used in the statute."

Back of such an opinion, which is fairly typical in so far as it illustrates a tendency of courts to belabor simple and undefinable notions with elaborate definition supported by learning, is the assumption of a man who constantly needs definition in order to obtain peace and certainty. Before the opinion, this man was in doubt about what a tomato was. Now he knows, and has the further advantage of a general guide in his struggle to differentiate between other fruits and vegetables. The great forces of government are here assisting him in the solution of his most detailed problems. A mere administrative tribunal might have decided the particular case without an opinion, but the Court refused to consider the problem without offering a guide to future conduct when similar problems arose, because the legal man is apt to flounder in confusion without such a guide.

The Legal vs. the Economic Man

THE economic man needs no such guide. If a problem is regarded as coming within the area of economics, the law should keep its hampering principles out of the picture. Economic man needs no such governmental instruction in

3. Morgan and Maguire, *Cases on Evidence* (1934).

order to make his conduct conform to economic law, any more than falling bodies need regulations to show them how to fall. Nothing but catastrophe awaits the legal system which attempts to gild the economic lily.

The economic man customarily operates in larger affairs, and the legal man in minor ones. Indeed the economic man is the chief justification for the failure of the law to define, plan, or interfere with matters which have a broad general scope. If the law attempts to plan such matters, it is doomed to failure because the economic man will automatically refuse to follow such plans of control. Even experiment in the economic field is undesirable. We cite in illustration a typical reaction of an economist.

From the pages of history Dr. Gus W. Dyer, professor of economics at Vanderbilt University and editor of the Southern Agriculturist, today drew the prediction that the New Deal is doomed to failure.

Dr. Dyer spoke at the opening of the two day convention of the Council of American industry at the Palmer House, which is meeting for the purpose of checking the effects of the labor section of the N.R.A., the rulings of the National Labor Board, the appraising of the substitute for the Wagner labor bill passed during the closing days of Congress, and to seek ways and means to promote peace in industry.

The policy of governmental restraint and direction of business, as exemplified in the New Deal, is a very old policy, Dr. Dyer said. He traced trials of the system in France and Germany in the seventeenth and eighteenth centuries and in England in the nineteenth century to their collapse.

Under the experiment in France, many of the principles of the New Deal were established, Dr. Dyer said. He pointed to holding gold, keeping grain prices up by law, stimulation of agriculture, establishment of banks to help business, establishment of land banks, increase in money supply and the adoption of a policy to sell as much as possible abroad and buy as little as possible.

"The independent laborers suffered through unfair competition of labor taken care of by the government," Dr. Dyer said. "The state exercised over manufacturers and industry the most unlimited and arbitrary jurisdiction. It was decided who should be allowed to work and what they could make."

This policy in France resulted in an increase in debts, taxes became heavy and burdensome, land values fell, the state was forced to borrow heavily and the state treasury was exhausted. Dr. Dyer suggested that New Dealers study this failure of their system in France.

The speaker also drew parallels from history to "the dream of those in charge of the Tennessee Valley project," stating that only those ignorant of the history of Utopias are under a hallucination that this is a new experiment.

"It may be that David Lilienthal, T.V.A. administrator, who is the prophet, interpreter and director of this new social dream, got his inspiration from his Hebrew ancestors who were wont to sigh of a land flowing with milk and honey," Dr. Dyer said.

He traced the history of the model colony founded in Indiana in 1824 by Robert Owen under the name of New Harmony: Fourierism, a social order sponsored by Horace Greeley and others in 1841, and another experiment, the new Ruskin School in Tennessee, in 1894.

"All these movements had their brain trusts," Dr. Dyer said. "It would seem that the brain trust is almost an essential feature in these movements in order that their quick failure may be guaranteed.

"The Tennessee Valley experiment is new only in one sense. That is that it is the first time that the taxpayers' money has been taken without his consent to finance the movement. It is a dream that has always walked and talked and danced and pranced in a spectacular way to bankruptcy and failure" (*Chicago Tribune,* June 25, 1934).

Here we have the economic man in operation. Note that formulated rules lead at the same time to oligarchy, fascism, and socialism, any one of which may keep us under its iron heel for centuries if it once gets started. Yet, at the same time, these rules will be such a failure that the project they are to govern will never really get started at all. Such is the penalty for violating the fundamental economic law against interfering with the natural order which governs economic automatons.

Turn from college economists to the *Saturday Evening Post* and we find the same attitudes expressed in the same way. They represent a blind faith in leaving things alone— a faith which can never be refuted because leaving things alone is the one alternative which mankind will never try. For example:

Since time immemorial autocrats and dictators have resorted to wage fixing. It has its lure too, as an immediate and humanitarian measure. But is it economically sound? It was designed to raise real wages,—that is, not wages in the terms of currency but to their power to buy more goods. All past experience has demonstrated that raising real wages by fixing nominal wages is like making a river flow upstream. It is the nature of profit to pass the increased wage to the consumer. Therefore it becomes necessary to try to restrict profits by fixing prices (*Saturday Evening Post,* June 30, 1934).

The author goes on to show that something called the Marxian creed is a product of Asiatic despotism, and that we are in grave danger of a return of Genghis Khan. He concludes:

The forces of history have given us but one choice. It is the choice between the Tartar State and the Anglo Saxon State, between cardboard villages and realities, between dictatorship and democracy. The former is paternalistic, the latter is free.

The same ideas are statistically expressed with great complication for those with a bent for figures. They are also philosophically expressed, for the consumption of the learned. Basically, however, the economists, orators, editors, and Rotarians are all saying the same thing, to wit, "Since our economic man is an automaton, it is wrong to interfere with his machinery."

In selecting illustrations we have purposely refrained from taking the more sophisticated examples of the juristic or economic art. We are not trying here to criticize economists or jurists, but attempting to illustrate the background of popular ideology which compels them to select certain symbols and ways of expression to make themselves intelligible. Some economists are able to write in the terms of the separate sciences of law and economics without being misled by that conceptual division. However, in most instances, the separate personalities of the abstract men of law and economics color our editorial writing, our law-review writing, and both our legal and economic opinions to such an extent that it is difficult for more objective writing to obtain an audience.

Turning back from the economic sphere to the judicial, we find that here the only solution is to constantly formulate and elaborate principles and directions. It never occurs to anyone as desirable that a judge should be free to work out situations practically, a freedom which we allow to arbitrators or even to administrative tribunals doing the same thing with a different attitude toward their task. Among lawyers, generally, short cuts to practical results are taken to indicate loose thinking. Disregard of procedural principles of a generalized character are supposed to lead to procedural anarchy. A suggestion that the situation be handled in a businesslike way without regard to form will seem to be an unjustifiable sacrifice of sound procedural principles to temporary convenience. The only method of reform permissible is by a general examination and restatement of general principles. It is regarded dangerous to allow the situation to work itself out without a constant attempt to formulate and clarify rules and directions.

The essence of this way of thinking is that the legal man is a born sinner who must be constantly guided by rules and inspired by principles. He can never be let alone. *Laissez faire* in this atmosphere is unthinkable. Trial courts are not to be trusted to use their common sense. Even appellate courts are not to be trusted to create their own procedure, because in that direction lies arbitrary and capricious action. They can only interpret and enforce the law. Everyone must be tied down in advance. Hardship must be accepted in particular cases because special exceptions wear away principles. The whole system must be as ponderous and learned as an old-fashioned sermon. Yet a similar attempt to restrict the bankers' decisions would smack of paternalism, socialism, or regimentation. It would be contrary to all of our best American traditions. Need we closely regulate the business situation, and struggle always for a better set of rules in spite of the tendency of human nature to pervert them? Again the answer is "No." For the banker, alive to his best interest, will work out the situation along the lines of free competition. Those bankers who fail to do this will automatically be forced to the wall. Those unfortunate persons who are forced to the wall with them will learn to trust only sound bankers. The only thing which we, as governors, need be watchful against is legislation which interferes with this admirable process. True, the present situation is far from solved from a social angle. But just as, when the matter is in court, the only thing to do is to perfect and elaborate the rules constantly, so, here, where the matter is not in court, the only thing to do is constantly to guard against the formulation of any rules whatever. Otherwise, paternalism, socialism, bureaucracy, regimentation, automatically follow.

Thus, these two abstract men, legal and economic, constantly appear operating in the same situation, deeply embedded in the unexamined assumptions of general popular thought. Clothe any situation with the atmosphere of the law, and it becomes our duty to formulate logical rules and systems. We achieve order and certainty—not now, but in the future—by this constant statement and restatement. On the other hand, clothe the same situation with a business or commercial atmosphere, and it becomes our duty to let it alone—to avoid artificial or man-made restrictions, to shun panaceas, to keep constantly in mind that every time man has attempted to control his destiny in an orderly manner he has failed. Social sin in the economic sciences consists of imposing rules to straighten out complicated situations. Social sin in the legal sciences consists in failing to work out logically a complicated set of rules.

In other words, just as the legal man is a sinner, the economic man is an automaton. All he has to do is to want things—which he cannot help doing. In getting those wants society will form itself. It will be led astray only by those who try to regulate. The legal man on the other hand is a born backslider. He constantly needs education. He must make laws, understand his man-made laws, and enforce them. This can be done only at the price of constant vigilance accompanied by profound learning.

The Sociological or Humanitarian Man

IT is obvious that these two ways of thinking about people in groups—one which assumes a man who must be constantly exhorted, and another which assumes a man who will operate to the best interest of everyone if only let alone—leave a whole set of ideals unrepresented and without a logical place in our organized learning and thinking. Such ideals as are left out of the picture may roughly be described as "humanitarian" and "practical." They are the ways of thinking found in philanthropy and business.

The thinking of social workers, businessmen, and politicians has been very difficult to formulate into abstract principles without making them too vague to deserve the name of a branch of learning. By this we mean that those who successfully deal with people in groups soon acquire a way of thinking which makes it almost impossible for them to write treatises on the principles of their craft. If one asks an economist how to run a government, he will have no difficulty in giving you a set of general principles. If you ask a businessman a similar question as to his function, he will look vague and puzzled until he finally comes out with some form of the slogan, "Work hard and be efficient." This is simply a confession that he has no definitely formulated principles which can be put into a book and studied. In the same way, if one asks a social worker or philanthropist the fundamental principles of their trade, they can only reply with an injunction to be as kindly as one can without making a fool of oneself.

In these branches of effort, business and philanthropy, there are many elaborate techniques to be mastered, but very few fundamental logical theories. Such fundamental theories as find expression, furthermore, are of the type which we call "inspirational." By this we mean that they are all right in their place, but must by no means be confused with learning or scholarship. Indeed, if a scholar, in economics or law, happens to get enthused about either humanitarian ideas or everyday practical ideas to such an extent that he begins to apply them to his own trade, he is immediately branded as a loose thinker by his brethren.

Yet, in spite of the difficulty of formulating humanitarian or practical ways of thinking, it has been necessary for scholars at least to try it. Modern education has come closer to life than the old education in which the classics predominated. Business and philanthropy demanded a place in our organized thought. In such matters names are of the utmost importance, and hence a new branch of learning called sociology, with its separate associations of professors, its separate departments, its separate classified literature, appeared during the course of the last half century.

The men who have been classified under this name have been a far more heterogeneous group than is found in either law or economics. There can scarcely be said to be any special form of training which makes one a sociologist. Nevertheless, our ways of thinking created a real emotional need for this new name. Something had to be done with philanthropists so that they would not interfere too much with legal or economic ways of thinking. Only by creating a separate logical area for them, and giving them at least a nominally separate task, could the lawyer comfortably ignore them. After this had been done, he could go about his own business and assume that intellectual problems which might otherwise have bothered him were being taken care of by the sociologist.

Necessarily, the way of sociology as an organized science has been difficult. Into this classification has been dumped everything that the law or economics found inconvenient to handle, since it was this very need for a general dumping ground which created the classification of sociology as a separate science. The sociologist did not have any particular abstract man whom he could postulate and on whom he could build a coördinated system. When he considered criminology (which is everything which concerns criminal law with which the criminal law refuses to deal), he came in contact with the legal man. When he studied such things as housing, and the care of the poor, he ran into the economic man. He was so close to the variegated, unclassifiable, tumbling stream of life that abstract formulas became very difficult indeed—and abstract formulas are the life of the social sciences so far as general scholarly acclaim is concerned.

Hence it became customary for sociologists to be regarded

with suspicion by their brethren in the law and in economics. Because they had no definite postulates, it was seriously questioned whether they were a branch of learning at all. Learning which touches life becomes confused, developing techniques rather than cast-iron theologies. Students, however, demand that they be given some concrete principles for their notebooks. They resent being asked to examine a living institution and think about it. This sort of pressure has led many sociologists to attempt to develop logically organized fundamentals. Some of them have fallen into queer ways. Methodology has been elaborated as an end in itself. Curious statistical studies have been carried on, because in statistics the mathematical mind can find peace. Yet, in the large, it can be said that the sociologist, in our American scheme of thought, has represented a sort of humanitarian man, intent to discover ways and means for the alleviation of human misery.

In more ancient days such troublesome problems were customarily referred to the church. Balanced against the injustice and suffering of this world the church postulated a future life where social, economic, and legal problems were reduced to a minimum. There was no emotional need for the logical solution of humanitarian problems in this world because they were all solved in the next. With the decline of the theological school, however, as a center of active intellectual interest, the vacuum in organized thinking about benevolent and humanitarian values had to be filled. As a result, that mysterious force which creates languages and common cultures (sometimes referred to as the "group mind") gave birth in our intellectual centers to a separate "science" of sociology.

The ways of thinking of the business world have, of late years, also demanded scholarly recognition. Business schools have become an accepted adjunct to great universities. Again, that way of thinking which demanded logical arrangement and preconceived fundamental principles, compelled the professors of the business habits of the time to call their subject a "science." The "science of business administration" has a congenial sound to the scholarly ear, and indicates that so far as possible it will avoid creating a mere "trade school." More freely translated it means that, in deference to scholarly thought, it will avoid studying business as it is, to study it as it ought to be, since the close examination of living institutions is the enemy of all logical classification. Yet the business-school professors were so close to life that the best ones refused to become sufficiently theoretical to avoid academic suspicion that they were tradesmen rather than scholars.

The school for the study of the science of practical politics has not as yet appeared over the horizon. In our thinking about politics we still are satisfied with preaching about a future life. We still think that we can educate a world so that politicians will no longer be influential in politics. We still think that we can tell the difference between a politician and a statesman. Social pressure will in the long run compel universities to study the world as it ought to be, and, therefore, until they recognize that there *ought* to be such things as political machinery, it is unlikely that they will deliberately educate young men in political techniques.

Relationship of Law and Economics in the Popular Picture of Society

THE relationship between law, economics, and sociology is one which is felt rather than defined. Indeed it is so clearly felt that there is little emotional need of defining the exact limits of these separate sciences. It is true that some students of jurisprudence have thought of economics as part of the law, but if so, as a separate and distinct part. There has also been a school of thinkers devoted to what they termed the economic interpretation of history; but this school had no doubt that the economic motive was a distinguishable factor in group thinking which could be separated from other factors and examined. Indeed the general consensus of opinion that there was a distinct difference between law, economics, and politics was so well accepted that few pondered on the difference between an economic and a political fact; just as few naturalists would be bothered to define the difference between a horse and a duck, since it is a difference which everyone should be able to recognize without definition.

The reason for the lack of necessity for defining or even thinking about the difference between law and economics was that the picture of society, in which these different sets of principles played a coördinate part, was fairly clear in the mind of the ordinary man. Intellectuals do not "think up" their own assumptions. They are compelled to use the popular assumptions which are at hand if they wish to be intelligible. Therefore, in order to understand the prevalent type of thinking about government which finds a separate place for law and economics, it is necessary to analyze the popular mental picture back of it. We have discussed the abstract men behind the governmental sciences. We will now examine the conception of social organization as a whole into which these governmental sciences fit. It is a picture which was accepted unquestioningly ten years ago. Today its sharp lines are wavering, and those who look at it are full of doubts and questionings. However, it is still in the background of our thinking.

The following is submitted as a crude picture of society which the common man holds without thinking, and which thinkers elaborate endlessly into legal and economic philosophies.

At the front of a procession, headed in the general direction of progress, come the economic and social sciences.

They are busy discovering principles which will lead to ultimate good. The adoption and successful operation of these principles are hindered by two things, usually referred to as human nature and politics. The principles are thus only partially effective. The margin of ineffectiveness is called lag. There is not very much that can be done about it except to denounce the politicians and to try to keep them out of politics. Behind the advance guard of political and economic theory, marches the law. Here there is another lag, because the law must move very slowly or it will fly all to pieces and become bureaucratic. (A bureaucracy, as we will show later, is a system of courts which does not use the terminology of the law, and prefers everyday forms of expression. This is supposed to make its conduct loose and unpredictable. It follows the whim of the moment rather than principle, and is bound by "red tape" instead of "procedure.")

Behind the law are supposed to march the institutions as they are, en route to becoming the institutions which they ought to be. They are kept in line by various types of preachers; economic, moral, social, and legal. They are constantly harassed by politicians and demagogues who try to delude them with unsound theories of one sort or another. The extent of the failure of institutions to keep up with the principles set for them is again referred to as lag. To the extreme rear, digging its feet into the ground and being dragged along, we find human nature, which cannot be changed. Occasionally it breaks loose, pulling the institutions after it. For example, it is often said that it is not the absence of government control over business that causes business depressions, because governmental noninterference is a sound principle. The real cause is human greed, speculation, and failure to realize how to act under a sound principle.

Another way by which this procession toward progress

may be broken up is by the introduction of unsound principle. Future tendencies of governmental action are supposed to be more important than present effect. Societies are not supposed to be able to get temporary advantage from an unsound principle and then to drop the principle. Governments should never do anything that they do not intend to keep on doing indefinitely.

The writer was recently informed that price-fixing by the Government was unsound in principle. He replied that the cling peach license in California seemed to have benefited that industry through price-fixing. The answer was made that it was only temporary and would not work in the long run; therefore the principle was bad. The word "artificial" is applied to any economic advantage arrived at in a new way. The idea is deeply embedded that the only "natural" rise in price is one that has occurred without governmental action. It is better to suffer under a sound principle than to thrive under an unsound one.

It is by means of this naïve set of concepts that economics and the law keep separated from each other and avoid the consideration of institutions as they are. Law schools escape studying the actual habits of judicial institutions. Schools of economics ignore the complex character of political institutions. They are able to do this by separating political from economic facts. For example, an economist who opposed the recent gold-purchase plan was asked if he had considered the effect of the plan on the farm strike. He replied that this was a political consideration and not an element in an economic judgment. The theory is that persons in power should follow sound economic principles and disregard mere political considerations. They should never follow sound political principles and disregard mere economic considerations. The fact that the latter method keeps politicians in power is simply a proof of the perversity of human nature, not a justification for giving paramount weight to political considerations. There follows from this the never-ending but always futile crusade by our best minds to take politicians out of politics by raising the character level of people in general.

Adjustment to Theories

IN times of prosperity, any economic theory that supports things as they are is generally regarded as sound. Persons who point out contradictions or logical difficulties are regarded with suspicion. Yet in times of depression, the sound economic theories get all mixed up and their tendency to lead in different directions becomes apparent to everyone. We have, for instance, a theory that a government should operate on the principles of balancing its budget. We have another theory that public works are a good investment in times of distress. We have a third theory that the Government should not interfere with business.

To satisfy all three of these theories at once, we go through the curious process of balancing part of the budget, which propitiates this particular god. Then we spend money for public works through the device of government corporations, because we have a theory that corporations may act on judgment rather than principle. We are inclined to restrict public works to things which we do not need—to satisfy the theory that government should not enter into business, which consists of producing the things which we do need.

At this point, however, the Economy League discovers that the Government is not actually balancing its budget, and that having two budgets, only one of which is balanced, is dangerous. It discovers that the public-works projects are self-liquidating only in name, and demands that they be restricted to those self-liquidating in fact. But because self-liquidating projects are businesslike in character, we again run into the notion that government competition in business stifles private initiative and is a step toward socialism.

In times of expansion we have no spiritual difficulties in getting the Government to add to the expansion. We do it by electing extravagant politicians and publicly complaining about them at the same time. We also encourage loose banking by the simple device of preventing governmental regulation except in its most superficial form, on the theory that government should not interfere with business. Thus the money gets out, and we keep our theories intact at the same time.

Examination of Theories

THE process of objectively examining the theories behind our own institutions, rather than of arguing their truth or falsity, at first gives us a shock. We can discuss savage taboos and understand them. Then we may use our information in guiding the savages. The same point of view toward our own institutions seems to undermine them. On the New York Post Office we find carved in stone the following sentiment: "Neither snow nor rain nor heat nor gloom of night stays these couriers from the swift completion of their appointed rounds." All this means is that mail will be delivered even in winter. So translated, however, it spoils the building. On the Washington Post Office is a much more elaborate motto indicating that mail is sent only to nice people for laudable purposes. Yet if this motto were so stated, it would affect the morale of post-office employees. They would become casual toward an institution which demands loyalty and devotion. In the same way we find that if an economic principle is examined too critically, it loses its emotional appeal as something which can always be relied on if let alone, and to which we therefore owe a blind loyalty and devotion. Once take this atmosphere away, and the utility of the principle disappears.

Again, the theory must be elaborated sufficiently so that those who choose to study it can honestly feel that they have an advantage over those who do not. For example, if a social worker wants the state to build houses for humanitarian reasons, that request simply shows the impracticability of social workers. An economist, by showing us that housing is an indirect way of furthering fundamental economic principles exactly like the sound old principles we are used to, and that it has nothing to do with humanitarian reasons except incidentally, makes us see that building houses may, after all, be economically sound. It is the same manner of thinking which in the law makes a humanitarian argument look lax and visionary, whereas the same argument couched in the heavy terminology of equitable remedies appears to be a pillar of a great structure.

Then, too, the theory must always be concerned with making precedents for the future, instead of relieving present inconvenience. Present inconvenience can be relieved only by relying on a theory of emergency,—which is the negation of theory. In war, principles disappear in favor of objectives. We do not refuse to win a particular battle because the methods might make a bad precedent for the next battle. But in times of peace, it is considered ignoble to sacrifice a principle of future conduct for a present advantage.

Where Does the Blame Rest?

A FINAL requisite of all governmental theory, whether it be founded upon the church, the law, or economics, must be some form of the doctrine of original sin. It is almost impossible for an economist who desires an audience to escape this. Our governmental principles involve an assumption of group free will. Therefore when times are bad it cannot be the principles which are to blame. It must be the fault of the American people for not following them.

The conception of group sin is not necessary if we are arguing that the principle is wrong. Thus inflation was the cause of Germany's recent difficulties, and not the action of the Germans in carrying it too far. If, however, we were arguing that the theory of inflation was right, we could do so by blaming the people who operated under it. Thus, in arguing that the gold standard is a correct theory, we point out that the recent collapse of the credit structure was not the fault of the standard but of the people.

Therefore it is not surprising that today economic dispute is filled with the doctrine of original sin. I cite some random examples. The *New York Times*[4] congratulates Dr. Sprague for his sound judgment in holding everyone who made business decisions in the past fifteen years responsible for the depression. Dr. Sprague spoke as follows: *"We were all miserable sinners, bankers as a class no more and no less than the rest of the community."* The editorial cites as additional support to this theory of economic sin, Alfred E. Smith, who used to be a Socialist but who is now in his homely way gifted with profound economic insight. Mr. Smith says:

The fundamental cause [of the depression] was as old as original sin. Stubborn human nature is basically responsible for the world's economic miseries and it is only by raising the general level of human character throughout the world that a new society . . . can be brought about. It can't be done by magic, fiat, hokus pokus or mere experimentation.

There seems to be something vaguely familiar in this economic discovery which reminds us of the words of an older set of governmental advisers: ". . . We have left undone those things which we ought to have done; and we have

4. Editorial, *New York Times* (Dec. 10, 1933).

done those things which we ought not to have done; and
there is no health in us."

The power of this simple argumentative device throughout the ages is unquestionable. It makes us satisfied with
what we have been thinking by showing that our theories
were not to blame. It prevents others from proving to us
that it is our theories that were wrong. It presupposes a
start of group free will. It is an essential dialectic weapon
in the armory of the preacher. It also stops experimentation. It succeeds in arresting discoveries. It successfully delayed the physical and medical sciences for hundreds of
years. It is today equally successful in delaying the techniques of social organization.

Element of Effectiveness

IN this situation we may draw a few conclusions as to what
are the necessary elements of an economic theory if it is to
be successful and effective in making whole groups of
people march in step. The requirements are somewhat
paradoxical.

If an economic theory is to perform this function it *must*
be false, because it must oversimplify, and thus ignore the
actual facts. The reasons for this are clear enough. In the
first place, the theory must induce everyone to believe that
he is working under the best possible economic arrangement. If he thought otherwise, those who were in less fortunate positions might make considerable bother, and we
could not answer them by calling them dangerous radicals.
We are entirely too sentimental to say to dissenters: "We
support the present economic arrangement because it keeps
us up, and you down." We must say that we support it because it is the only theory which is consistent with the laws
of God (if the ruling institution is a church), with the emotion of patriotism (if the ruling institution is a nation in

time of war), or with a whole set of fundamental things like the law of supply and demand, nongovernmental interference in business, the superior efficiency of private enterprise, the gold standard, or the national credit, if the ruling institution bases its justification on the argumentative technique of modern economics. We must be able to say that the institution is in tune and in rhythm with certain fundamental laws or principles which exist independently of itself, and therefore any unfortunate results are mere accidents. Of course this is never true; yet we must believe it, or our economic theory is ineffective.

In the second place, the theory must induce us to think that no other institution is as good as ours. This is not difficult—indeed, it is difficult to escape believing it. But we must express that belief elaborately enough so that we think we are proving it instead of just saying it.

In the third place, the theory must be simple enough for everyone to understand. For example, the economic theory in favor of private banking must arise from deep-seated and very simple emotions. The largest bank in Chicago at the end of its lobby has a motto to the general effect that America has a system of banking which in strength and soundness surpasses any other system in the world. Here we have economic theory effectively in operation. Its position in the lobby gives it a dignity which by implication cites the writings and learning of all sound economic thought.

Under this set of ideas we have made great progress in business organization and technique. The reason has been that the whole effect of the picture has been to allow businessmen to progress by experimentation. Economic philosophy has not required businessmen to be learned or theoretical. It has split the agencies of control over society into something very like the spiritual and temporal government of the Middle Ages. The great industrial baronies may be said to represent the temporal government. They have exercised the really important powers over individuals, so far as their livelihood is concerned. Yet the arbitrary nature of those powers, the wastefulness of the experiments by which business has developed, and the extremely practical and day-to-day techniques of American business have all been concealed by the fundamental principles of law and economics. Law has set up moral ideals for business and dressed huge organizations in the clothes of small individuals. Economics has excused the law from doing anything more than dramatizing these ideals, by the invention of greater and more fundamental principles even than those of the law. In so far as the development of productive capacity is concerned, this disorderly system of industrial feudalism has succeeded beyond the wildest dreams of fifty years ago. However, it has imposed on us a way of thinking which makes it very difficult for us to realize the benefits of that productive capacity. Production and transportation seem to have grown beyond the limits of control through the competition of individuals. The only centralized agency of control which at present exists is the Government. But the Government has become so tied up with the principles under which it gave business unrestricted freedom that it can with difficulty exercise toward the problem of distribution the same trial-and-error method which American business used in solving the problem of production. We are now struggling to formulate a philosophy which will give a more centralized power the freedom to learn from experience. This philosophy must be woven out of the terminology of the older way of thinking.

The Union of the Legal and Social Sciences

THE fact that the underlying phenomena back of both law, economics, and sociology are the same inevitably occurs to every student of any of these subjects sooner or later. Those who have faith in the validity of principles regardless of facts are not particularly troubled by this realization, because their concern is with principles, and their belief is that those who deal with the real world are under a duty to make it conform with the principles enunciated by the thinkers. For the failure of doers to perform what thinkers decide ought to be done, such thinkers do not consider themselves responsible.

This is the attitude of the so-called "legal mind." Thomas Reed Powell of Harvard has described that attitude as follows: "If you think that you can think about a thing inextricably attached to something else without thinking of the thing which it is attached to, then you have a legal mind." The legal mind is probably in the majority because people as a whole demand order and classification in their thinking, and the only way to get it is to exclude a disorderly world. When social phenomena are considered without intellectual molds, the world appears to be a very untidy and illogical place, just as the individual mind appears to be more untidy and illogical to a psychiatrist than to a moralist. Therefore, those legally minded persons who insist that if we only keep trying long enough the world can be made rational, or else it is its own fault that it stays irrational, believe that law and economics should be studied by different persons, and not mixed up together.

Of late, however, there have been many calling themselves "realists" who demand that we unite these subjects because they deal with the same things. Much has been written pointing out this necessity, and the arguments in favor of such a union are almost impossible to answer. However, our ways of thinking have gone on pretty much as before because the result of uniting legal and social sciences is to take away many of the faiths on which our present social organization depends. We require the belief that there are order and certainty, and the possibility of positive long-range prediction about legal and economic affairs. We do not like to believe that social therapeutics is only a series of experiments and guesses. But when we examine legal and economic theory objectively we find that it consists, not in definite predictions, but in a battleground on which there is no unanimity, and in which political expediency finally dictates results. Therefore such a union is not popular.

Of course there is no actual predictability to law or economics. In these times of depression, economists are as unable to agree as lawyers. In such a matter as governmental spending, for example, there is a complete lack of accord as to, first, whether the policy is sound, and, second how the money should be spent. Each man's plan can be made to appear dangerous and uncertain beyond a possibility of a doubt. In the same way the theory that we should let everything alone can also be shown to be unworkable and foolishly utopian. Of course physicians disagree about their diagnoses, but the disagreement is of a different character. They recognize that they are giving different guesses, on complex phenomena about which only guesses are possible. Hence they do not clash upon principle so much as on what they are observing. Further than that their object is to alleviate the disease at the time. They are not concerned so much with what diseases the man may have next year.

It therefore appears that the union of the separate sciences of law, economics, and sociology is impossible because such a union would destroy the utility of these sciences as rational proofs of popular faith. It would result in a series of observations like the following: No economic theory can possibly explain a depression in any other way than by blaming society for not following the principles which made up that theory. Predictions cannot be made on the basis of either legal or economic theories because there are so many of them and there is no objective method of choos-

ing between them. The predictions of the most respected
economists of the time are usually wrong, because the most
respected economists reflect all of the more firmly held
popular delusions. The predictions of radical economists are
also usually wrong because they reflect the firmly held delusions of their own group. The most accurate predictions of
what action the Government is going to take are usually
made by politicians or newspaper writers, and do not extend
very far into the future. Such people, however, are not ordinarily called either economists or legal experts.

A series of observations like the foregoing could not be
accepted as a branch of learning. They would simply tend
to destroy those faiths which are necessary for the proper
functioning of government. Today, when they are frequently made, and half believed in by large numbers of
people, we are experiencing the paralyzing effect of lack of
popular faith in institutions.

Therefore he who seeks to unite the legal and the social
sciences *fails to recognize* that the climate of opinion which
created them compels them to be kept apart. Such efforts
are like the efforts to change a language. Language changes,
but the factors which mold it come up from the picturesque
phrases of the people, not from the grammar of the scholar.
In the same way economic and legal theories change only
when popular attitudes change.

Therefore, the first lesson to be learned by the objective
student of governmental theory is that, when he desires to
step into the moving stream of events as an actor, he must
accept the legal and economic theories of his time just as he
accepts the language of his time. He will find, in the vo-
cabulary of current theory, principles through which he may
support any cause. If he thinks it useful to shock people, he
may use radical theories as a means of advocacy. If he desires to soothe, he may dress up the same proposal in con-

servative theory. His choice of theories cannot be made on any other ground than that of expediency in gaining the ends he desires. Legal and economic theory, whether radical or conservative, can never make him a prophet. They may, however, make him a successful advocate.

CHAPTER V

Spiritual vs. Temporal Government

IN the last two chapters the separate sciences of law and economics have been discussed without reference to particular situations. In this chapter we will consider the impact of these theories and symbols on the confusion of a great depression.

In times like the present, when institutions fail to function adequately, we rush to theories and principles as guides. Questions as to the soundness of the law or the prevailing economic doctrines rise to the level of popular debate. Everyone becomes a reformer; everyone becomes a social planner. Constitutional law and economics are dragged out of the technical publications, which no one reads, to appear every morning in the local newspaper and every evening over the radio. Popular newspapers expound the Constitution. Sound economic theory and fundamental law are explained by everyone to everyone else. The separation between politics and economics is broken down and issues such as budget-balancing, public works, inflation, foreign trade, and indeed all the theories of current economics are submitted to the people by political conventions. Bitterness and intolerance increase because partisans are compelled to argue about matters which formerly were taken for granted. There is nothing so annoying to a conservative as the questioning of a conservative axiom which he takes for granted. Thus in such times political opponents appear as dangerous and subversive characters attacking the very foundations of government by substituting communism, fascism, and the like. The very theories which formerly constituted conflicting explanations of practical institutions, contributing to loyalty and reverence for an established order, become sources of fear and confusion.

When institutions function adequately, the theories which support them also appear to be adequate, because they are never called upon to solve practical problems. The very success of the institution prevents anyone questioning its underlying theory. It also makes the theory less of a hampering force because the failure to question it leads to a lack of discrimination in applying it. It thus remains vague and does not stand in the way of the practical adjustments within the routine of the pattern of the institution.

When, however, institutions fail to exercise the social control which we expect of them, and we rely on principles to tell us how to fill the gaps, both our actions and our principles appear chaotic and confused. Yet we can never completely escape trying to follow our symbols of government, even though we know they are leading us in all directions at once. No better illustration of this fundamental axiom of government can be found than in the political thought and action of today.

In 1933 we were faced with a situation in which an industrial feudalism was unable to take responsibility for ten million unemployed, where it was unable to operate at full productive capacity, and where its goods had piled up without any outlet for distribution. In these most important respects it failed to function as a governing force, and a government based on the tradition of inaction and noninterference was forced to rush in to fill the vacuum. This loss of power was the result of a surrender, not of a revolt. Institutions adapted to handle old problems were faced with new ones for which their organization and ways of thinking were completely inadequate. They were therefore unable to exercise control, and retreated in disorganized terror.

For a time the retreat was complete. Bankers rushed to the Government demanding that it do something so that depositors would again have confidence in them. Industrialists sat quiet while legislation was passed which was intended to prevent them from cutting each other's throats. Farmers even permitted control over their crops, because their old institutions were incapable of exchanging them for a decent amount of industrial goods. Yet the words "New Deal" describe the process better than the term "Revolution." The central notion was that the same old cards should be redistributed so that the same game could go on. There was no revolt of those who suffered most from the depression, the unemployed. True, that problem was considered as most important, but the emphasis was on the creation of more purchasing power so that bankers and industrialists and farmers could again be safe. The ancient symbols and traditions have never been deserted by even the most radical of those who have exercised power during the depression. We have not witnessed a revolt of the downtrodden, but a panic on the part of the well-to-do.

The New Deal included few, but only a few, of the phenomena which accompany what we are accustomed to call a revolution. There were parades by a suddenly hopeful middle class. There was a sudden burst of confidence in intellectuals, giving rise to a temporary respect for what was called a brain trust. But the old institutions surrendered only a little of their independence to give themselves a breathing spell. When the crisis was over they began the political struggle to get that independence back. It was an emergency which they thought confronted them, not a social change.

However, though the panic on the part of the industrial feudalism was gone, there was little evidence of its capacity to solve problems of unemployment and the distribution of goods. There was only the hope that these problems would solve themselves, and a fear of consequences if the Government be permitted to solve them before that hope was realized. That hope was not strong enough to stop the questioning of legal and economic axioms to which conservatives looked for guidance.

Therefore, contradictory assertions of great lawyers and economists have filled our press for three years. They are similar in their high moral tone, in their great earnestness and assurance, and in their complete confusion. The legislation which was the result of such debates necessarily had the same characteristics of morality, earnestness, assurance, and confusion.

No other result was predictable. The duration of such a period of contradictory movements depends upon the time required to create new institutions which will fill the gaps created by the failure of the old ones. Until these new institutions are established—and they do not appear full grown except by violent revolution—a situation is created where the great principles of law and economics are forced to live up to their pretenses as guides to human conduct. In this rôle they are a source of confusion, yet there seems no way of escaping this confusion—at least there is no escape so long as men insist on believing in a logical and rational society.

The physical and mechanical problem of distribution of goods today is hopeful. It is obvious that we have sufficient resources to take care of everyone. It is also obvious that we are wasting those resources and depleting the nation for our descendants. Over a billion acres of land have become the subject of dangerous erosion. Floods are increasing yearly in severity and economic loss. Mineral resources are being depleted. Even an exhaustion of bituminous coal under present methods is prophesied by engineers. The avoidable waste is 150 million tons a year—enough to supply the entire German Empire. In 1933 over a billion cubic feet of gas was blown into the air daily in the Texas Panhandle (the equivalent of 40,000 tons per day). The waste of gas for twelve years in California was one third of the total production. Our methods for the extraction of oil are scandalous in their inefficiency. And, in the meantime, millions are suffering for want of fuel.

Even larger than the waste of our fixed resources is the waste of our productive capacity. Our national income, in terms of goods valued in dollars, shrank from about eighty billion in 1929 to about fifty billion in 1934. It is easy to estimate that if the human energy and productive technique available had been put to work it might have increased thirty billion instead of decreasing. Such facts can be understood by everyone.[1]

Thus, from the point of view of actual and tangible wealth, the picture of the future might appear to be rosy. It seems that it may be easy to support the population in 1960 at a higher level than ever before. The mechanical means of stopping waste are at hand. Estimates of land resources indicate that fewer people in the future will have to undergo the drudgery of farming to give us a better national diet. The possibilities of industrial production seem unlimited. Cheap labor is available in foreign countries. Japan is offering us the benefits of coolie labor in giving us goods for a minimum of our surplus raw materials, and thus releasing our own labor supply for housing projects and better living generally. Other nations are willing to work for us on the same terms.

The ideological picture, however, is gloomy and dispiriting. Cheap foreign goods threaten to ruin industry. Where is the "money" coming from? Old people are increasing, and their pensions which will cost only 136 million in 1936, threaten to rise to over a billion in twenty-five years. Unemployment insurance seems about to mount to such staggering figures that we are doubtful if business can meet

1. *Report of National Resources Board* (Dec. 1, 1934, U.S. Govt. Printing Office).

the drain. From the platform of our ancient symbols there seems to be no way to support the population at all in 1960, without embracing something like communism and thus turning ourselves from free Americans into Russians. Gloomy as this picture is, we must therefore cling to our ancient symbols and take refuge in prayer and letting things drift. In such a delicate situation it is dangerous even to suggest reforms.

Yet old symbols, as guides, never operate as they do when their function is only to hold working institutions together. They lose their power to suppress new notions. This was illustrated at the beginning of the depression in the wide acceptance of all sorts of new ideas. Technocracy became overnight a national term. Here was a theory of the distribution of plenty done up into statistical terms. The Townsend plan, the EPIC plan, the various forms of share-the-wealth plans followed. However, the very existence of such plans creates their own reaction. They seem to undermine everything we have been used to. The fanaticism of their followers creates equal fanaticism for budget-balancing, rugged individualism, and the Constitution. The result is even more confusing because at this stage in social thinking those who take up the new theories do not reject the old. Thus the Townsend plan and the EPIC plan, and even inflation were only alternative methods of balancing the budget and of realizing the dreams of the constitutional fathers. Everyone distrusts direct methods of solving the problems immediately at hand. Everyone is more interested in future tendencies than in everyday needs. Everyone is thinking in the terms of some moral philosophy and wants good people rewarded and bad people punished.

Therefore the legislation of the depression partook of all these attitudes. The direct practical way of taking care of the needy was to distribute a decent subsistence to them without regard to its effects on their character. This, however, was the one thing that could not be done. The dole must be only temporary. It must not be large. We must invent things which will make government-spending conform to the ideals of a time when there was no government-spending. Hence we observed the frantic efforts to make relief look like productive employment, and the equally impassioned attacks on the fictitious form of employment that followed. We saw waste, quarrels, worry, accompany all the variations of the eternal conflict between radicals, liberals, and conservatives about the moral clothing in which relief for unemployment should be dressed.

The public-works program fell under the same confusion. The practical idea that the Government should spend as much money as it needed for public projects which would be useful, became confused with the idea that public works were a method of creating character, of priming the pump, of stabilizing productive-goods industries or consumer-goods industries, of breaking up large corporations by creating yardsticks for them—indeed, anything rather than a simple and direct way of creating needed improvement. The symbolic effect of public works became more important than their practical need. Hence public works, which started as a practical scheme, became most vulnerable to attacks based on practicality and common sense.

It is interesting to speculate what might have been the results had we been able to link spending and public works to an adequate sentimental ideology. If we had been able to conquer Chicago, and improve it as a national asset, we might have been more sensible in our operations. It is interesting to compare what we were able to do in the Philippines under the ideals of a humanitarian imperialism. In 1898, at a time when no one was accustomed to big figures, we were able to spend what has been estimated at four hundred million dollars in conquering and improving the Philippines. The humanitarian work done in these islands by the United States is amazing. Disease was reduced, social work carried on, living conditions made better, until the population doubled under the improved conditions. The story of American improvement in the Philippines is a story of heroism and self-sacrifice on the part of pioneers, unselfish in their interests. Yet it would have been psychologically impossible at that time to have spent an equivalent amount of money on our own poor. The reason was that in the ideology of the time, the spot on the map which represented these islands was considered a national asset. Hence we were not "spending" the money. We were investing it. Every American felt richer because the Philippines belonged to the United States. There was an asset to balance the debit. The imperialistic ideal coupled with our natural humanitarian impulses permitted us to treat these primitive people better than our own. We were not afraid of ruining their character because we did not think of them as equals who had characters to ruin. Therefore we were able to do many sensible things for the comfort and peace of our little brown brothers, in spite of all the difficulties which this ideal involved us in, in other and quite separate respects. One wishes that it were possible to consider our own country as an asset today. If so, the budget might be balanced by calling expenditures for improvement investments instead of debts. The idea is frequently put into words, but unfortunately it has not the emotional meaning to give us confidence in following it.

The result of all of these conflicting ideological forces is reflected in the confused picture of the New Deal legislation. Most prominent was the N.R.A. because it unified under its slogans more of the contradictory ideals which were generally accepted than any other piece of legislation. It satisfied the demand for action, and gave a discouraged people the emotional release of marching in parades. The act itself did not create a blue eagle, nor command the imposition of a war psychology, but the times did. Subconsciously the act was based on the ancient ideal of a social compact, which has lurked in the background of our thinking for a hundred years. Warring, competitive businessmen were supposed to meet together and agree on an orderly state just as Rousseau's savages did. Once they had agreed, the contract became law. The great illusion that men become reasonable when sitting around in conference, aided by statisticians, lawyers, and economists spread over the whole legislation like a great rainbow. Here was the hope of the future, because here was a reconciliation of all the conflicting desires of both the small and the large businessman of capital and of labor. With such a background, parades, symbols, and slogans were inevitable.

But there was also a moral and legal ideal to be represented. The old notion that loss should follow fault, and that virtue and wisdom should be rewarded, was the heritage of our common law for centuries. It was represented by lawyers and courts. Hence lawyers drew up the Securities Act, and relied on the judicial process to make the investment market, that tangible symbol of the creation of capital, conform to ancient principles. It appeared to us important that prudent men be protected from losing their money and that foolish men should take care of themselves. Hence the facts about all investments should be disclosed, so that if a man lost his savings it would be his own fault. The depression was supposed in part to be the result of moral delinquency. When moral delinquency becomes an economic factor, it is the function of the trial court to step in.

Of course there was much more to the Securities Act than this simple moral issue. What we are concerned with here is the symbol which it represented in the public mind when it was passed. Small investors who had been caught in the stock market felt avenged and more secure. However, those investment bankers who were sure of their own rectitude reacted violently. Amendments were made after the crusading zeal which accompanied the Act had spent itself. The result is an administrative machine, capable of exercising centralized power over all stock exchanges, and preventing the anarchy which formerly had made self-discipline on any one exchange almost impossible. Thus a moral urge to punish the blameworthy became translated into a practical and a going institution. The moral urge led only to confusion. The arguments pro and con about the merits of the old act will never be settled. They have been forgotten. The new administrative machine is gradually acquiring competence, and as it does, the debate on theories dies away. The time will come when even those who became enraged and gnashed their teeth at the awful inquity of the original act will be able to see that it was a necessary step in the creation of a new practical institution to fill a gap. The only path of *orderly* social change leads through a confusion of principles. Clear-cut and logical systems suddenly imposed bring the violence of Russia, Germany, or the French Revolution.

Practical common sense was to some extent represented by the Agricultural Adjustment Act. Here was a scheme which recognized that farm prices must be raised to a parity with other prices to enable farmers to get for their products enough manufactured goods to enable them to live in comfort. The scheme recognized also that in a world where price is dependent upon scarcity, it is necessary to produce scarcity in order to raise prices. It recognized that such a course could not be permanent, and that for every temporary alleviation of the farmer's lot new problems would be created. The alternatives, for example in the South, were the creation of a new problem of share croppers without any fixed place in the economic scheme, or the possible collapse of the financial structure of the South because it no longer had a cash crop. The operation of the scheme was a dangerous gamble. Standing still seemed to be an even more dangerous gamble. At least the plan did provide for a huge distribution of cash where it was obviously needed. And so the Agricultural Adjustment Administration took the plunge.

Because the plan was practical, and administered by realists, its practical aims were more nearly accomplished than those of any other of the New Deal legislation. Yet it became the most vulnerable of all from the point of view of both the ancient and the newer ideals. The notion of the destruction of goods seemed so utterly silly to those who thought of government as rational—the admittedly temporary nature of the relief seemed so completely irresponsible to those who believed in long-time planning; the new problems created by the change in the farmers' position were so painful and unexpected—that the plan created the most intense bitterness and the kindly and practical Secretary Wallace was hailed as a public enemy. His speeches and explanation were the frankest and most realistic of any man in public life, yet he was attacked as the most dangerous doctrinaire theorist.

The labor legislation showed the same confused difference to ancient ideals. A man from Mars might be of the opinion that an orderly government should not permit pitched battles over wages, to the loss and suffering of entire communities, any more than it would permit public disorder over the payment of debts, or the settlement of any other civil litigation. However, the notion of compulsory arbitration was as uncongenial to labor as it was to capital. The great labor organizations grew up as fighting and bargaining organizations. Compulsory arbitration would destroy their purpose by taking away their power to call strikes. Collective bargaining fits in with the accustomed habit of a series of labor wars and armed truces, which is the way we think of a dispute over wages as opposed to a dispute over a debt. Therefore, collective bargaining is the pattern which labor legislation has been compelled to take.

The monetary legislation, both on the conservative and radical side, was all based on the ancient ideals of the quantity of money as the key to distribution of goods. Both inflationists and noninflationists believed the same things about money. They only desired different results.

The symbols of taxation became hopelessly confused. To those who were compelled to act, and who could not shift the responsibility by sitting back and praising the utopia of *laissez faire,* taxation seemed the only way to set up assets against the debits caused by unavoidable government-spending. The ways in which other financial institutions balanced their budgets by creating assets, were ideas alien to government bookkeeping. Hence, there seemed no other acceptable way of distributing purchasing power to one trained in that ideology. It all worked out in theory. However, the symbol of taxation is not a pleasant one like the symbol of finance. It appears as an aggressive act of the government to take away money by taxation, even though coupled with a promise of future benefits. It is a benevolent act to take away money and return a share in an organization, even though the promise of future benefits is the same. All tax programs produce unpleasant associations and bitter hostility, and for that reason falter under conflicting pressures. The avenue by which J. P. Morgan produced order in the steel business by creating a huge paper asset to balance the money he paid for control, was closed to the Government because it is not the traditional way of governments to create assets. It seems right and proper that governments should have to go on their knees to bankers. The story of Rothschild is a romance which has such appeal that it makes a popular movie. The avenue of taxation was made difficult by the ancient idea that a government which taxes heavily is necessarily a hostile and selfish government.

Like a great Delphic oracle, representing all that was good and reasonable about our ancient ways, stood the Supreme Court. Here was supposed to be definite principle in its final form. Yet this great body shared all the confusion of the other branches of government and was further handicapped by the fact that theoretically it could never take back anything it said without suffering a loss in prestige. It split with great bitterness on the constitutionality of the currency legislation. It dodged for two years the necessity of saying anything about the National Recovery Act, or the Agricultural Adjustment Act. It was able to do this because of a tradition that it should never decide any current issues in any case where the Court itself did not rule as a matter of law that it was forced to decide those issues. There was an opportunity to talk about the power of the Government under the commerce clause in the Nebbia Case,[2] in which the right of a State board to fix milk prices in New York was upheld. Later, in the famous hot oil case (*Ryan* vs. *Panama Refining Company*[3]), the validity of an N.R.A. code seemed directly involved, but through a complicated accident and the use of some ingenious legalisms, the Court was able again to dodge the question. Gradually the National Recovery Act grew ripe for the judicial harvest. In 1935 it had few remaining defenders. The reaction to the parades and enthusiasm had set in. The various compromises to conform to the notion that social compacts may be made by warring groups who sit down and reason together had made the administration of the act a maze of inconsistencies. When this occurred the Supreme Court struck and struck hard, destroying not only all the absurdities which had clustered about this legislation, but also the great administrative machine which might have had the beginnings of some form of unified social control to fill

2. *Nebbia* vs. *New York*, 291 *U.S.* 502 (1934).
3. 293 *U.S.* 388 (1935).

gaps where control was needed.[4] No one knows, of course, what this far-flung administrative machine would have developed into. However, the idea that institutions grow just as business enterprises grow is foreign to our judicial thinking. No institution which is based on wrong principles can ever grow up to be anything but wrong. The character of the institutional infant is supposed to be irrevocably fixed by the formula of its baptism.

The action of the Supreme Court emphasized a new set of symbols; it dramatized the fear that a government which assumed responsibility for gaps left by the failures of an industrial feudalism was gradually pushing on toward a Russian or a German culture. The word-symbols for this idea —regimentation, bureaucracy, fascism, and communism— were what the Court was credited with saving us from. Since the decision, like the legislative action of the Government, went in all directions, it received support from all directions. We were confronted with the spectacle of the conservative *New York Herald-Tribune,* and the radical Oswald Garrison Villard both hailing the decision with approval. William Randolph Hearst, Clarence Darrow, the *Chicago Tribune,* the American Bar Association, Huey Long, and Senator Borah all thanked God for the Supreme Court, each making the decision a symbol of a different point of view. The unanimity of such diverse people was the unanimity of those believing in different utopias, all of whom condemned a practical organization which conformed to no utopia. The N.R.A. had enlisted nation-wide enthusiasm when it had a little utopia of its own. It lost that enthusiasm when its dreams were disappearing and it was beginning under the pressure of hard necessity to build up a practical administrative organization.

4. *Schechter Poultry Corporation et al.* vs. *U.S.,* 55 *S. Ct.* 837; 79 *L. ed.* 888 (1935).

After the decision, the thought of the conservatives expressed itself in ways of which the following was typical.

This country is threatened by a highly simplified and definite attack from within. This attack is known to have been made by a set of adroit, determined and utterly unscrupulous men. It puts the question up to us, will the nation continue to develop and meet its emergencies and overcome its difficulties by means of a republican form of government supported by a free people, or will it deliver itself into the hands of an intellectual oligarchy that will inevitably lead our government into a dictatorship? (*New York Herald-Tribune,* July 7, 1935.)

The thought of the radicals expressed itself in a movement for a new political party which could think simply and directly and ignore the symbols and traditions of the past. Yet even the new political party was still bound by the same symbolic fetters as the conservatives, as is evidenced by the speech of Senator Nye at a preliminary parley for a new party. The Senator said:

"Don't make the mistake of trying to cover too much territory and try to change the structure of the nation over night. We must divorce ourselves from communism or anything that smacks of communism. Three weeks of communism in practice in America would disprove its theory" (*New York Times,* July 7, 1935).

We are not here attempting to give an accurate account of the progress of the New Deal, but simply to illustrate the pattern of thought which always occurs when practical and organized institutions fail to control practical situations, and we attempt to find our way out of the wilderness by the guiding light of great principles. In such patterns there is usually some legislation of which people vaguely approve, or which they do not dare to attack, which may constitute the beginnings of a practical solution of social problems.

That kind of legislation is as conflicting in its ideals as any in the forefront of the political battle, but it seems to muddle along. Of such a character was the Social Security bill of 1935, and therefore it is worth analysis.

This bill attempted to meet the problems of old-age pensions and unemployment insurance. When the bill was introduced no one dared deny these ideals. It had taken years before the notion of the beauty of private charity was given up. A former administration had insisted that the relief of suffering in drouth stricken areas in the South was not the business of the Government. Relief had to be given under the fiction of loans for crop purposes. The humanitarian ideal was regarded as soft and impractical, and old symbols were thought to be the only sure guides. However, as the gap in control widened, the older symbols of private charity began to be examined. It was discovered that the problem was not a humanitarian problem at all, but a problem of distribution of purchasing power so that industrialists could sell goods, so that recovery might come; and, finally, so that we might later go back to private charity. As such the bill took on an economic aspect. It escaped the heavy political cannonading. True, everyone was disappointed in it, but the thinking was so confused that the symbols of bureaucracy and regimentation did not work so well in attacking it. It compromised with all of the accepted ideals of everyone, including the budget-balancers. The result was a curious conglomeration from any rational standpoint, but it was nevertheless important as the first legislative recognition of a problem which people had come to believe not even business recovery would solve.

The bill began by providing old-age pensions, though at a minimum subsistence level. Here was a recognition of an obligation coupled with the notion that impecunious old people should not live too well even in a land of plenty.

But the humanitarian notion that old people are entitled to more than a minimum of subsistence could not be ignored. Therefore an enormous insurance company appears, to which the workmen contribute up to 3 per cent of their pay. Now we are on familiar ground. We would be shocked at the idea of giving a man a decent living in his old age unless we made him go without something in his youth to obtain it. However, under the notion of insurance, there is no limit to the amount which it is morally right for a man to live on when he retires. Therefore the symbol of an insurance company allows us to live at peace with our moral ideals, and still support systematically a vast class of people who are now supported in a haphazard way.

It did not matter that an insurance company on such a scale has no meaning whatever. It was estimated that the reserves will amount to over thirty-two billion dollars in thirty-five years. There was no way in which the Government can invest these reserves except in its own bonds. Hence these bonds can never be retired because they constitute the only insurance reserve which the Government can have. There is no way in which the Government can pay interest on these huge reserves, under the current bookkeeping, except by taxes. Hence the bill in effect meant the same thing as if funds had been provided for by direct taxation. Nevertheless, in the ideological confusion of the time, this scheme was the only way in which we could create a claim in favor of old people. An unworkable bill which conformed to the old ideal of insurance as the backbone of the social order escaped attack. We were in the stage of fumbling for recognition of the problem. We were not yet ready actually to solve it.

Even the contribution to the fund is more or less fictitious because a tax on all pay checks can be nothing more than a tax on industry. Actuaries produced figures which prove that the bill is actuarially unsound. Constitutional lawyers threw doubt on its constitutionality. Yet it failed to receive its merited abuse in the public press.

Added to old-age pensions in the bill was unemployment insurance. This was based again on the symbol of building up insurance reserves and required a graduated tax to 3 per cent on the employee and to 3 per cent on the employer. Both divisions of the bill contemplated a total tax of 9 per cent, not on profits, but on pay rolls. Yet in a time when Roosevelt's "soak the rich" program of taxation was arousing hysterical protest, this far greater tax remained comparatively unnoticed.

The Social Security bill was unworkable in the ideological frame it had to assume. It was full of impossible social bookkeeping. As it was set up it appeared that the burden of the aged and the unemployed in the future might be greater than the nation could bear in spite of the fact that in terms of tangible goods to distribute it seemed certain that there would be enough to go around. But the important thing about this bill was its acknowledgment of a social obligation dressed in the ideas of a time before such a social obligation was recognized. It presented the hope that as the old symbols of the bill got in the way, they would be discarded for more direct methods and that we could afford to go through the period of confused bookkeeping necessary while the new institution which was to distribute these goods struggled to get itself into working order.

Such is the confused pattern which legal and economic principles weave in times when an industrial feudalism declines to take responsibility for ten million without employment, when goods pile up and cannot be distributed to those who need them, in short, when established institutions fail to perform the organizing functions required of an orderly government.

There is no escape from such periods of ideological confusion, though they may be less pronounced where nations do not insist upon being logical about the symbols which justify their institutions. Probably the English, who are untroubled by the lack of symmetry and the obvious pretense of their Government, escape from symbols more readily, without losing their emotional value. No one has ever been able to define the exact relationship of the Bank of England to the Government of England. It is not like our private banks, and yet it is not logically what we conceive a government bank to be. The English King serves much the same emotional purpose as a symbol of something above the actual government as does our Supreme Court, without getting very much in the way of experiment, or throwing a shadow of doubt across all legislation. An unwritten constitution is a contradiction in terms which can never be satisfactorily explained to a man with a bookkeeping mind. And thus the English have become notorious for that mysterious process of "muddling through," which seems successful, and yet antithetical to all principles of rational government. Americans, however, have faith in written documents, and in sharp delimitations of functions and power. They refuse to muddle, and thus prolong their period of confusion.

What then is the structure of an efficiently organized society? It appears to be one where theories and ideals protect its institutions from criticism and permit them to function with confidence without either guiding them or interfering with them. This requires social control to constantly resolve itself into separate institutions which do not collide with each other—one concerned with the practical organization of men into productive groups and the other with the embodiment of spiritual ideals. Where the spiritual government allows the practical institutions the most freedom, there we find the greatest progress and development.

In this essential element of a stable government, we find

the reason for the persistence of the ideal of *laissez faire* in times of peace and plenty. It is the philosophy which gives practical institutions freedom to operate without constantly tripping over their own ideals. Of course the great institutions do not let laws of supply and demand alone, nor are they interested in observing the ideal laws of free competition either intranational or international. Free trade and fair competition have been only utopias which justified business enterprise in insisting that a central government let it alone. They were useful utopias, because they deflected and consumed the energies of liberals and radicals. Reforms in stable times are directed only at making an institution conform to its own ideals, an essentially impossible task because of the nature of both institutions and ideals, but a very necessary ritual. Thus the battle of principles goes on at a level which does not permit the spiritual government seriously to interfere with the operation of the great temporal institutions. They protect themselves against the efforts of reformers to eliminate social injustice by dressing up the doctrine of *laissez faire* in technical and scholarly language so that reformers will believe in it and try to make it happen. Wherever the reformers are successful—whenever they see their direct primaries, their antitrust laws, or whatever else they base their hopes on, in actual operation—the great temporal institutions adapt themselves, leaving the older reformers disillusioned, like Lincoln Steffens, and a newer set carrying on the banner.

This is the inevitable fate of government in a moral society. It is a result of the paradox that only going institutions can do the work of the world, and only contradictory moral theories can comfortably insulate them against their humanitarian impulses. Practical institutions cannot develop if constantly hampered by an awareness of these theories. For example, our great industrial development could

hardly have taken place if its leaders had followed the logical and moral principles of the day. Legal, humanitarian,
and economic principles were all violated by those who
created our industrial empire. They built on their mistakes,
their action was opportunistic, they experimented with
human material and with little regard for social justice. Yet
they raised the level of productive capacity beyond the
dreams of their fathers.

Nor could that industrial development have occurred had
its leaders been cynics. Man can never escape from his
moral self, and a cynical position brings the futility of disillusionment. Man is under the constant necessity of putting
on ceremonial robes and watching himself go by. All the
wealth of Midas will not make man happy if he cannot
strut. Therefore our industrial leaders are of necessity good
and pious men, who belong to our churches, and who agree
with our liberals and even our radicals that the admitted
government must be a moral government of principles and
not of men.

Thus society is able to suppress its humanitarian instincts
by looking at the suffering of its unfortunate members
through the darkened windows of fundamental economic
theories. If we can escape the feeling of moral responsibility, human misery ceases to trouble us. When we believe
in the Malthusian explanation of the slums, the slums cease
to constitute a problem. Ideals of rugged individualism prevented us from being too sympathetic with labor. A fatalistic attitude toward politics, not unlike the Malthusian
theory of the slums, enabled us to look at a corrupt political machine with only an occasional worry.

These philosophies which justified letting practical institutions alone during our industrial development were
impregnable so long as our practical institutions were in
control of the industrial situation. Yet no matter how impressive their scholarly defenses, such philosophies always

crumble when practical institutions cease to govern. In such circumstances new institutions arise which are forced to struggle in the confusion created by the conflict of old theories.

We can observe through the ages a succession of spiritual governments, each appearing foolish and devoid of common sense after the practical institutions which operated under them had ceased to perform adequately their practical functions. There is a marked similarity between the partnership of the feudal states and the church during the Middle Ages, and the relationship of great corporations and our National Government at Washington. The medieval church, like our modern constitutional government, was the repository of the ideals of the people, and was unconcerned with the distribution of goods to them. It was the only important government to the idealist of the time, because it represented government as it ought to be. All else is transitory and of only temporary significance.

Of course, however, the lines defining the scope of the spiritual government are never clearly drawn. Spiritual power is always seizing temporal dominion, and in that dominion is compelled to act practically. Hence it is necessary to build a *sub rosa* practical government under the spiritual government, which has been called many things, throughout the ages, but which today is called politics. Politics can be and is practical, but it pays for this power in a loss of respectability. The more fixed the principles of the spiritual government, the more written the constitution, the larger gap there will be which must be filled by this *sub rosa* institution. We achieve comfort, and reconcile ourselves with the conflict between politics and principles by constantly dedicating ourselves to the task of getting rid of the political machine, or the political boss. The old idea of original sin comes to the front to keep us from becoming too discouraged. Sin must always exist, but righteous man must always fight against it. We never get rid of the political machine, but we can satisfy our moral conscience by preaching about it, and giving an occasional demonstration of good works.

Our spiritual government today centers in the judicial system. Here is the bulwark of all the older symbols and theories both legal and economic. Here is the stage on which the ideals of society are given concrete reality. Therefore it is to the courts that conservative men turn when new ideas in government cause them mental distress. It is in this great institution that the new and the old must somehow be reconciled if we are to achieve confidence and stability.

The ritual through which courts work, the stage on which they present their miracle play, is the trial. Without an understanding of that peculiar institution, no one can adequately discuss the progress of those conflicts of ideals represented by such opposing terms as the *rule of law* vs. *bureaucracy, freedom* vs. *regimentation, individualism* vs. *socialism*. Because the trial is regarded as a method of enforcing laws, its significance is usually overlooked. Actually it is the hub about which popular ideals of government revolve. It therefore becomes necessary to discuss in detail the functions of the civil and the criminal trial in making concrete the moral and economic notions which bind society together.

CHAPTER VI

The Criminal Trial

THE center of ideals of every Western government is in its judicial system. Here are the symbols of all those great principles which give dignity to the individual, which give independence to the businessman, and which not only make of the state a great righteous protector but at the same time keep it in its place. The psychological reasons as to why the settlement of disputes should furnish the stage for the daily enactment of the miracle play of government are beyond the scope of this book. Suffice it to say that in nearly all countries, and even among primitive tribes, the king as a judge between two disputing parties has been the symbol of power. When Henry II consolidated the courts in England, he consolidated the kingdom. When the barons at Runnymede struck for their independence, it was a jury of their peers (which meant to them an ancient baronial court, not our modern trial by jury) and the writ of habeas corpus which they wrote into the Magna Charta. China, without unity, has been a country without an organized and philosophically founded judicial system. Yet even in that disorganized country, the symbols of what business organization there is, are found in the tribunals set up by their guilds of merchants or bankers.

It is a common belief that courts are an efficient way of enforcing the law, and of settling disputes. This is because these are two of the important ideals of the judiciary, not because it is actually true. When we really want a dispute efficiently settled we turn to arbitration. The good lawyer from time immemorial has been the man who keeps his client out of court. When we want laws administered efficiently we turn to administrative tribunals. Wherever courts exist, we find that the delays and technicalities of the judicial system have been the subject matter of satire, humor, and constant but ineffectual efforts at reform. The effective procedural reforms in this respect have been accomplished by turning parts of the judicial task to bodies which we do not dress up in judicial robes or ritual. Jeremy Bentham's labors on behalf of reformed procedure led to the passage of codes which became fully as artificial and technical as the old common law. The explanation for this does not lie in any defects of the code, but in the nature of the institution which represents a set of ideals among which efficiency is of only minor importance. It is in this institution that we find concentrated to a greater extent than in any other, the symbols of moral and rational government.

Law as a philosophy is the property of scholars; as a technique it is the property of lawyers. For litigants, law is something to keep away from unless they are armed for a battle. To the great mass of people the language of the theories of law is unknown. It is not the doctrine but the public judicial trial which symbolizes for them the heaven of justice which lies behind the insecurity, cruelty, and irrationality of an everyday world. In the public trial we find the government speaking ex cathedra. Other actions of the government may be subject to political attack or may be called corrupt or foolish. The action of a court in a trial cannot be so considered without seeming to endanger the very fabric of the State.

The judicial trial thus becomes a series of object lessons and examples. It is the way in which society is trained in right ways of thought and action, not by compulsion, but by parables which it interprets and follows voluntarily. Yet there are two distinct kinds of object lessons—civil and criminal; the difference between them is hard to define, but easy for the ordinary man on the street to feel. For the businessman who needs a feeling of security from the encroachments of those who are appointed to enforce the law, the civil trial is most important. It exists to give the man of affairs a sense of security in his commercial relationships both from attack by his fellows and intermeddling of the government. However, it is too complicated in its rituals and terminology to appeal to the great mass of people who need to believe in the law. For most persons, the criminal trial overshadows all other ceremonies as a dramatization of the values of our spiritual government, representing the dignity of the State as an enforcer of law, and at the same time the dignity of the individual when he is an avowed opponent of the State, a dissenter, a radical, or even a criminal. So important is the criminal trial to the whole ideological structure of government that its disappearance in favor of an efficient and speedy way of accomplishing the incarceration of persons supposed to be dangerous to the social order, is always a sign of psychological instability of a people. Thus, when great masses of people are marching in step to some fanatically held ideal, which excludes all lesser ideals, as in the case of war, or revolution, the criminal trial becomes a mere form or a gesture toward the tolerance of bygone days. Society thinks it knows exactly what it wants to do, and hence has little patience with a process which gives dissenters from the social order a chance to air their opinions, or justify their antisocial acts. So we find war psychology creating the court-martial, since the objective of social discipline is one which is easily understood, and brooks no contradiction. Revolution produces the secret investigation as a natural consequence of a great morality which swallows up all lesser moralities.

The criminal trial is a consequence of security, because only when men are secure are contradictory social values tolerated. It appears as an incident to the enforcement of the law and the efficient investigation of issues of fact. One of its greatest difficulties is its necessity to appear as an efficient means of enforcement and working order, and at the same time bring into sharp relief various deep-seated popular moral ideals. Generally the ideal of law enforcement and efficient investigation are in direct conflict with these ideals. Often the ideals themselves are in conflict with accepted social behavior. In such cases the mental conflict between what the group thinks it ought to do, and what it actually does, must be reconciled by the conviction of some offenders and the acquittal or the failure to prosecute others. To illustrate how fundamental to group psychology is the function of the criminal trial we need only observe it in primitive societies.

For example, among the Melanesian tribes, sex relations between members of the same clan are forbidden. This taboo is violated with great frequency, very likely because both romance and tragedy center about forbidden things, in primitive as well as in modern societies. There are various forms of magic against the evils which are supposed to follow from the violation of this great principle of the clan. These are effective, however, only in private. If an offense of this character is denounced publicly, banishment or suicide follows. The trial symbolizes the ideal that the clan is like a big family, with the same sort of loyalties. The suicide of the person publicly indicted dramatizes this ideal in the most gripping way possible. Spectators return to their homes convinced that the ideal of a clan as a big family has been properly and publicly acknowledged through human sacrifice.

This sort of process has nothing to do with the "enforcement" of a rule. It has significance because people desire not compliance but a symbol which reflects this notion of the closeness of the ties of the clan. When enforcement rather than drama is actually desired it is left to policemen. Trials become short and summary. It is where dramatization of ideals is required that the trial becomes important.

We observe the same thing in modern society. The writer once lived in a small town where prohibition was almost a religious issue. As is always the case with great moral symbols, a large number of believers had liquor in their homes. This fact was treated as is all conduct which is not in accord with great moral principles; it was preached about on Sunday, and during the week served to make the process of taking a drink a very romantic affair. A professor in the university, for reasons irrelevant here, acquired an enemy. One morning his house was searched and wine found in the cellar. Criminal proceedings immediately followed. The professor was discharged by a board of trustees, many of whom also had liquor in their cellars. Some of the board were a bit sheepish about it, both because they were violating the law themselves, and because they knew the prosecution had its origin in personal spite, but in view of the publicity, they did not see anything else they could do. After all the university must stand for the best moral ideals of the community. To retain the professor would be to flout these ideals in public and thus irreparably damage them.

After the arrest and discharge, bootlegging went on as before, and drinking among the respectable became even more romantic. It had all the appearance of a dangerous undertaking, without any real danger, and served to introduce an element of excitement and release into communities which would otherwise have been very dull indeed. Morals were vindicated, and life went on.

Prosecutions of this character perform the same function on the Melanesian indictment—proving two ideals: first, that we had prohibition; and, second, that no one is above the law. In this respect we are as primitive as the savages, or, to put it in another way, the savages are as civilized as we are. Illustrations could be piled up without end. The occasional Mann Act prosecution proves our dislike of prostitution, without in any way affecting that ancient institution. The Insull trial shows that we dislike customary methods of finance without committing us to a government control which would actually prevent those practices. The jury acquittal is a *sub rosa* admission that if we look be-beneath the symbols those practices are inevitable under the system. The ceremonial trial never is, or can be, an efficient method of settling disputes. Of course efficiency is one of its ideals, but there are others equally important which must also be dramatized. Therefore, if we want real speed, or efficiency—in other words, if results are more important than the moral lessons which are to be taught by the process—we move the settlement of the dispute into a less symbolic atmosphere. We find this atmosphere in what we call administrative tribunals. Yet in a climate of opinion which demands the comforting belief that there is a "rule of law," the administrative tribunals never quite satisfy us, and the ceremonial trial continues as a method of resolving all disputes concerning which philosophical argument is possible.

For example, the Securities Act is probably not as efficient a method of protecting investors as a more drastic system of administrative control would be. It relies in part on penalties to be enforced by juries. Yet drastic administrative control of the machinery of investment was not politically possible at the time the act was passed. No one wanted to give up the moral ideals involved in a free market where it was possible for fools and their money to be parted. Therefore the criminal trial was used to provide a symbol that trading was to be made moral, and that honesty was the only policy which could be successfully pursued in an industrial free-for-all conflict. Had we been emotionally ready to give up the conflict, the criminal penalties would have been relatively unimportant and the administrative control far more effective.[1] If we had recognized that it was just as important to prevent fools from losing their money as investors, we would have abandoned the notion that investment safety could be increased by a full disclosure of the facts.

Out of the mass of ideals and attitudes which make up our spiritual government two stand out as primarily important, in connection with the criminal trial. They are the ideal of a fair trial and the ideal of law enforcement. These two deep-seated notions constantly conflict with humanitarian sentiments, with practical considerations, and with each other. Out of that conflict comes a large part of our elaborate judicial system, the form of much legislation, most of the crusades, countercrusades, vice inquiries, good-government movements, and appeals for human dignity and freedom which make up so much of our thinking about government. Without an appreciation of the significance of its ideals, the criminal trial becomes a maze of inconsistencies; but with an understanding of their function even the inconsistencies take on a real meaning in the emotional life of our times. Therefore it is important to observe their operation in some detail.

The Ideal of a Fair Trial

THE notion that every man however lowly is entitled to a trial and an impartial hearing is regarded as the cornerstone of civilized government. Before this notion considerations of efficiency in the administration of the law must give way. Even a criminal caught in the act is still entitled to present his "defense" to a tribunal which must be ignorant of the event. This ideal is as old as Western civilization, and

---

1. Though criminal penalties actually are of comparative unimportance in the Securities Act, the legislation was heralded to the public as penal legislation.

its significance in our culture is tremendous. It involves the humanitarian notion that the underdog is always entitled to a chance. It gives us a sense of security against what we are accustomed to call "mob rule." So persistent is it that once the symbol of a "fair trial" has been violated, the matter is never quite ended until the ideal is vindicated. Every legal device intended to establish judicial finality was employed in the Mooney Case, yet the justice of that trial was an important political issue in a campaign fifteen years after Mooney had been sent to prison.

The ideal of a fair trial can be studied in operation better than it can be defined or described. It can be observed more objectively if the example taken is a trial removed from the prejudice of our own time. The trial of Jeanne d'Arc, in 1431[2] offers us an excellent mirror in which we see reflected our own ideas of what a fair trial should be. Here was an attempt to create a record of dignity and impartiality, made by judges who at the outset were moved by political pressures. The effect of the sincere attempt to create a fair trial record was to change the original partisan attitude of the judges to one of sympathy. It is a lengthy and carefully prepared record in which the trial judges took great pride because it represented in their eyes the fairest and most dignified judicial procedure possible; and because it showed that in spite of the obvious guilt of the defendant, no opportunity for her to present her case had been neglected or slurred over.

During the years that follow this trial we find this case condemned as an outstanding example of hypocrisy by a partisan court. Yet the fairness of the proceedings is evidenced by the fact that most of the evidence on which her fame rests is found in the trial record itself. Her guilt is clearly established. An open-minded reader can scarcely es-

2. W. P. Barrett's translation, *The Trial of Jeanne D'Arc* (1932).

cape the conclusion that Jeanne was setting herself up as a moral authority above the heads of the Church. That this was heresy at the time, few would deny. Of course we may criticize the law of heresy as outrageous, and a commentary on the intolerance of medieval government. Naturally in our more enlightened age we consider prosecutions for heresy as examples of bigotry, and very different in character from refusing citizenship to a minister of the gospel who declined to fight in a hypothetical future war, or from sentencing a Boston bookseller for disposing of one of the works of D. H. Lawrence,[3] or from punishing a man named Gitlow[4] for making anarchistic addresses. Such distinctions have their unquestioned merit and are so well settled that they need not be argued here. We only wish to point out that they are irrelevant to a criticism of the judicial process itself. A fair criticism of the trial of Jeanne d'Arc must proceed on the assumption that the medieval court was compelled to represent the prevailing ideals and phobias of its era. As commentators on the judicial process of this medieval court, we must therefore refrain from blaming it for the governmental philosophy of the Middle Ages.

Judged by this standard, the record of the trial of Jeanne d'Arc shows all the restraint and all the judicial attitude of the best-conducted trials of our own day. It is a record of which a modern prosecutor might well be proud. The conventional requirements of due process familiar to us are all present, though under different names: we find a preliminary hearing; an indictment which discloses to the accused the nature of her offense in elaborate detail; a trial in which the evidence is fully disclosed and opportunity is given to the accused to meet all relevant issues; an appellate review

3. *Commonweath* vs. *James A. De Lacey*, 271 *Mass.* 327 (1930). See also "Massachusetts and Censorship," 10 *Boston University Law Review* 147 at 182 (1930).

4. *Gitlow* vs. *People of New York*, 268 *U.S.* 652 (1925).

of both the law and the evidence; and a permanent written transcript of the entire proceedings.

We find missing only one of the modern requirements of a fair trial, the representation of the accused by counsel. Nevertheless, if we let the record speak for itself we find a certain fairness in the questions asked and full opportunity for the defendant to deliberate on her answers. In fact the absence of counsel seems to impel the court to be less brutal in its questioning than is now permitted under cross-examination. Jeanne avails herself very well of her opportunities. Her answers show astuteness and legal skill. Her great fault lies in the fact that she has the courage of her convictions, and those convictions are that she is in closer touch with the Deity through her Voices than even the Lords of the Church themselves. She is setting her conscience, as represented by her Voices, against the fundamental theories of ecclesiastical government; and such presumption will seldom be permitted in any organized society properly mindful of the prestige of its institutions.

The deliberations of the University of Paris, whose entire faculties were requested to review the proceedings, proceed with inevitable logic. The Faculty of Theology is very skeptical about Jeanne's "Voices," stating that they are either lies, or else that they proceed from the diabolical spirits Belial, Satan, and Behemoth, with which terms the ancients described what we now call dangerous radicalism. The Faculty of Degrees points out truthfully enough that if this woman was sane (and there is no reason to believe that she was insane, even according to our modern right and wrong test), she had separated herself from obedience to the Church militant. Inasmuch as the Church militant is unfamiliar to some, it may be helpful to point out that Jeanne's attitude was much the same as that of the late socialist Eugene Debs who was sentenced for separating himself from obedience to the Government. The chief difference between them was that Jeanne believed in killing people to further her peculiar ideas and Debs did not.

The method of appeal in Jeanne's trial is admirable in its simplicity as well as dignified in its procedural form. It appears to be discretionary, just as appeal by certiorari is discretionary in the United States Supreme Court today. Yet it is entirely free from procedural traps because the court itself takes the trouble of getting up its own Appellate Record. No judicial doctrine prevents the appellate court from reviewing all the facts as it did in the Sacco-Vanzetti Case. No philosophy concerning the nature of proceedings in error hinders the court from going into the merits.

The effect on the conduct of the judges of the ideal of a fair trial is most illuminating. As the trial proceeds one detects the change of attitude due to the orderly and rational procedure which they have adopted. At first we suspect that for reasons which might well be described by the insidious word "political" these judges would have been delighted to convict Jeanne. Natural human emotions of sympathy are submerged in the desire to get rid of her. But as the trial progresses, the court becomes more and more sympathetic with the heroine; and as it is made more and more evident that respect for the law compels them to convict no matter how they feel, it becomes no longer necessary for the court to suppress its feeling of regret. The court becomes more paternal in its attitude. When the question of torture is raised, "to restore her to the way of knowledge and truth," these judges, accustomed as they were to such methods of salvation, decide after a long conference (with some dissenting votes) that torture is unnecessary. And at the end we believe that final sentence was imposed with real regret, because of judicial necessity, rather than celebrated as a political victory.

Had the "substantive law" of heresy been in Jeanne's fa-

vor, this dignified and logical process might even have compelled acquittal, in spite of the motives which inspired the prosecution. For the ritual which we today term "due process" is powerful in its emotional effect on a court which follows it. A "political" conviction is difficult to obtain without using a form of procedure by which the court escapes looking at the facts. On the other hand in trials where conviction is certain, courts may more willingly give the accused the advantage of every protection because of the fact that these protections can do him no good. To a certain extent it may be said that the judicial protection of accused persons by way of preliminary hearing, the orderly taking of testimony, and the right to appeal have crept into the law, not to free innocent persons, but to make judges feel that in the trial of the unquestionably guilty there has been offered every fair means of defense. In such cases even new safeguards may be afforded in order to give the judges the comforting feeling that not they but the law is punishing the defendant. Nor is this to be condemned as hypocrisy because the emotional effect of safeguards thus invented may have a powerful restraining influence in later and less obvious cases.

The appeal to the University of Paris was an additional safeguard in this case. The appellate courts did not try to escape the consideration of evidence by relying on presumptions in favor of the court below as the California court was compelled to do in the Mooney Case. It could and did consider and review all of the facts.

Yet of Jeanne's trial it has been said that "rarely has injustice taken the light of justice to this degree." There is a very subtle fallacy behind this judgment of the judicial process. It assumes that these judges did not believe in the law which they were enforcing and that the formulations of the doctrines of heresy which they invoked were not among the compelling forces behind the decision. Such a judgment forgets the impelling force of dignified and rational procedure upon the judges who invent it.

The trial may be compared with that of Eugene Debs and Benjamin Gitlow in our own day. Debs made speeches inconsistent with the purposes of a militant government in time of war. Gitlow made them in time of peace. Both had fair trials and full appellate-court consideration. Both convictions were sustained with judicial regret—the one, on the theory that the war could not be carried on if Debs were allowed to talk; the other, on the theory that peace could not be secure if persons like Gitlow are allowed to talk. The prosecuting attorney might have ignored either or both of these men without serious consequences. It is doubtful if even Debs could have stopped the war, and it is not at all clear that even Gitlow's sentence postponed the depression. Yet once these cases were in court, the conviction of these men could confidently be predicted in any country which adopts the prejudices of Western civilization. No judicial machine is likely to question the underlying assumptions of the government which it supports, however regrettable those assumptions may be.

Courts, in the long run, can probably be true to their judicial character only if they frankly expose on their records for the judgment of the future all the relevant facts of the cases which they decide. Only in this way can the assumptions on which the decisions were based be examined. The fact that Jeanne d'Arc was rehabilitated on the trial record itself is the best evidence of the character of the proceedings. A fair trial can never insure a fair result, but it can at least afford an opportunity for consideration of all the circumstances. This is the most important contribution which trial procedure can make to our judicial process. Where a court allows all the relevant facts to appear on the record, we may well forgive unfortunate results caused by human prejudices. Where a court denies this, seeking safety in presumptions and ancient doctrine, leaving to outsiders the burden of disclosing all the facts on which it should have acted, thus making such outsiders who desire to complete the record appear as attacking the court itself, and, through it, the State, then only is the rather splendid ideal of a fair trial in danger.

Yet in spite of all this, the trial of Jeanne d'Arc is generally regarded as an outstanding example of judicial unfairness. Paradoxically enough, this is because of its attempt to be fair. It permitted all of the good qualities of the defendant to shine through the record. Had Jeanne been stabbed in the dark, it would have been only another assassination, and the evidence on which the Maid was made a saint might have been lost to the world forever. But the record was so carefully and meticulously prepared, and all the arguments in favor of Jeanne were so carefully set out and answered, that as soon as prosecutions for heresy no longer fitted into popular prejudices, this trial, so eminently fair, appeared to be unfair.

Indeed it is the most important function of the ceremony of a trial to leave a record by which we can examine the injustice done to well-meaning and harmless persons through the blind phobias which from time to time make themselves part of the law. And it is most important for the observer to distinguish whether the trial itself was fair, not whether the phobia was unreasonable.

Fair trials are difficult to obtain except where the judicial institution is confident of itself and its own powers. Only a feeling of security on the part of the judiciary can create an atmosphere where the underdog is given a chance. If the Alabama court in the Scottsboro Case dared to say that as a matter of principle negroes were not entitled to sit on juries, and that negroes who had intercourse with white women were to be treated as white men who committed rape, we would find a calm atmosphere about the trial which is now completely lacking. The negroes might be convicted but the trial would have been fair. The Southern court, however, did not have that confidence in the reasonableness of its conduct which permitted it to spread it frankly on the record. Therefore the trial became a maze of attempts to keep relevant material out of the record. Blunders occurred so obviously against the accepted form of a trial that the Supreme Court of the United States reversed the case.[5]

Yet the cultural value of the ideal of a fair trial is advanced as much by its failure as it is by its success. Any violation of the symbol of a ceremonial trial rouses persons who would be left unmoved by an ordinary nonceremonial injustice. Thus the Scottsboro Case gained nation-wide attention. The defendants may finally be hanged, but the cause of tolerance has been dramatized in a way no one will quite forget. Harmless anarchists may be shot by the police in a strike. Liberals will be sorry and forget. But let them be unfairly treated by a court, as happened in the Mooney Case,[6] and, before the dissatisfaction has died away, the prejudice or phobia which created the unfair atmosphere of the trial will receive a public analysis and examination which otherwise it would not get. Even Germany, caught in an absurd phobia, was compelled, by the persistency of this dream of what a trial should be, to attempt to spread their case upon a court record in the trial of those accused of burning the Reichstag. That attempt made Germany a somewhat better place in spite of the cruelty with which the proceedings were conducted.

It is of course true that all the machinery surrounding the ideal of a fair trial has its social cost in delays, technicalities, and injustices in the judicial process. It is equally true that

5. *Powell* vs. *Alabama*, 278 *U.S.* 45 (1932), *Patterson* vs. *Alabama*, 294 *U.S.* 600 (1934).
6. Henry T. Hunt, *The Case of Mooney and Billings.*

in times of public fear and intolerance this machinery is seldom strong enough to prevent the conviction of weak and harmless persons. Yet the cultural effect of these failures on mass psychology is probably worth everything it costs because of its contribution to the ultimate survival of a great humanitarian ideal.

The ideal of a fair trial, of course, is constantly in conflict with other ideals. As an example of this the writer recalls a conversation with a great law teacher. Jake Factor, a notorious resident of Chicago, was resisting extradition sought by English authorities. He was represented by Newton D. Baker, who was successful in getting the United States Circuit Court of Appeals to deny extradition.[7] (Their opinion was subsequently reversed by the Supreme Court of the United States.[8]) The law teacher expressed dismay that a man of Mr. Baker's prominence at the bar should defend a member of the underworld. He was reminded that the Bar Association had gone on record against the practice of criminal law by a class called "shysters" and, therefore, persons like Mr. Baker should be urged to defend criminals, since every criminal is entitled to a defense. His reply was that while perhaps this might be so, the defense should be conducted in a less belligerent manner, and should consist only in a cold presentation of the possible points involved. The answer was then given that if Mr. Baker had done this, he would probably have lost the case, and this would be a breach of loyalty toward his client.

In the same way, in every criminal prosecution we see a number of absolutely contradictory ideals marching side by side: an attorney should not take cases the winning of which imperils the forces of law and order; every criminal, however, is entitled to a defense; criminal lawyers, however, should not resort to mere technicalities; nevertheless they

---

7. *Factor* vs. *Laubenheimer,* 61 F. (2d) 626. (*C.C.A.* 7th 1932.)
8. *Idem,* 290 *U.S.* 276 (1933).

should do everything legally possible for their clients. Involved in these contradictory statements we have the notion of fair trial; law enforcement; attorneys as agents of their clients; attorneys as officers of the court; the right of a criminal to have the full protection of all the law; the undesirability of his taking advantage of technicalities; the impropriety of a court ignoring a technicality because only the legislature can change the law; the query as to what, after all, is a technicality (since everyone always brands as technicalities any procedure which reaches a result he does not like).

In addition to the notion of fair hearing, the ceremonial trial must dramatize the impersonal application of logical rules to facts. Here we have the contradiction between the ideal of a permanent unyielding law which must be enforced without respect to persons, and the ideal of justice, which can never ignore persons. This conflict is resolved as most conflicts are resolved, by inventing a devil who can be blamed for the inconsistencies of the system. In the American trial the part of the devil is taken by the jury. We are constantly defending the jury as the best device for securing "Justice" ever invented, and at the same time attacking it and seeking to limit its functions. The defense always refers to juries in general as an institution protecting our liberties, etc. The attack always centers about juries in particular types of cases, considered as an unpredictable body, moved by emotional considerations, and not careful of the fundamental principles of the law because of ignorance, prejudice, etc. Yet the jury continues as the great symbol of justice, in spite of constant proof of its inadequacy in particular cases.

Actually, of course, the reason for the existence of the jury[9] is to absorb the criticism of the numerous unsatisfactory re-

9. Cf. E. S. Robinson, *Law and the Lawyers* (1935), p. 293, discussing the jury as a method of conflict resolution.

sults in the trial of cases, and thus to deflect it against the judicial system itself. When Insull is acquitted, we blame the jury if we do not like the result. We cannot blame the law, because according to law there was a question of fact to be left to the jury which the law had no right to decide.

In civil cases the ideals and symbols are more complicated and therefore the jury does not play as prominent a rôle. In the criminal law, where the issue revolves around notions which the common man thinks he understands, the jury is found an inseparable part of the system, even in continental Europe. Waivers of juries are much more difficult in the field of criminal law—constitutional guaranties are stronger—because here we have simple and understandable symbols, and therefore need a very simple and understandable devil. Even in continental Europe, where the jury is not used in civil cases, it retains its position in the criminal law.

It is not alone the fact that the jury is a great shock absorber in that area where ideals conflict with actual results, which gives the system its power to resist practical reform. Much of its strength is due to the romance and color which is centered in the jury trial. More efficient methods of judicial investigation can easily be imagined, but none more picturesque. When a great government treats the lowliest of criminals as an equal antagonist, strips itself of the executive power which it possesses, and submits the case to twelve ordinary men, allowing the judge only the authority of an umpire, we have a gesture of recognition to the dignity of the individual which has an extraordinary dramatic appeal. Its claim is on our emotions, rather than our common sense. We feel that our conception of human equality needs this concrete institution to give it reality.

To those who believe that legal institutions are following a logical pattern, the criminal trial is a very confusing phenomenon. Reformers who seriously believe that the judicial process should seek a rational solution of the problem of crime are able to show that it is a complete failure. The rules of evidence are not an efficient technique of investigation, and it is easy to prove that they are only the rules of a game. The definition of criminal responsibility which courts are forced to use does not square with the ideas of modern psychology. The criminal sentence of the defendant to the penitentiary does not reform him. On the contrary, by shutting him off from the world, and giving him nothing to do but to brood over his past experiences, it prevents any effective reform of his character, as has been demonstrated by students of criminology time after time.[10] Those who think that the judicial process should be a cold-blooded method of removing criminals from society are also always able to prove that the criminal law is a failure. Of course while the criminal is in jail, he cannot commit further crimes; but society is unable to follow the cold-blooded logic which would require courts to sentence dangerous persons to jail for life, or to execute them. A jail which incarcerates dangerous persons permanently is just as utopian an idea as a jail which gives them an opportunity to shake off old habits and develop different personalities. We may make futile gestures toward both of these ideals, but popular psychology will not permit any consistent pursuit of either policy. When steps are taken to make the criminal forget his past habits by substituting new ones, popular indignation rises because the penitentiary is being made a pleasant place, and this is used as an explanation of that crime wave which can always be discovered at any time by anyone who is looking for it. When, on the other hand, drastic sentences are imposed, humanitarian ideals always prevent them from being carried out consistently. Thus we swing from one emotional posi-

10. One of the most penetrating discussions of the effect of penal sentences on the criminal is found in Frank Tannenbaum's, *Osborne of Sing Sing* (Univ. of North Carolina Press, 1933).

tion to another, with the net result that just about as many criminals are graduated from our penitentiaries each year as are incarcerated. Our criminal system offers a course of education in crime, and neither reforms the criminal nor cuts off the supply of new ones.

None of these results can be attributed to the criminal trial, because the only function which the criminal trial can perform is to express currently held ideals about crime and about trials. It can act as a brake against a popular hysteria which insists upon following any one of the ideals to its logical conclusion, but it can only accomplish this by emphasizing some competing ideal. Thus in prohibition times the ideal against searches and seizures was given a new emphasis in response to a popular demand, and thus the courts appeared as the great bulwarks of individual liberty. But it is an error to consider courts as an enforcing agency. Actually, in the play of conflicting ideals in the trial, we have a great stabilizing agency. In the confusion so many different moral values are represented that everyone is more or less satisfied that his own ideals have not been entirely ignored.

This position makes the judicial process constantly open to the attack that it is behind the times, because it never quite lives up to any of the ideals of the times. Actually, however, the criminal trial is probably more up to date than any part of the legal process. Overwhelming evidence of this is found in the enormous appeal which such trials make to the public. They permit the public to argue and discuss all the various contradictory attitudes about crime and criminals, since these different rôles are all represented by the various persons connected with the trial, with tremendous dramatic effect.

Obviously, therefore, the public administration of criminal justice is not a method of controlling crime. It is rather one of the problems which must be faced by those who desire to control crime. Without the drama of the criminal trial, it is difficult to imagine on just what institution we would hang our conflicting ideals of public morality. It is hard to imagine government except in the light of a protector of decency and morals through a series of parables which are a guide to the honest and a terror to the outlaw. To treat criminals with common sense, one must classify them as insane. Only in this way can we adopt genuine therapeutic techniques without appearing to tear down the foundations of our society.

CHAPTER VII

Law Enforcement

GENERALLY and vaguely opposed to the ideal of fair trial is that of the sacredness of law enforcement. The place which this notion occupies in our ideas of government is amazing. For example, in 1928, when the country was about to plunge into a depression, a poll of leading businessmen showed that they considered the most dangerous American problem to be lack of respect for law. No one knows quite what they mean by law enforcement or respect for law, and the contradictions involved are the subject of endless discussion. Its intricacies provide a fascinating riddle, like the problem whether a father should harbor his son who is a murderer instead of turning him over to the police. Out of it, a constant succession of dramas can be spun.

It is, however, more than a mere parlor discussion. Its institutional effects are tremendous. The whole form and organization of the administration of criminal law are molded by our interest in, and insistence upon, the validity of this ideal. It represents the feeling that criminal justice is impartial and impersonal, that principles instead of personal discretion control both judges and prosecutors. Its conflict with other ideals is never ending, and always fraught with intense dramatic interest. Indeed an understanding of the conflict between this ideal and others is essential to a comprehension of the way government operates. We will begin with the analysis of a typical situation.

A few years ago the Massie trial in Honolulu was occupying the attention of the civilized world. A lieutenant in the United States Navy had killed a native Hawaiian suspected of criminal assault upon the Lieutenant's wife. The Ha-

waiian had been tried for the offense and acquitted, but the
Lieutenant's family and many of the public still believed in
the guilt of the accused. Everyone connected with the case
became world figures, and there were few dinner tables in
America where the merits of the case were not argued pro
and con with great heat.

The reason for the emotional significance of the case was
that it dramatized two ideals—first, law enforcement, and,
second, a code of personal honor above the law. Both ideals
are emotionally necessary for the average American, and
therefore he refuses to give up either. Since every right-
thinking man believes that law should be enforced impersonally, those who argued for Massie's acquittal appeared to
their opponents as against law and in favor of lynching. On
the one hand law does not permit exceptions for non-
legal reasons. Therefore the freeing of Massie leads to the
supposed danger that all murderers may be turned loose on
sentimental grounds. On the other hand there is the feeling
that no red-blooded American should permit an assault of
his wife to go unavenged. Those for whom this chivalric
notion is paramount refuse to consider Massie as a criminal.
In the hopeless mental confusion that results men turn to
the Law for an answer.

The Law solves the problem by accepting both ideals,
and relegating one to a *sub rosa* position. The defense in
the case is insanity. No one really believes that Massie was
insane, and the alienists who testify for him at the trial are
regarded with suspicion because Massie does not look "insane" to the man of common sense. However, the alienists
perform a useful function in reconciling the conflict between law enforcement and personal honor. They absorb
the blame. Under the protecting mantle of the notion that
they are applying scientific principles, alienists consider all
of the mitigating circumstances which would otherwise be
excluded, and discuss them before a jury. In this way the

conflict between personal honor and the law is fully presented and the jury given an opportunity to acquit if it desires. Both of the conflicting ideals are recognized, and the interest in the case gradually dies down. If Law Enforcement could be treated as a useful emotional value which had only a limited application like Santa Claus, or football in college—if we did not feel we had to mold our entire system to be consistent with it—much of the elaborate argumentative technique which surrounds criminal law would disappear. However, it is so important to our institutions that it cannot be so treated. Its universal application must never be denied in public. Therefore the ceremonies which attend its observance, and which conceal the escapes from its implications, become very elaborate indeed.

The creed of Law Enforcement was stated by President Hoover in connection with the famous Wickersham Commission as follows:

The most malign of all these dangers [to the State] today is disregard and disobedience of law. . . . Our whole system of self-government will crumble either if officials elect what laws they will enforce or citizens elect what laws they will support. The worst evil of disregard for some laws is that it destroys respect for all law. . . . If citizens do not like a law their duty as honest men and women is to discourage its violation; their right is to work openly for its repeal.

The idea that a prosecuting attorney should be permitted to use his discretion concerning the laws which he will enforce and those which he will disregard appears to the ordinary citizen to border on anarchy. The fact that prosecuting attorneys are compelled to do this very thing is generally ignored, or, when attention is called to it, regarded as evidence of some kind of social degeneration which must be preached away in public speech and judicial utterance. Nor does the fact that the actual conduct of the ordinary citizen constantly contradicts this ideal seem to weaken public faith in it. During Prohibition, politicians could drink in private, but they had to come out for law enforcement in public. Disorder must be curbed by law enforcement. If laws are not enforced, disorder will be presumed whether it actually exists or not. Therefore failure to enforce laws is disorder in itself. The idea is essentially a religious one, and we are acclimated to a wide conflict between practice and utterance in the realm of such notions. Even those who regard the ideal as impracticable, so far as their own conduct is concerned, consider it good for the public in general.

The effect of such notions on general human conduct is slight indeed. But the effect on judicial institutions, their verbal technique, and their procedural structure is very important. It is difficult either to understand or to reform criminal law or procedure without taking the underlying assumption of law enforcement as an ideal into consideration, because it will color the interpretation of any attempted change.

It is important to keep in mind that we are concerned with Law Enforcement as a sort of creed, and not with the enforcement of any particular rule. When, by imperceptible gradations, emphasis is changed from the purpose or merits of a rule itself to the notion that the very prestige of government depends on enforcement as a kind of ceremonial, to be observed even toward obnoxious legislation— when the enforcement becomes directed, not to preserve public safety or convenience, but to justify a moral attitude toward law regardless of public convenience—then the common-sense idea with which we started has become the mystical ideal called Law Enforcement.

The first important thing to be noted about Law Enforcement is that while it always appears to be very closely related to the problem of public order and safety, actually it has very little to do with it. Its effect is rather on the public utterances of those interested in the criminal law and on the appearance of the judiciary to the public. In order to understand this we must recognize that there are two very distinct problems of criminal administration: first, the keeping of order in the community; and, second, the dramatization of the moral notions of the community.

The first is primarily a police and prosecutor's problem, little concerned with, and only incidentally affected by, any governmental philosophy. General satisfaction with or acceptance of the economic system, plus a good set of policemen, is probably more important in preserving peace than any code of criminal law. Given reasonable approximation of such a condition, the problem of the police and prosecutor is the suppression of the occasional dangerous individual. For this purpose the ideal that all laws should be enforced without a discretionary selection is impossible to carry out. It is like directing a general to attack the enemy on all fronts at once. It conveys no idea whatever as to what the prosecution should do. The prosecutor therefore must look at the criminal law, not as something to be enforced because it governs society, but as an arsenal of weapons with which to incarcerate certain dangerous individuals who are bothering society. He will be confronted with a long line of offenders caught in the net who are unimportant, but who must be disposed of. His choice will be either to make reasonable compromises with them, or else to clog the machinery with relentless prosecution of comparatively harmless persons. There also will be dangerous and important criminals who are sentenced under some minor count because there is not sufficient evidence to convict them of the crime for which they are apprehended, and whose ignorance of the strength of the prosecutor's case makes them believe a guilty plea to a lesser offense is a wise compromise. Or they may be restrained under some en-

tirely different law dealing with the income-tax or va-
grancy statutes, because it is more convenient. The fact that
there are more laws than he can ever enforce is not a handicap but an aid to the prosecutor because it gives him so
many offensive weapons against any particular individual.
Obsolete laws may be revived and used for purposes that
their authors never dreamed of, to sink into obscurity again
when the particular individual has been put behind the
bars. The prosecutor wants to win cases, and to restrain
individuals. The ideal of law enforcement, distrusting bargaining, demanding uniform sentences, and putting the
emphasis on laws rather than on individuals, sinks into the
background.

The second function of criminal law administration, to
dramatize the moral notions of the public, is probably the
most important function of the criminal courts, as distinguished from the prosecutor, because they work in the limelight of public observation. We may illustrate this by two
cases, one in which Al Capone, against whom no sufficient
evidence of bootlegging or racketeering had been found,
was sentenced under a tax law;[1] and another in which an
admitted whiskey ring, against which there was all sorts of
evidence, was freed by the Supreme Court of the United
States.[2] In the Capone Case a compromise was at first reached
on perfectly justifiable grounds, known to the Federal judge
and approved by the Attorney-General of the United States.
Subsequent advertisement of his good fortune by Capone
himself made this compromise impossible because it con-
flicted with the ideal of law enforcement. It became necessary, and under the circumstances quite justifiable, for the
Federal judge to repudiate the compromise and to an-
nounce from the bench that there could be no bargaining

1. *Capone* vs. *U.S.*, 51 F. (2d) 609. (*C.C.A.* 7th 1931.)
2. *Go-Bart Importing Company* vs. *U.S.*, 282 *U.S.* 344 (1930).

with the Federal court. The expediency of this announce-
ment from the point of view of the dramatic function of
criminal courts is obvious in spite of the fact that statistical
studies indicate that it would be quite impossible to conduct
the criminal business of the Federal court without something which can only be distinguished from bargaining by
logical hairsplitting. Capone was then sentenced for violation of the income-tax laws, but the penalty was obviously
based on his supposed violations of other laws. The prestige
of the State seemed somehow involved in his conviction.
There was a general impression that an acquittal would
cause respect for the law to suffer a very serious setback,
leading to all sorts of vaguely imagined calamities. The
actual incarceration of Capone may have had some effect
on the criminal situation in Chicago, but certainly very
little elsewhere. Yet the case was considered of the utmost
importance on the criminal problem all over the country;
it was hailed as a triumph of law enforcement. People generally felt better because of the emotional significance of this
vindication of Law against its enemies. It was as important as a spectacular victory in a war, in which someone
who wore epaulettes and bore the title of general had been
captured.

In the same way when the admitted whiskey ring was
freed by the Supreme Court of the United States because
of an invalid search, we were furnished with a symbol of
the conflicting ideal that government should not enforce
laws by unreasonable searches no matter what they find. A
moment's reflection would indicate that the temper of the
police commissioner is of much more significance on governmental interference with rights of respectable citizens
than appellate-court utterances. The testimony of any district attorney will bear out the assertion that persons who
consciously rely upon these utterances are almost always

criminals who deserve to be convicted. Third-degree methods may flourish even in an atmosphere of appellate-court condemnation. But the function of courts here is not directed toward the practical solution of the problem with which they can have little to do. They are engaging in a public ceremonial in celebration of an ideal. For this purpose, the more deserving the accused is of punishment, the more striking is the exemplification of the emotional lesson. Thus the prestige of the government in enforcing laws is vindicated in one case; while a ceremonial in memory of individual freedom from law enforcement is celebrated in another. The task of keeping these two shows going at the same time without losing the patronage or support of the Constitution for either is then left to the legal scholar. The result is the development of criminal law, as a body of fundamental principle, with conflicting details which are puzzling to persons who do not understand the unexamined popular assumptions that lie in the background.

The dramatic ideal of "Law Enforcement" as it has become part of the political consciousness of today shares the frailty of all ideals in that, when reduced to logical statements instead of being expressed emotionally or poetically, it disappears. The best statement which we can make of it would run about as follows. Laws (particularly criminal laws) are peculiarly sacred things. Whatever their merit intrinsically or by whatever political chicanery they may have been passed, they must be respected or enforced. Laws must be respected because, as President Hoover said, if any single law is not enforced it leads to disrespect for all laws which in turn leads to the nonenforcement of all laws. The original notion of respect for a "law" which is above the king was invented as a justification for revolt against constituted authority acting in an arbitrary way. Under Prohibition, it became the emotional compulsion *not* to revolt against constituted authority acting in an arbitrary way. Under the New Deal, on the other hand, "respect for law" justified revolt against particular laws in the name of individualism.

These circular notions, sometimes learnedly and at other times oratorically or poetically expressed, are constantly molding our criminal administration and our ideas of its reform. In the struggle over. Prohibition they compelled the wets as well as the drys to demand enforcement. So fixed was the notion in the popular mind, that parents often hid commonplace liquor violations from their children because they were unable to formulate a philosophy which would justify their conduct even to themselves. They did not want to be a "malign influence" causing disrespect for government. A politician who today would publicly advocate the disregard of any law would be a dangerous radical, because such an open statement of a well-known fact would disturb the structure of our Government.

It is curious to note that as the ideal of law enforcement becomes more and more abstract and mystical it has less and less to do with actual enforcement. This is illustrated by the fact that it attaches itself to some laws and not to others in a way which seems almost accidental. Generally, the laws or the instances which cause the most violent emotions of law enforcement in the public mind are those of the least social significance. The creed is notably absent in so-called civil cases, and even from criminal penalties in the field usually designated as civil law. We do not find it attached to negligence, breaches of contract, public-utility rate-making, corporate mergers, unfair competition, etc. Attorneys who arrange devices by which their corporation clients may avoid the implications of such laws are able to maintain positions of impregnable respectability. If they assisted in the operations of a bootlegging syndicate, their social positions would be much less secure. To a man from Mars, however, unaccustomed to our emotional atmosphere, it might seem that the prestige of the State might just as well be involved in public-utility-rate-making provisions as in the occasional incarceration of a bootlegger. The important difference which he would fail to see is that the case of the bootlegger is much simpler, less important, and more easily understood by the man on the street, and therefore offers better material for drama in which conflicting ideals are alternately demonstrated.

It is also curious to note that the creed generally attaches to laws which are not only not enforced but which cannot be enforced. It has surrounded rules regarding chastity of priests in the Middle Ages, card playing by members of the Methodist Church, and prohibition violations in our own day, all of which appear to have been impossible ideals, with an importance and with a vast body of expository logic which the actual social effect of these rules would hardly seem to warrant. The creed has made relatively insignificant laws grow like snowballs, adding enforcement provisions to provisions which are to be enforced, penalties to penalties, speeches to appeals to civil consciousness at public mass meetings, oratory to scientific reasoning until other social problems are completely forgotten in the turmoil. Among criminal laws the public emotion which was expended over prohibition enforcement has been ten times that involved in the more serious crime of murder. And even in murder cases the issue of "Law Enforcement" becomes acute only in such cases as that of Lieutenant Massie who killed the ravisher of his wife under circumstances which raise grave doubt about the justice of the law's penalty.

This attitude has very significant effects on political theory, on legal procedure, on the treatment of convicted criminals and the general problem of crime.

Effect of the Ideal of Law Enforcement on Political Theory

ONE of the most interesting results of this attitude on political theory is the generally accepted and constantly recurring slogan that we have too many laws. Learned people are always counting the laws and claiming that their number is a menace because they cannot all be enforced. No policeman can learn all of them and therefore he cannot know what to "enforce"; no citizen can keep from unwittingly committing "crimes." There appear to be 13,672 sections in the Missouri code, 15,532 in Michigan, 15,367 in Ohio, and eight volumes in New York. (To make the argument more impressive, "civil" and "criminal" statutes are usually lumped together.) Many speeches and numerous articles are formulated on this theme whenever the talk turns to the administration of criminal law. And yet one is not accustomed to hear complaints made about dictionaries because they contain so many words which are never used, thereby causing disrespect for words. The prestige of the church does not appear to suffer because there are so many texts in the Bible upon which sermons are never preached, or so many hymns in the hymnbooks which are never sung.

Obviously these constantly reiterated warnings about the number of laws do no more than illustrate the conception of law enforcement and its general unanalyzed acceptance. They lead to practically no tangible results. It seems to be a permanent characteristic of criminal codes that they are palimpsests, with one thing written over another, with few things ever repealed. The theory that this can be cured by education does not seem to have worked out, because with the increase in legal training the process has only been accelerated. No way has yet been discovered of preventing moral attitudes from persisting long after they are in direct conflict with human behavior. Most unenforced criminal laws survive in order to satisfy moral objections to established modes of conduct. They are unenforced because we want to continue our conduct, and unrepealed because we want to preserve our morals. However, so far as the effect of the number of criminal laws on policemen or the prosecutor is concerned, they are more apt to be a help than a hindrance. Such persons are trying to apprehend individuals who at the time happen to be considered dangerous to society, and the wider the selection of laws which they have, the more chance there is of conviction. Of course this power in the prosecutor to dig up obsolete laws, or to use laws passed for one purpose (such as the income-tax law) to accomplish an entirely different result may be viewed with alarm. However, it is the very creed of law enforcement which increases the number of laws. Given a law which is not enforced, we must pass other laws to enforce that law, and still others to make effective the laws to enforce the law. Hence the same attitude which causes fear because there are so many laws which are not enforced, also causes the multiplication of enforcing laws. Take away that attitude, as has been done in the case of so-called "blue" laws, and they appear to die a natural death without bothering anyone, even though they are not repealed.

It may well be that we would be "better off" with less elaborate codes, but we are interested here only in pointing out the factors which cause elaboration. When codes are revised in the interests of simplicity and clarity it is usually done by lawyers. They bring to their task another ideal: that there is some use for all legal concepts, and that everything may always be reconciled with everything else—a wordy process for which the legal technique seems preeminently adapted. Hence codes appear to be increasing in size rather than diminishing, and general preaching that laws should be either enforced or repealed is not adapted to the purpose of simplification.

Effect of the Ideal of Law Enforcement on Criminal Procedure

THE chief difficulty which arises from the above ideological conflict is that procedural reforms are undertaken without taking it into account. This leads to proposals for change without examination of the standards by which we are judging the judicial institution. Thus we find attempts to raise both the salaries and dignity of police-court judges, and, at the same time, attempts to take away police-court business from high-salaried and dignified courts. We find some who condemn grand juries because the grand jury requires too many persons to interest themselves unnecessarily in the criminal process, while at the same time expenditure of more money is advocated to interest a larger number of citizens in the problems of the criminal court.

One of the most frequently applied standards is based on the unexamined assumption that courts are business institutions which are engaged in some sort of production (presumably the production of justice measured in statistical terms by the number of convictions). A comparison with the United States Steel Corporation is invoked. Speed and efficiency are the tests resorted to. Cases of rare occurrence, even though spectacular, are assumed to be of minor importance because they do not stand out in the mass statistics which grow out of all efficiency studies. We thus lose sight of the dramatic functions of the court because of the idea that courts are business institutions which should enforce law in a "businesslike" way.

The results of the ideal of law enforcement on the procedure of prosecutors, officers, and judges will be briefly described.

(1) It compels the necessary compromises of criminal cases to be carried on *sub rosa* while the process is openly condemned. Probably the difficulty with our compromise system and the technique of obtaining pleas of guilty, today, lies in the fact that concealed practices have a bad odor. In civil cases we find compromises actually encouraged as a more satisfactory method of settling disputes between individuals than an actual trial. However, if the dispute (even though it is in fact only a quarrel between individuals), finds itself in the field of criminal law, "Law Enforcement" repudiates the idea of compromise as immoral, or as at best a necessary evil. The "State" can never compromise. It must "enforce the law." Therefore open methods of compromise are impossible.

The same notion is a factor in preventing adoption of the very sensible Continental practice of combining civil and criminal penalties in one suit. This could not be done without bringing out in the open the possibilities of compromise of criminal cases by securing civil reparation. So long as civil cases are accompanied by one ideal and criminal cases by another, we will find great difficulty in combining them, no matter how sensible the result.

(2) The doctrine of mitigating circumstances pleaded at the trial of a criminal case also falls afoul of our law-enforcement creed, because the recognition of such circumstances means that some violations of the same law are to be treated differently from others. Therefore, while the State in its sentencing or in its pardoning function may take these things into consideration, they are certainly matters which jurors or anyone concerned with the stern impartial process of "trying" the accused must not know. Thus our process attempts to outlaw the "unwritten law." But since the unwritten law can never be ignored at any stage

in the proceedings, we find it creeping into the trial in devious and highly diverting ways. The only effect on the contested trial of that enormous body of literature devoted to criminal responsibility and criminal insanity is that it permits mitigating circumstances to creep into the evidence dressed up as facts to which scientific and impartial testimony may bear witness. The search for definitions of legal sanity, while it may express public morality, is pathetic in its failure to solve the trial problem of keeping emotion out while letting science in.

And now comes the latest and most entertaining development of all, the parade of psychiatrists and alienists before the bewildered jury. Since they are "scientists" every believing person expects them to agree, if not now, at least some time in the future when the court or some impartial body selects them. No practical person expects anything of the kind. In practically all cases where the issue is contested they serve only one function, which is to permit evidence of mitigating circumstances to be brought before the jury. Read the records of the Remus Case[3] and the Massie Case,[4] and you will find that the attorneys knew exactly what they were about. The problem disguises itself as a problem of the treatment of insane persons. The actual cases where expert testimony is introduced are cases of persons whom the man on the street would call sane. Most cases of insanity are, in general, dealt with by prosecutors before trial, and statistics are not necessary to prove the assertion that the prosecuting attorney does not ponder over the argumentative technique of *mens rea* (i.e., criminal responsibility) in order to make up his mind whether to prosecute or to turn an offender over to the insane hospitals. The confusion is created, not by faulty definitions of criminal responsibility, but by the conflict of the ideal

3. *In re Remus,* 119 *Ohio St.* 166 (1928).
4. *Massie Case,* Hawaii, 1931–32.

of law enforcement with the ideal of mitigating circumstances. When this problem is solved in some other way, and not before, the conflicting psychiatrists will disappear from our criminal trial.

(3) The ideal of Law Enforcement conflicts with the older concept of individual freedom from governmental interference which is not less tenaciously held, and which has become increasingly pressing as Law Enforcement has been preached. Before prohibitionists sought to distract attention from the merits of the prohibition law to Law Enforcement as involving the integrity of government, the problem of search and seizures was a minor one. Thereafter, searches and seizures became the weapon of attack which could be used against prohibition enforcement. For every "dry" speech on the dangers of disobedience, there was a "wet" oration on the dangers of invading the privacy of the home. Reflected in the courts the figures are startling. In six states selected for the purpose of study we find 19 search-and-seizure cases appealed in the 12 years preceding Prohibition and 347 in the 12 years following.[5]

Because the creed of law enforcement has a habit of arising out of laws which are impossible of being enforced, it seems to be more of an influence in this country today than in any other. England seems to have escaped it through a tradition of private prosecution. There, the prosecutor may take the position that it is a matter within his discretion as to what laws he will enforce and what laws he will leave to enforcement at the expense of private individuals who are complainants. This furnishes a logical escape from the demand of any small minority that their preference for any given legislation be turned into governmental action, which is not open to a prosecutor in this country.

5. J. D. Jennings, "Search and Seizure" (Student Essays 1931–32, Yale Law Library).

Effect of the Ideal of Law Enforcement on the Treatment of Criminals

A MOST interesting effect of the creed of law enforcement on the treatment of criminals is the recurrent wars on crime which keep appearing in this country. Such wars are generally not the result of increasing disorder but rather a consequence of a public notion that laws are not being enforced.[6] It is difficult to appraise the effect of these crusades on the actual problem. The writer suspects that in general their chief contribution is to inject an element of interest and excitement which actually hinders a scientific treatment of the problem of crime. It is unquestionably true, that while a war on crime is being prosecuted, disreputable characters in large numbers are rounded up and subjected to a certain amount of inconvenience. On the other hand, wars on crime beget a large degree of intolerance and emotion which confuses the practical solution of the problem of crime. Newspapers and periodicals invariably start an attack upon the humane treatment of prisoners, and efforts at rehabilitation in prisons receive a severe setback. The notion is drummed into the public that one of the chief causes of crime is leniency in the treatment of criminals. Statistics are produced showing that the most effective

6. "CLUBWOMEN URGED TO AID CRIME DRIVE. *Justice Official Tells the State Federation of Federal Efforts To End Violations. City Lottery Faces Fight. Mrs. Clare J. Hoyt Calls on Delegates to Buffalo Convention to Seek County Reform. (Special to the* New York Times) BUFFALO, Nov. 12, 1934. A plea for cooperation between women's clubs and local agencies for a war on crime was made by Hugh H. Clegg of the division of investigation, Federal Department of Justice, at the opening of the annual convention of the New York State Federation of Women's Clubs today. Mr. Clegg accompanied his plea with mass crime statistics. . . . During the afternoon workmen put in place the huge mural by Hildreth Meiere of the Beaux Arts Institute of Design. The painting, done for the World's Fair at Chicago, shows 'woman's emergence from the home' " (*New York Times,* Nov. 12, 1934).

method with criminals is to treat them rough. The parole system is attacked because paroled convicts are congenital backsliders. Pictures are published in popular magazines showing prisoners playing football, singing about the piano, and having a high time generally, and the public is asked if it is possible to obtain law enforcement by coddling law violators. In this way crusades on crime, by emphasizing the problem as one of instilling fear of, and respect for, the law in the minds of professional criminals, tend to keep our administration of criminal justice from developing any new techniques whatever.

The results of any policy of undue severity are to induce a reaction toward leniency. Thus it is that wars on crime are always followed by protests against third-degree methods, and proposals for more lenient treatment of criminals, so that having gone too far in the direction of harshness, we swing back into a hit-or-miss type of humanitarianism. Much can be said in favor of the effectiveness of keeping the professional criminal in jail for life. The only difficulty is that the human race is so humanitarian that a consistently harsh policy which would remove all dangerous persons permanently from society, is just as utopian as the wildest scheme of making criminals better by petting them. In spite of all our recurrent, highly publicized wars against crime, and our demands for a sterner administration of justice, the same number of persons continue to graduate from our penitentiaries as enter them. Harsh treatment within the prison therefore simply has the effect of throwing the criminal back in solitude to relive his past and plan revenge for the future. He is neither kept away from society permanently nor is he finally released with any better background. He is simply given an education in crime, and goes out in the world with his former tendencies sharpened and emphasized.

Progress in the field of criminal administration is difficult so long as we persist in regarding the problem as primarily one of law enforcement and respect for law. We would have the same unfortunate results in our insane asylums if we regarded the problem in the same way and conducted crusades against insanity to bolster the moral fiber of those who were still sane. So long as a purely moral attitude is taken toward the problem of crime, criminology will swing back and forth from too much humanitarianism to too much blood and iron.

Of course, even if we treated the problem of crime as we treat the problem of insanity, progress would be slow. If we took the attitude toward insanity today that we take toward crime it would be easy to show the entire failure of all of our techniques in caring for the insane, just as we can show the failure of the parole system. Statistics could be gathered to show that in spite of all the progress in learning about mental disease, there are still more people in the insane hospitals than there were fifty years ago. The percentage of cures of various typical kinds of insanity could be used to prove there was no use doing anything to such people except to keep them in strait jackets. Yet the fact that people are well treated in asylums is never considered one of the causes for the increase of insanity since it took away the impelling motive of fear from those about to go insane. Thus we could prove in terms of social cost that our treatment of the insane had been only an unnecessary burden on the taxpayer, without tangible practical results.

However, fortunately in the case of insane people we simply do not worry about such arguments. We have ceased to regard the problem as a moral one. We are not concerned with the exemplification of moral lessons to the rest of the community. Hence in a slow but fumbling way we are unquestionably developing our knowledge of the treatment of mental disease.

Our treatment of the criminal problem, however, is

founded on the notion that the particular offender should be utilized as a moral example to the community. Our aim is "law enforcement." We use each offender to illustrate the fundamental principles of criminal justice. Therefore, not only are we failing to develop techniques, but anything other than continuation of the struggle between humanitarian motives and a policy of blood and iron in the future is improbable. There is nothing in particular to be done about this, excepting to recognize it as a fact and to note its inevitable contradictions with other equally important social ideals in order to appraise and predict more accurately the results of various proposed reforms. Civic wars on crime, indulged in by forward-thinking and right-minded men and women must be accepted as social phenomena which cannot be avoided, but which do not contribute to better knowledge of the criminal problem. They are obstacles to change rather than movements toward a solution of the problem of crime.

Law Enforcement and Political Government

THE attitudes which we have just been describing are peculiarly dramatized in the courts, but their effects spread over all government activities. Publicly recognized government is unable to act efficiently in practical affairs and at the same time conform to the ideal that laws should be enforced without partiality and regardless of consequences. This is generally true of all governmental ideals, as we have pointed out in a previous chapter. However, a fixed belief in the ideal of law enforcement hinders and delays the activities of public bodies, more than any other popular illusion. Thus we cannot conduct public works on a large scale, and we have difficulty in administering relief. Our only recourse is the creation of a *sub rosa* organization which we call a political machine. The comparatively greater importance which political machines have in the United States than in England is an illustration of our greater emphasis on the creed of law enforcement.

The political machines which do the work of our Government are not composed of bad men. Their ethics are dictated by their task. That task, however, is antithetical to the ideals of an impartial law above men. Therefore the political machine, though based on faiths and loyalties as all organizations must be, does not conform to publicly accepted government morality. Political machines are drafted into the part of the villain in the piece, and receive the hisses of right-thinking people. Yet in spite of these hisses every reformer, if he desires to take any other than a critical part in government, is forced to play the political game, and conform to its undercover standards. If civil servants in England are less political than ours, it is not because of the perversity of a single man called Andrew Jackson, nor because of the villainy of the group of men who surrounded Boss Tweed. It is because in England that great source of practical confusion, i.e., rigid and logical enforcement of laws, is not permitted to interfere to the same extent with practical activity.

It is amusing to listen to the oft-repeated demand that we should obtain for ourselves a civil service like England's, because the demand is generally made by the born worriers who think that an impending moral chaos will inevitably follow any public deviation from a written constitution, or written laws, or a written structure of government—the very persons who are the fountain from which *sub rosa* politics owes its constant refreshment, and whose blind logical ideals compel the actual stream of control to retreat underground.

So long as such attitudes are near and dear to us it is impossible for public government to escape red tape. Just as the judicial compromise of criminal cases must be done in whispers behind closed doors, so similar compromises in other fields become the task of politicians. Today, as the Government is forced into activities which were formerly those of private business, it flounders because of the notion that any deviation from established rules is corruption or else leads to corruption. Ask any of the long-suffering pub-lic servants who boil with indignation at the petty restrictions imposed by the Comptroller-General of the United States in his doctrinaire and humorless auditing of their accounts. The enormous expense caused by the necessity of circumventing the ritual of this high priest is known to everyone who has attempted to make any department of the Government operate like a common-sense organization. The T.V.A. desired to establish a fair standard of public-utility rates. It was compelled to urge an amendment in Congress which took its auditing from the power of the Comptroller-General, in spite of the public criticism and suspicion which such action threw on it. Its only other choice was to use those *sub rosa* methods of the petty poli-tician which no auditing can circumvent. This is only an isolated example of the working of the ideal of Law En-forcement in practical affairs. It has given us a government whose public morality and logical symmetry outshine that of any government of the world. It has also elevated the plain uncultured foreign-born politician to a position which he could obtain in no other country in the world.

With the workings of this ideal in political government the courts have little to do. They represent it in its ideal moments, purged of all its dross, represented by a figure of a blind justice holding the scales and unable even to see what is in them. The American criminal trial is not the cause of our worship of the Law Enforcement ideal but rather the temple where the most frequent celebrations in its honor are held.

The moral of this chapter is not, we hasten to say, that

right-thinking people begin to get rid of these basic ideals of Law Enforcement and fair trial by preaching about the foolishness of the human race. Nevertheless, there is a moral the discussion of which we will postpone until the final chapter.

CHAPTER VIII

Trial by Combat

IN the summer of 1935 screaming headlines announced that the N.R.A. had been declared unconstitutional. The members of the vast organization spread all over the country found themselves without salaries and without a place in the scheme of things. Accepting the decision as "law," the public was greatly puzzled to explain how an unconstitutional organization could have existed unchecked for two years. Blame was variously apportioned to Congress, the President, the executive officers of the Government, the brain trust, radicals, and others, but it occurred to no one that the Supreme Court of the United States might possibly have had something to do with the delay. New laws were advocated to move litigation faster and moral lessons were read to everyone except the Court. It was assumed without question that it would have been impossible for the Court to have said the law was unconstitutional any sooner than it actually did.

President Roosevelt sent up a trial balloon in which he accepted the decision in its broadest interpretation as preventing any further exercise of national power over commerce than we were accustomed to in the "horse and buggy" days. He told people that his hands were tied. Immediately, another storm of criticism arose because it was heresy to claim that such a good constitution interpreted by such a learned court could tie anyone's hands. To interpret the N.R.A. case in this way was simply another attack of a different kind on the Constitution. The public wanted to think of the Constitution as tending to restrict such things as tyranny and bureaucracy without interfering with any necessary exercise of national power.

Upon the failure of this trial balloon the President took the opposite course and urged laws about which there was some doubt in the light of the N.R.A. decision. Immediately, conservative newspapers began bitterly to remind the President of his oath to support the Constitution. The *New York Herald-Tribune* printed the President's oath to support the Constitution, and under it, as a complete contradiction, his very sensible statement to Congress that the only method of determining whether a doubtful law was constitutional was to pass it and let the Supreme Court decide.[1]

Finally, when lawyers began to study the decision, it appeared that it might be given either a broad or a narrow scope and that actually no one could predict the next case with any certainty. Disturbed by this the *New York Herald-Tribune* recommended that a commission of experts be appointed to study the decision and that the President take their advice on the exact limits of his powers.[2]

This strange situation brought into the limelight by the public interest in New Deal legislation is repeated every day on a smaller scale whenever judicial sanction in legislative or business practice is required. Courts owe their prestige to the idea that they are constantly making the law more and more certain. They owe their power to the fact that they never clarify total situations. They leave the cases which are just around the corner always undecided, and thus compel businessmen and legislators to be constantly in fear of their judicial veto. This is a characteristic of judicial government. Without it we would scarcely have what people call a government of law. Other countries perhaps do not extend the process so far as the United States, but the situation above described is inherent in any judicial institution.

1. Editorial page, *New York Herald-Tribune* (Friday, July 12, 1935).
2. Editorial, "Plenty of Time," *New York Herald-Tribune* (June 2, 1935).

The trick by which this strategic position of the courts is maintained is the institution of civil trial by combat which is developed in this country probably to a further extent than in any other. An analysis of this institution, technical though it may be, is necessary for an understanding of how government operates.

As the criminal trial dramatizes law enforcement as a creed, so the civil trial dramatizes the moral beauty of the noninterference of government in private affairs. Enforcement of the criminal law by policemen is a public duty; enforcement of civil rights by policemen, or even administrative officials, tends toward bureaucracy. The whole ideology, and procedural organization of the civil trial is designed to insulate the court and the Government from taking the initiative in enforcing or even protecting the civil rights of individuals. Even the existence of injustice is preferred to the active participation of the court in private or business affairs.

This rôle of the civil trial as a symbol of individual freedom from active interference by the government, makes it a most important factor in preserving conservative traditions in the face of new regulatory legislation. It achieves its obstructive power not by opposing the Government, so much as by declining to decide general problems, or to give sweeping directions. In this way, courts obtain a power to keep litigants guessing; a condition which would be impossible in a body charged with the actual enforcement of law.

At no time were the effects of the civil trial as a method of furnishing object lessons in government more marked than in its relation with New Deal legislation. A series of acts was rapidly passed, the general effect of which was contrary to all traditional ideas of the function of government in business. Businessmen were in a panic, and ready to surrender any control that was necessary. Conservatives who insisted that the legislation was unconstitutional were brushed aside, and many of them accepted with public lamentations the distressing fact that the Constitution was gone. The Supreme Court of the United States, that great symbol of the power which limited the encroachment of Congress in private affairs, was silent.

Yet the judicial system, by virtue of its brooding silence, hung like an ominous cloud over those who were attempting new forms of control. So long as the public was marching enthusiastically in step with New Deal policies the Court managed to avoid the issue. At first it relied on the word "emergency" which committed it to nothing permanent. In a case involving the action of a state legislature which had given a moratorium on mortgages,[3] the right to use such power in an emergency was upheld by a close vote. A second case involved the unheard of right of the New York legislature to delegate to a board the authority to fix the price of milk.[4] In the minds of the public the case involved the constitutionality of much of the national legislation. Yet the power was upheld, without comment on the validity of any national legislation. The Court was still silent on the National Recovery Act, and in its decision appeared to be completely unaware of the fact that a whole country was marching in step to what might be unconstitutional legislation. Yet no one seemed to consider this strange. Before the decision many had thought that the New York Milk Case did directly involve the constitutionality of the Agricultural Adjustment Act's license for milk with which the New York action might easily conflict. However, after the decision came down, everyone seemed to think that the Court had answered everything which it legally could answer under the circumstances.

3. *Home Building and Loan Assn.* vs. *Blaisdell*, 290 *U.S.* 398 (1934).
4. *Nebbia* vs. *New York*, 291 *U.S.* 502 (1934).

There followed the Hot Oil Case,[5] which directly involved an N.R.A. code. At last the constitutionality of the N.R.A. code regulating oil would be decided, and by inference all N.R.A. codes. Yet the Supreme Court succeeded in dodging that question by a feat of intellectual legerdemain which was so transparent as to tax the credulity of that man from Mars, if not the man from America. Due to a clerical error a clause had been omitted from an amendment signed by the President, and during a brief period officials had been enforcing provisions which the President had actually approved, which he thought he had signed, but which did not bear his physical writing. The mistake was immediately corrected. Counsel stipulated that they did not wish to take advantage of it. Yet this was of no avail. The Court said that they had no question before them to decide. They went further and even criticized the Government for carelessly putting the case beyond the Court's power to decide. There had been passed a declaratory judgment act in the meantime which seemed almost to compel a decision, but the Court ignored that opportunity also. The same court, which later read the Government a long moral lecture on the power of Congress to excuse gold payments on bonds,[6] refused to clarify the situation by even a hint on the constitutionality of the N.R.A. Later, the case against the Weirton Steel Company, involving the N.R.A. labor provision, was brought up to the Court and dismissed by the Government,[7] without a word from the Court, on the traditional assumption that the Court did not have power to retain cases on its own dockets. Finally, after the N.R.A. had lost all its friends, when people had ceased to march to its

5. *Ryan* vs. *Panama Refining Company,* 293 *U.S.* 388 (1935).

6. *Nortz* vs. *United States,* 294 *U.S.* 317 (1935).

7. *U.S.* vs. *Weirton Steel Co.* (D.G. D. Del. No. E-1060) (Feb. 27, 1935).

tunes, when radicals and conservatives alike were tired of it, the Court declared it unconstitutional.[8]

Then there arose the great public bewilderment referred to above as to how an act which had been unconstitutional from the start could have been enforced for two years. Something seemed wrong somewhere, but not in the Supreme Court. On the contrary, never did that great body appear upon a higher peak of eminence than at that time. It was the fault of the counsel for the Government because they had not forced the Court to act sooner in impeding their cherished plans. The humor of putting the responsibility for seeing that an act is beheaded upon the persons most interested in having it continue, never occurred to anybody.

However, this was not all. Not only did the Supreme Court escape criticism for delaying the decision for two years, and making it only when it had become quite safe to do so, but its decision left no *certain* way of telling whether any of the other acts pending before Congress were constitutional. There was the Social Security bill, the Guffey bill, setting up a miniature N.R.A. for the coal industry, the Wagner Labor bill, amendments to the T.V.A., and others. The decision had changed the opinion of no one on these acts, but only made the fight more bitter. The new legislation was pressed with renewed vigor. And yet out of it all the Supreme Court arose as somehow or other the highest and most ultimate pinnacle in government. Its delphic pronouncements were so broad that they terrorized the advocates of the new legislation and so full of loopholes that they filled opponents of the legislation with a great uneasiness.

Here is a government of symbols in its most rarefied es-

8. *Schechter Poultry Corporation et al.* vs. *U.S.*, 55 *S. Ct.* 837; 79 *L. ed.* 888 (1935).

sence. The Court had played its hand with great skill, and emerged triumphant as an institution. The Constitution was more revered and feared than ever before. But still no one quite knew just what had happened,—what was constitutional, or what unconstitutional.

The method by which this strategic position of a court is maintained is by the application of Anglo-American legal theory that only the particular and narrow issues brought before the courts by contesting parties be made the basis of judge-made law. This theory, briefly outlined, is as follows:

The Civil Trial

A COURT is not supposed to regulate situations merely because regulation is badly needed. A court should never approve, disapprove, or clarify an entire set of rules governing a general business situation. A court should never answer questions. The limits of the power of the courts in this direction is to produce parables out of which further arguments may be spun.

What the issues of a case are, depends upon a printed record, beyond the limits of which no court should go. Statements of law on assumed facts, a familiar procedure to continental judges, are supposed in this country to indicate loose judicial thinking. The court may be aware, as men of common sense, that the parties desire a general rule to be adopted or rejected, or the parties may even stipulate that such is their desire. Nevertheless, the court is powerless to discuss the rule or principle if the actual facts in the record do not raise those precise issues in a way prescribed by technical rules.

Typical Results of Emphasis on "Issues"

THE most frequent illustration of this attitude is found in the repeated exhortation of appellate courts that counsel stay within the record. The doctrine of judicial notice becomes at times a convenient escape from this limitation, but counsel can never know how far they may rely on it. Oral arguments are filled with remarks which indicate how fixed the attitude is in the minds of the court. For example, in the New York Milk Case,[9] a case designed to test the constitutionality of far-reaching power of the State to fix milk prices, counsel was asked by a justice to point out where in the record it appeared that the defendant was a milk dealer, on the theory that the mere fact that he had sold a quart of milk might be insufficient. It was apparent that the sole purpose of the case was to test the power of a state to fix prices. There was a deliberate attempt by counsel to exclude all other issues. Yet the assumption in this question was that a careless omission in the record might make it impossible for the Court to make a decision for which vast interests were anxiously waiting.

Actually this rule does not prevent a court from taking notice of matters outside the record where it wants to do so. Thus in the recent Lake Cargo Rate Case, the entire coal industries of Pennsylvania and West Virginia were awaiting an interpretation of the Interstate Commerce Act. A bitter dispute was in process of litigation. The Interstate Commerce Commission had been enjoined from establishing a certain differential in rates between West Virginia and Pennsylvania coal mines. Entirely outside the record of the particular case the Interstate Commerce Commission had made an order which temporarily approved a compromise rate to preserve the *status quo* while an appeal was pending. Instead of deciding the question which it had required so much time and effort to bring before them, the Supreme Court took judicial notice of this compromise rate as a reason why they were powerless to decide anything.

9. *Nebbia Case* see footnote 4 *supra*.

The case they said had become moot. In commenting on this case Mr. Harvey Mansfield says: "So ended, in a grand anticlimax, five years of litigation, pursued at a cost, to all concerned, of millions of dollars."[10]

The regulation of its own administration by the court must generally be made at the risk of the parties involved. In the recent receivership of the Interborough Rapid Transit of New York, Judge Manton's right to appoint the receiver and supervise the receivership proceedings was questioned. The matter assumed the proportions of a public scandal. The Supreme Court of the United States, after an appeal, finally indicated that Judge Manton had acted in doubtful taste, though not without jurisdiction.[11] It suggested his withdrawal. This very sensible solution, of advising Judge Manton, had been obvious from the first. The mails were open between New York and Washington, and the trains were running on regular schedules. Only tradition prevented an immediate judicial intervention by the Supreme Court

10. Harvey C. Mansfield, *The Lake Cargo Coal Rate Controversy* (1932), p. 133.

11. *Johnson* vs. *Manhattan Ry.*, 1 *F. Supp.* 809 (S.D.N.Y., 1932), 61 *F.* (2d) 934 (*C.C.A.* 2d 1932), 289 *U.S.* 479 (1933); see Note (1933) 46 *Harv. L. Rev.* 503; (1932) 42 *Yale L.J.* 279. See also Frankfurter, *New York Times* (Oct. 14, 1932, p. 18).

The chronology of events is as follows. On August 26, 1932, Judge Manton appointed the receiver of these vast properties. After the matter had gone to the Supreme Court, Judge Manton in a memorandum opinion on June 28, 1933, stated that he would continue to act in the case. Thereafter an affidavit of bias and prejudice was filed by the Manhattan Railway Company. It was stricken from the files by Judge Manton on August 2, 1933. Thereupon a petition for a writ of mandamus and prohibition was filed in the Supreme Court of the United States by the Manhattan Railway Company. An order restraining action in the matter by Judge Manton pending hearing on the petition for mandamus was signed by Mr. Justice Stone on September 21, 1933. Shortly prior to the hearing of the petition Judge Manton withdrew from the case. Thus the matter of what judge should sit on the case was litigated for over a year. The inconvenience resulting to investors and creditors because the judicial system could invent no sensible way of settling disputes quickly between its own officers can easily be imagined.

without trial or appeal, without public battle between members of the Federal court. Yet matters involving millions of dollars had to remain up in the air until the case could be presented to the Supreme Court in the guise of legal issues presented on a record.

The outcome of the case was amusing. Inasmuch as the Supreme Court advised, rather than commanded, Judge Manton adopted an attitude of defiance. It began to look as if the whole matter would have to be brought before the Supreme Court again in the same cumbersome way by means of additional proceedings, when the Judge decided to withdraw. Thus a matter purely of judicial administration is embalmed among the parables in the Supreme Court reports, instead of being part of its minutes and correspondence. The man on the street is somewhat puzzled as to why this administrative question could not have been frankly and informally answered by the Court without so much controversy as to the way in which it was asked.

Not only is a court given every chance to escape decisions by declaring cases moot, but other difficulties are placed in the way of formulating precise issues by those who desire to test the constitutionality of acts. The theory is that the cases must just happen. They are not to be planned in advance. This theory does not permit a coherent or planned scheme for judicial participation in government regulation. Nothing can be determined in advance except by the elaborate fiction of enjoining threatened action, and no one can ever surely tell whether the fiction will be allowed to pass or whether it will be challenged.

The Department of Agriculture was engaged in negotiating a milk agreement and license in the State of New York. The Attorney-General of New York examined the cases and announced that the proposed action by the Department was beyond the national power to regulate commerce.[12] The Government proceeded with its negotiations but there was no way to obtain judicial approval or disapproval until the license was completed and in actual operation. The courts are a necessary part of the system which finally approves marketing agreements, licenses, and codes. Yet their participation in this system is based on a sort of catch-as-catch-can philosophy.

For example, the case of *Hillsborough Bank Corp.* vs. *Yarnell*,[13] in which a Florida judge decided that the Agricultural Adjustment Act was unconstitutional, was appealed. During the pendency of appeal it was desired to modify the license under consideration in that case. The following unanswerable questions arose: (1) Would the proposed modification of the license make the original case moot? (2) Assuming that the Agricultural Adjustment Administration wants a decision on a new license, must it depend upon the irrational processes of chance and a determined litigant for that decision, or is there some way of getting the new license into the old record? The appellate court sent back the case on a procedural question and nothing vital was determined.

Such difficulties may be multiplied indefinitely. They all reflect the same fundamental attitude. The function of the judiciary is to stay aloof from investigation and regulation. Rules and regulations must emerge only from contests. Each battle is a sort of war to end wars, because it will aid in the development of principles which will make future contests unnecessary. Regulations made in advance after investigation of a total situation, rather than a particular case, are not judicial functions. They are turned over to administrative tribunals with a lower place in the governmental hierarchy. Each new extension of this power to regulate is regarded as a step toward bureaucracy. Bureaucracy must

12. See *New York Times* (March 6, 1934, p. 1).
13. 70 *F.* (2d) 435 (1934).

be curbed by the courts, but this can only be done by decisions approving or disapproving action or threatened action which has damaged, or is about to damage, some particular person. The rules themselves can never be reviewed as a whole by any judicial body, because review of regulation as a whole is not a judicial function.

Assumptions Underlying the Search for Issues

THE suggestion that a court should be permitted to speak without a contested case before it, has been met with an air of shocked surprise by such persons learned in the law as the writer has interviewed on the subject. It is considered dangerous in spite of the fact that in large areas of judicial participation in business, such as consent receiverships, this is exactly what the courts have been compelled to do. Courts for a long time have regulated insolvent business on the sensible lines of control instead of the romantic technique of battle. The difficulties have arisen only because the older tradition keeps courts from exercising enough control. Today, when something of the same type of regulation is being imposed upon solvent business, the notion of groups of individuals getting up plans and regulations for the approval of the court becomes a necessary development. Yet we still prefer a two-party injunction suit to test the operation of a code to a more sensible impartial examination at the request of interested groups who are not necessarily fighting each other. The reasons for this preference are worth examining.

The philosophical rationalization of why courts may not be trusted to clarify rules in confused situations, except by the hit-or-miss method of the occasional decision after a contest, is of course contradictory. If one were compelled to summarize the assumptions underlying the ideal of a lawmaking body, which never speaks except to settle a combat properly brought before it, the result would be somewhat as follows:

1. Every trial should be a contest over issues presented by the parties, and not an investigation of what the facts were which created the necessity of the suit.

2. If one party loses on a technicality it is his own fault because he is supposed to know the rules. Simplicity of rules is obtained by not permitting courts to clarify these rules except by penalizing one of the antagonists. To permit any-one to find out about them in advance would destroy the idea of a combat.

3. Courts are not permitted to plan their participation in a new situation, such as was presented by the recovery acts, any more than they were permitted to plan their participation in arbitration, rate-making, or administrative law. This participation is rather to be determined by a series of battles. Each particular battle is a war to end war.

4. Rules governing human conduct will be better and more consistent if only a small section of that conduct is considered at a time. It is a mistake for a rule-making body to consider a situation as a whole.

5. The best way to avoid litigation is to make the power to promulgate rules and regulations exclusively dependent upon litigation.

6. Courts should keep their eyes fixed on the past and follow precedent. Legislatures should look to the future, and disregard it. Thus the two extremes will correct each other, if courts in making their decisions will only keep future policies in mind, and if legislatures will only have more respect for the past. Thus the legislative and judicial functions will nicely balance each other, provided we set up enough administrative tribunals actually to do the work required.

These assumptions are reconciled with practical efficiency by the notion that courts are more apt to formulate or apply rules soundly if the opposite sides are prevented from sitting around a table together in friendly conference. Mutual exaggeration is supposed to create lack of exaggeration. Bitter partisanship in opposite directions is supposed to bring out the truth. Of course no rational human being would apply such a theory to his own affairs or to other departments of the government. It has never been supposed that bitter and partisan lobbying assisted legislative bodies in their law-making. No investigation is conducted by hiring persons to argue opposite sides. The common law is neither clear, sound, nor even capable of being restated in areas where the results of cases are being most bitterly contested. And particularly with reference to administrative regulation does mutual exaggeration of opposing claims violate the whole theory of rational, scientific investigation. Yet in spite of this most obvious fact, the ordinary teacher of law will insist (1) that combat makes for clarity, (2) that heated arguments bring out the truth, and (3) that anyone who doesn't believe this is a loose thinker. The explanation of this attitude lies in the realm of social anthropology.

Methods of Avoiding Trial by Battle

DEVICES exist for escaping from this ideal that a court is permitted to speak only after a contest on definite issues, but they are not important enough to change the general effect of the attitude. Advisory opinions are given in some states, but they are infrequent. Since most of the present regulation is national, they play little or no part in the present administrative difficulties. The idea that courts should answer questions of law so that parties would not have to act at their peril was embodied in the Declaratory Judgment Act. Authors of declaratory judgment acts have been careful to make them only a minor pleading reform. They insist upon issues and an actual controversy as prerequisite to declaratory actions. Hence the old question as to whether a case or controversy exists must be decided anew each time the declaratory judgment statute is invoked. There are various limitations, purely technical and all aimed to prevent courts from actual approval of general regulations under the declaratory judgment statutes. So thoroughly conservative have been the reformers who advocated this legislation that it is very doubtful to the writer whether the declaratory judgment acts have done any more than add a new common-law writ. The very fact that this procedure has surrounded itself with such an enormous body of learned literature, philosophy, and cases during the brief period of its acceptance in this country indicates that the framers of the acts have been anxious not to depart from the traditions of the past. Declaratory judgments which approve or disapprove of entire codes of administrative regulation are nonexistent. Declaratory judgments which are aimed at informing a trade group just what they may expect from a contemplated course of conduct are so rare as to be negligible.

It is not surprising that the declaratory judgment has not been received with enthusiasm in the Federal system. The fundamental difficulty with this device in a situation requiring regulation is that it makes the parties rather than the court the judge of what the issues are and when they shall be decided. If the Supreme Court were forced to approve or veto legislation immediately after its passage it would be thrown into the same political turmoil as surrounds the legislature. It would lose its aloof and strategic position, and thereby its priestly power. For this reason courts instinctively reacted against carrying the declaratory judgment to its logical conclusion of quickly answering questions of law. They have continued to emphasize the importance of contested issues in order to maintain that separate and independent power which distinguishes them from legislatures.

Arbitration, a frequently used escape from the judicial hunt for issues, has similarly met with such confusion when it encountered legal tradition that the drafting of an arbitration agreement has become technical and full of pitfalls.

Perhaps the most useful and extensive device for asking the court questions has been the injunction. In testing the recovery acts its use has been frequent. It is a common method of appeal from administrative bodies. The idea of a contest is preserved by the phraseology. A large discretion is given upon the principle that it will never be exercised unless the injury is irreparable.

The technique of corporation reorganization has gone far in escaping the limitations of precise issues. Here the court works through receivers, committees, and masters. Yet even here the influence of the ideal is felt in the reluctance to abandon the notion that the perfect legal analogy to selling a railroad is the judicial sale of a farm to a hostile creditor. The limitations of the record also make it difficult for the court to exercise a continuing supervision of related transactions after the reorganization plan has once been approved.

The ideal of trial by combat, dramatized over and over again by courts, expresses individual freedom from regulation. The part it plays is supposed to be the antithesis of bureaucracy—the villain of the piece. It hampers regulation of competition and encourages businessmen to fight each other for business. It encourages litigants to fight each other to obtain law. It withholds legal rights from those who will not fight. Legal rights might become cheapened if they were handed down to those who do not spend time and money to obtain them. It is beneath the dignity of a court to become part of regulatory machinery unless it develops into a fight between two or more parties. This being the ideal, we find courts presenting a series of miracle plays to give it a theatrical development. In the memory of the present generation the moral lesson of the judicial miracle play has been that rugged individuals are not regulated. Instead, they fight for their rights. In this battle they expect government to let them alone.

The Strategic Position in which the Ideal of Trial by Battle Has Placed the Judicial System

In a society of clashing ideals and rapidly changing conditions, courts are expected to preserve the fundamental principles of the ancient order. Far-flung governments from the time of the Roman Empire have found the judicial system the most convenient instrument to preserve the unity between the past and present. They have used it as a stage to show that the great ideals of our fathers are still the most real and important. The most sacred ancient ideals of the Federal system in America were the antithesis of regulated social control. Therefore such regulation as practical necessity from time to time forced on the Government, was made the duty of a system of lesser courts, called commissions. In these bodies a different technique, the technique of conference and investigation, took the place of trial by battle because they were more concerned with results than with symbols.

As regulatory bodies expanded in power and influence, the weight of all our philosophy and our judicial drama was aimed at keeping them on a lower plane. Principles of freedom did not find their habitation in surroundings where man is being directed for his own good. The Lord in Milton's *Paradise Lost,* confronted by the same problem, decides it is better to allow man to fall than to take any active steps to help him out. He conceives his function to preserve man's free will by judging him only after he has sinned. To prevent sin by divine regulation would be to create a heavenly bureaucracy. Here we have poetically expressed the ideal of the common law.

The acclaim given to *Paradise Lost* because of its ponderous way of expressing this ideal is not dissimilar to the acclaim given to legal scholars for performing a similar function. Milton and Blackstone thought very much alike. The same type of thinking is found in Hegel, in his elaborate development of the notion that out of the combat of thesis and antithesis comes synthesis on a higher plane.

It was in such an atmosphere that the judicial system at first rejected the ideal that the proceedings of such bodies were their concern. Issues which required practical investigation rather than philosophical learning obviously were not "judicial."

However, this administrative technique began to spread rapidly to problems so important that courts could no longer ignore them, and there arose the necessity of finding philosophical formulas which would make it possible to avoid the methods of investigation and conference and at the same time to assert judicial supremacy over decisions arrived at by these methods. The notion that they could decide only contested issues put the courts in an admirable strategic position. It gave them a constant escape from being rushed into interpretation of regulations at unpropitious times. It enabled them to take pot shots at specific regulations without ever being forced to assume responsibility for the regulatory scheme as a whole. The court could always refuse to review because the commission's decision was either final, or entitled to great weight on questions of "fact." It could always take questions of fact back into its power of review by using the doctrine that certain facts were "jurisdictional" and, therefore, required judicial determination. It could then throw these very jurisdictional facts back to the commission in cases (such as railroad rate decisions) where the evidence was too complicated for the judicial technique by declaring that the court need go no further than to ascertain whether there was typical evidence. It could escape all these formulas at once and regain jurisdiction by declaring that whether the commission acted in an arbitrary manner or whether they properly applied the law was solely a judicial issue. It could avoid talking about the matter at all by compelling the litigant to exhaust his administrative remedies, and escape from this rule in turn by stating that it might not apply to cases of unusual hardship. The court could invoke doctrines of estoppel and waiver if the litigant attempted to try out the regulatory scheme in an experimental way, and ignore these doctrines when review was desired by taking advantage of the fact that the seamless web of the law of estoppel and waiver was constructed on the general lines of Swiss cheese. By using injunctions to review the commissions, the court could add to these doctrines of administrative law all the loose formulas of equity which sound in discretion and good conscience. In this way to the two-story structure of law and equity was added a third story of administrative law, and the whole structure was equipped with noiseless elevators and secret stairways, by means of which the choice was always open either to take a bold judicial stand or make a dignified escape.

By these means courts were able to apply criteria to administrative tribunals without ever being compelled to elaborate as a complete whole what the criteria were. Thus was maintained great supervisory power with a minimum of executive responsibility. A new and curious legal science known as administrative law grew rapidly. Although it was the most important of the subjects in the legal field, because it contained the procedure for the treatment of the most important problems, it did not lend itself to the typical law-school treatment. The American Law Institute never even attempted to restate it. Its comparative immunity from efforts by conventional legal scholars to clarify and classify it made administrative law an admirable method by which courts could keep a dignified distance from bodies which investigated and regulated instead of refereed.

The judicial position taken in the great areas of governmental regulation which include rates, zoning, workmen's compensation, taxation, and unfair trade practices preserved the illusion that the decision of fundamental principles of jurisdiction was the more important and dignified duty, and that actual regulation was a minor affair. It kept constantly before us the idea that administrative bodies, even when they acted as judges, were only quasi-judicial. However, the philosophy and argumentative technique required to maintain this idea became so complicated as to defy orderly statement. It was easy to imagine a more efficient method of review of administrative bodies, yet to put it into practice required a restating of fundamental concepts which would have given courts more direct responsibility. If the courts had been able to look at administrative agencies as they did at their own masters, referees, or receivers, elaborate formulas of administrative law, in so far as they described a method of review, would have been unnecessary. Under a scheme of discretionary review the courts would probably have let commissions alone because this is the history of discretionary review. The judicial system might not have split up into a double-headed affair. It would have had the efficiency of a rational appellate organization in dealing with matters of regulation to which the older technique was not applicable.

The spectacle presented to the public of an administrative review similar to the approval of a master's report would have made the courts appear to approve or disapprove administrative regulations as they were formulated. It would have taken away their opportunity to talk in parables, and made them responsible for definite rules. The court would thus have appeared to be an investigating body, and not an arbiter of combats. We were accustomed to attack regulation by contrasting it with a type of government which we designated as judicial. This could only be done by keeping the judiciary apart from regulation. The strategic advantage of the position which the vague ideal of *stare decisis* limited to precise issues, permitted courts to appear as the last refuge of unregulated individualism. For this purpose it was worth all the confusion which a separate science of administrative law threw upon the actual procedural situation.

The Problem Today

THE strategic position which the judicial system occupies on account of its ability to create a cloud of hampering uncertainty was never better illustrated than during the operation of the recovery legislation of the Roosevelt Administration. A magnificent effort at administrative control was launched, but as it proceeded it began to be halted at every turn by uncertainties as to what the courts were going to do. An elaborate group of administrative tribunals rapidly took form, but in the scheme there was no definite place allocated for judicial intervention. No one knew just at what point administrative remedies were exhausted, or when judicial review was permitted. The scope of judicial review was uncertain, and all over the country conflicting results appeared.

Since the favored method of reviewing any of the code provisions to determine its reasonableness was by injunction, we found trial courts compelled to tie up, and cast doubt upon, an entire working arrangement in order to give an effective decision against a single code provision. Business could not wait on the slow process of appeal, and hence in most instances where lower courts issued injunctions the entire code was rendered practically inoperative. The Government was fearful of the results of appeals, and hence many codes limped along with half-hearted attempts to enforce them hindered by the fear that some final decision would render everything which had been done void from the beginning.

There was no provision possible under the system for the experimental operation of a code. Its provisions were either valid or invalid from the start. There was no way by which groups of diverse interests could present a plan before a court in such a way as to permit the court to go into all the relevant factors. Codes therefore had to be valid or invalid on the analogy of books rather than on a present investigation of facts. After over two years of operation of the administrative regulations imposed by the New Deal no one could positively affirm how far the Federal Government could regulate. Then the whole structure was torn down by a single blow which left the regulatory powers under other acts as doubtful as before.

In the face of all these unknown hazards created by the necessity of enforcing regulations through the medium of the civil trial, regulation by the Government faltered, lost direction, and became discredited. Whether this was a fortunate or unfortunate result will never be known. It has become apparent that many of the regulatory schemes proposed by the Government were ill-conceived and doomed to failure, even if they could have been enforced. Yet the existence of the tradition of judicial review by means of contested trials confined to narrow issues undoubtedly prevented the experimentation which might have followed the failures of some of the administrative methods had they been pursued with confidence. Therefore it can be plausibly argued that the institution of trial by combat was one of the most important factors in keeping the tradition of governmental noninterference alive during a time when popular enthusiasm was willing to accept greater governmental regulation than ever before.

It is important to note that it was the peculiar institution of trial by combat, rather than any particular constitutional decisions, which kept the conservative tradition alive. The decisions at the beginning were favorable to the Government. It seemed almost as if no court would dare impede a scheme which looked so promising and was backed by so much popular support. However, it was impossible for any court to go beyond the narrow limits of the case before it, and therefore no general plan of government regulation could possibly have been approved before the reaction set in. Thus in the struggle between two ideals which took place in the first two years of the Roosevelt Administration, the one representing governmental regulation of business, and the other representing governmental noninterference with business, the latter maintained its prestige and effectiveness at least in part through the operation of the judicial system and its peculiar method of trial. Both ideals are still competing for supremacy, and each has its separate system of tribunals. Governmental regulation is represented by administrative law, and individualism by the formal judicial system. We are building up a double-headed system, similar to the law and equity courts of an earlier day, with the two sets of courts paralleling each other and clashing in a haphazard way; the one, a symbol of a law which is above government, and the other, a symbol of efficiency and control.

The unfortunate part of this method of judicial control is that in order to affirm a principle the court may have to destroy a great organization without giving it a chance to develop or mend its ways. This happened when the N.R.A. was declared void. Useful organizations do not arise full grown. They are a product of growth, and of trial and error. Not even Henry Ford could have put his present organization in running order except over a period of years. Governmental organizations must go through a similar process. To attain efficiency, they must be allowed freedom to grow and change. The famous chicken case destroyed an organization which was slowly growing into something workable. Practically everything which the Supreme Court was most concerned about was disappearing in any event. Government's control of prices was on the wane. Its desire to meddle with little businesses was being strictly curbed. The Government was just being compelled to wrestle with the problem of making the great organization fill some real need. The Supreme Court relieved it of this problem, and permitted it again to wander in the field of popular political generalizations; but this meant that the growth of the organization from a chaotic mess into a unified and disciplined body had to start all over again under some other of the schemes that were then being advocated.

Man is a peculiar animal. He desires logical unity. He hates change. There is a great emotional need for him to prosecute social changes in terms of ancient ideas. This takes time. It requires experiment. It means that he must go in different directions at the same time, until the conflicting pressures of the past and future slowly resolve themselves. He must plan in order to give himself faith and purpose, even though he knows that nothing comes out as planned.

He must experiment, even though he knows that one successful experiment is bought at the price of countless failures. The alternative is the sudden change, in which all familiar landmarks disappear in the cruelty and injustice which new doctrinaires, suddenly elevated to power by the disappearance of older symbols, never seem unable to avoid.

In times of change, what should be the functions of the Supreme Court? What dangers can this venerable institution guard us against? It is our most important symbol of government. It should be the concrete dramatization of the ideal that there is a power which prevents government action which is arbitrary, capricious, and based on prejudice. It may or may not be that had it developed without the power to declare laws unconstitutional we might have had all the advantages of a flexible government without losing the advantages of a symbol of the law above the king. That question, however, is not worth discussing. We did not develop that way, and the power to declare laws unconstitutional is now inseparable from the prestige and power of the Court. One cannot build up in a day the kind of traditions which surround this great institution, and therefore one must accept the institution as one finds it. Sudden changes in its power and function cannot be made, after it has reached its maturity, any more than great branches can be cut off an ancient tree. The practical question, therefore, is not one of changing its power, but of how it is to exercise that power.

There is no formula for the exercise of such a power. Yet a judge who recognizes the evanescent nature of any form of social bookkeeping will hesitate to interfere with any exercise of governmental power which is sincere in its purpose and honestly designed as an experiment in social welfare. When the Court stands guard over any legal or economic theory, or over the form of our governmental structure, they are taking a gamble on the continuance of that theory, the outcome of which the Court cannot be wise enough to predict. The history of the Supreme Court of the United States is spotted with decisions declaring invalid unemployment insurance, income taxes, Federal employment agencies, railway pension schemes. None of these decisions has turned back the stream of events. Each of them has only added its quota of confusion.

A court which recognized the place of legal and economic theory would be freed from the fear that "an impending moral chaos"[14] could possibly be the result of any conceivable decision which the court could make. He would realize that in times of social change the greatest danger is from intolerance of the ideas of others, and from the neglect of the splendid ideal of a fair trial. Vested property interests will either be strong enough to control the political situation, or so weak that not even the court can maintain their privileges. But the lowly and oppressed, the fanatical idealists who desire to speak their theories in public without undergoing martyrdom have no protection in the entire system other than the Court.[15] It is here that the Court can take a bold stand without gambling on the future, because the ideal of a fair trial for the oppressed has survived every dictatorship that the world has ever known. Chief Justice Taney by his decision in the Dred Scott Case damaged his permanent reputation. Yet he is remembered with admiration for his courage in granting a habeas corpus in the Merriman Case, even though that decision was ignored by President Lincoln. In the celebration of legal and economic theories the Court should be equipped only with prayer books and collections of familiar quotations. In the protection of those seeking a fair trial it should be armed with a sword which it dared to use with courage. Here is a func-

14. Full quotation: "Loss of reputation for honorable dealing will bring us unending humiliation; the impending legal and moral chaos is appalling." From Mr. Justice McReynolds' dissenting opinion in the *Gold Clause Cases,* 294 *U.S.* 240, 317, 330, at p. 381.

15. In the case of *Herndon* vs. *Georgia, 79 L. ed.* 871 (1935), a negro was sentenced for proclaiming communist doctrine. The Supreme Court of the United States refused to review the decision of the Alabama Court because of a technicality. In the excellent dissenting opinion of Mr. Justice Cardozo, the failure of the Supreme Court to live up to the ideal of protecting minorities from intolerance, and the exposure of the trivial nature of the technicality on which the instant case was decided is brilliantly discussed.

tion for which the grand old ceremony of trial by combat is eminently fitted. It should be used for such purposes rather than as an instrument for hit-or-miss conservative social planning.

CHAPTER IX

Courts vs. Bureaucracy

A VAST literature has grown up in the last fifty years which explains the difference between a government of laws exemplified by court decisions in contested cases, and a bureaucracy. This literature includes general philosophical discussions of the fundamental differences between courts and administrative tribunals, and also particular detailed tests by which they can be identified and classified as the one or the other. In spite of the fact that no satisfactory philosophical or practical solution has ever been found to explain the difference, most thinking people feel that there is a fundamental distinction here of the utmost importance in government. The fact that such a feeling exists has molded our ways of thinking about government, and resulted in many significant legislative and judicial habits based on the belief that the differences between courts and bureaus are fundamental. Among other things, it has led to a double-headed system of law in which courts are given one function and administrative tribunals another. The attempted distinctions between the two are becoming of increasing argumentative importance, both judicially and politically, as the ideals of individualism and governmental planning continue to clash. In order to understand the operation, today, of either political government or legal argument, it is therefore necessary to examine the philosophical distinction between courts and bureaus and the practical effect which the prevalence of that philosophy has had on the operation of our governmental institutions.

The Difference between Courts, Quasi-Judicial Commissions and Bureaus

IN general it may be said that the courts, both in England

and America, exemplify the Rule of Law, which is the antithesis of "bureaucracy." No other institution is deemed fit to take the final responsibility of representing the law. For example, when Theodore Roosevelt suggested that the decisions of the Supreme Court declaring laws unconstitutional might be subject to recall, he was met by a rebuke from that elder statesman Elihu Root which read as follows:

We must choose between having prescribed rules of right conduct, binding in every case so long as they exist, even though there may be occasional inconvenience through their restraint upon our freedom of action, and having no rules at all to prevent us from doing in every case whatever we wish to do at the time. . . . A sovereign people which declares that all men have certain inalienable rights, and imposes upon itself the great impersonal rules of conduct deemed necessary for the preservation of those rights, and at the same time declares that it will disregard those rules whenever in any particular case it is the wish of a majority of its voters to do so, establishes as complete a contradiction to the fundamental principles of our Government as it is possible to conceive. It abandons absolutely the conception of a justice which is above majorities, of a right in the weak which the strong are bound to respect. It denies the vital truth taught by religion and realized in the hard experience of mankind, and which has inspired every constitution America has produced and every great declaration for human freedom since Magna Charta—the truth that human nature needs to distrust its own impulses and passions and to establish for its own control the restraining and guiding influence of declared principles of action.[1]

Like inspirational preaching, the above leaves many questions unanswered. Why, for example, should a court be so much more careful of our freedom than an administrative tribunal? Is it actually a fact that administrative tribunals

1. Quotation from Root in Thayer, *Recall of Judicial Decisions,* Sen. Doc. No. 28, 63d Cong. 1st Sess. (1913), p. 9.

are notoriously arbitrary in their actions, while courts usually follow sound principles? Indeed, given a body of men who are empowered to settle disputes and to lay down regulations, how can we tell when they are a court, which will give us a rule of law, and when they are a bureau, which will exercise arbitrary power. If we follow the conventional literature of explanation, we find that the difference is something like this:

Courts are bound by precedent, and bureaus are bound by red tape. Of course courts are forced to follow precedent, even when it leads to foolish results, because of their solemn obligation not to do anything in the future very much different from what they have done in the past. But bureaus in allowing themselves to be bound by red tape (an impersonal rule of conduct) do so out of pure malice and lack of regard for the fundamentals of freedom, because they have taken no oath not to violate the rules and analogies of the past. Therefore they are much worse than courts because courts only act unreasonably when they cannot help it, and bureaus act unreasonably when it is in their power to do differently. This is brought out very clearly in a typical editorial, "Bernt Balchen Discovers Bureaucracy":[2]

According to a ruling of the department of labor Bernt Balchen, Admiral Byrd's pilot in the flight over the south pole, cannot receive his citizenship papers. Balchen, a native of Norway, declared his intention in 1927. It is held that he has failed to meet the condition of five years' continuous residence in the United States. The Byrd antarctic voyage took him out of the country, although he was on a ship flying the American flag, was an invaluable member of an American expedition, and in a region to which there is an American claim because of the exploration and occupation of it by Americans, this region being Little America.

The bureau of naturalization explains that it cannot proceed

2. *Chicago Tribune* (June 24, 1931, p. 10).

on the assumption that Little America is American soil. That would be trespass on international questions where it has no sanction. So far as the bureau is concerned, Balchen was out of the country and technically has not complied with the law of naturalization. The upshot is that, unless a way of modifying this opinion is found, a man whom the country would like to have as a citizen cannot soon become one simply because he took an invaluable part in an enterprise of which the country is proud.

This editor has a definite notion of the superiority of judges sitting as *courts* over judges sitting as *bureaus*. While, of course, instances can be found where courts have acted just as outrageously, a close examination of such decisions always shows, nevertheless, either that they were forced into such action by a greater principle, such as the one against judicial legislation, or against hard cases being allowed to make bad law, or else that they were wrong according to the principles of the common law, in which case the decision does not count and we may ignore it.

If, on the other hand, the judges sit, not as a bureau or department, but as a commission with quasi-judicial powers, the danger is not so great. Nevertheless it represents a tendency which deserves careful scrutiny, and we must be at all times cognizant of just where it is leading us. The suspicion that has greeted commissions to which have been entrusted matters of public importance never quite disappears until the commission has been firmly established, and the dangerous tendencies of such movements are constantly talked over for a long time afterward.

The distinction between a bureau which is a very bad sort of thing and a commission with quasi-judicial powers which is well enough in its place, is that the commission, while not exactly a court, is nevertheless more like a court than like a bureau. Therefore if we are very watchful of these commissions and see that the inevitable mixing up of the three great branches of the Government—the executive, legislative, and judicial—occurs only on lower levels, and in comparatively minor matters such as the valuation of rail-roads, the fixing of rates, workmen's compensation, bank-ing, taxation, trade regulation, zoning, immigration, irriga-tion of arid lands, drainage, insurance, and similar things which do not involve the great principles of freedom (as, for example, a suit for libel and slander, replevin, or criminal conversation does), we may escape this new form of despotism. It is particularly important, however, to have a law court in the background ready to keep in check each commission which has been given quasi-judicial powers, because in this way the powers which had become so mud-dled when passing through the commission, again become separated and run in clear and separate streams; and every-thing becomes less arbitrary and personal and more subject to the fundamental rules of law.

Thus, in spite of their cumbersome way of approaching problems, courts appear to have found a way of acting which has brought them overwhelming prestige and re-spect. They seem to have induced the feeling, even among persons who know nothing of court methods and have never been inside a courtroom, that there they will find protection. Even when they fail miserably to give protection to someone who seeks it, such is their demeanor and atti-tude that he, or at least his friends, feels that it was not the fault of the court that protection failed. Perhaps it was the fault of the legislature, perhaps of the jury—at least the court did the best it could; and had it done otherwise it would have, in some mysterious way, imperiled the whole system of protection to others. Commissions, composed of experts, can be violently criticized by editorial writers. But if the matter is appealed to a nonexpert court, sitting on the same question and using the same criteria, it appears to be settled in the only way possible under the law. Our quarrel is, then, with the law, which we must respect until it is changed, and not with the court which applied it. Courts are protecting the liberties of Englishmen though in 1927 they committed approximately five thousand persons to jail for nonpayment of debt.[3] The imprisonment was the fault of the law and not the court. It is true that the Parliament in 1869 had abolished imprisonment for debt, but this did not include judgments which the debtor had the means to pay yet wilfully refused to pay. The difficulty, that it was entirely too easy for the creditor to establish the fact that the debtor had the means to pay, is only a procedural fault for which no court can be held to account. It must simply do the best it can with procedure as it finds it. Therefore the Right Honorable Lord Hewart of Bury, Lord Chief Justice of England, was quite right in ignoring such details as this when he wrote his book on *The New Despotism* in which he pointed out the dangers from the arbitrary actions of men who judge cases sitting as bureaus instead of as courts, and who are thus creating a new form of despotism in England.

The paradox which is in course of being accomplished is, indeed, rather elaborate. Writers on the Constitution have for a long time taught that its two leading features are the Sovereignty of Parliament and the Rule of Law. To tamper with either of them was, it might be thought, a sufficiently serious undertaking. But how far more attractive to the ingenious and adventurous mind to employ the one to defeat the other, and to establish a despotism on the ruins of both! . . . The old despotism, which was defeated, offered Parliament a challenge. The new despotism, which is not yet defeated, gives Parliament an anaesthetic. The strategy is different, but the goal is the same. It is to subordinate Parliament, to evade the Courts, and

3. *Criminal Statistics, England and Wales* (1927). This figure does not include imprisonment for nonsupport or bastardy cases. Including these cases, the total is 12,132. See "Imprisonment for Debt," (1923) 68 *Sol. J.* 178, (1928) 72 *idem* 676.

to render the will, or the caprice, of the Executive, unfettered
and supreme. The old King, as Rudyard Kipling sings in "The
Old Issue," sometimes reappears under a new name.[4]

It appears from this that bureaus, even though given absolute power to enforce the decrees of other persons in the
government, do not use that judgment in enforcing them
which is so characteristic of courts. They do not, on the
one hand, check the government in its wilder flights of
regulatory fancy, nor, on the other hand, are they able to
carry out the decrees of the government efficiently because
they are too bound down by that particularly silly form of
rule and precedent known as red tape. Courts, on the contrary, do not concern themselves with red tape, but only
with procedure and substantive law. Both may sometimes
be antiquated, but that is never the fault of the court,
whereas the red tape is always the fault of the bureau. Applying this principle to the cases of the persons imprisoned
for debt, we at once see that if it had been done by a bureau
it would have been an annoying invasion of personal liberty
accomplished in an arbitrary way. When it is done by the
court, even those in jail realize that it is not the fault of
the court, but the fault of the legislature which forced this
procedure on the court. Thus it appears that even when
courts refuse to protect the freedom of individuals they act
from such high motives that everyone should respect them
for their integrity.

From this we may reach our final definition of just what
courts, commissions, and bureaus are.

1. A court is a body of judges whose decisions are either:
(a) right, (b) caused by the fault of someone else (usually
the legislature), or (c) unfortunate but unavoidable accidents due to the circumstance that no human system can
be perfect.

4. Hewart, *The New Despotism* (1929), p. 17.

2. A bureau is a body which, if it happens to make a wrong decision, has no one to blame but itself, and if it happens to make a right decision, offers us no assurance that it will do so again.

3. A commission with quasi-judicial powers is halfway between a court and a bureau.

In other words, a court is a body toward which we take an attitude of respect because we use it to symbolize an ideal of impersonal justice. A bureau is a body which has little symbolic function, and which therefore is entitled to no greater respect than are the individuals composing it. A court escapes criticism, just as the church used to escape criticism, because it cannot be criticized without seeming to attack the whole governmental structure. Since its functions are primarily dramatic, the court is necessarily compelled to escape as far as possible from actual contact with society. It succeeds in doing this by elaborate procedural rules, and by isolating appellate courts through a system of appeals which are both difficult and expensive. Such a process automatically compels the arbitration of many disputes—and more important than that—it compels the establishment of commissions toward which we do not take the attitude of reverence due a court, wherever efficiency rather than ceremony is desirable. This is not a conscious process. It it the result of a climate of opinion in which courts which become practical and efficient cease to look like courts.

Bureaucracy as a Political Symbol

In its attempt to make philosophic distinctions between the functions of courts and administrative tribunals, the law is reflecting a general public ideal which heretofore has seemed a part of the most fundamental structure of our Government. An examination of the use of this ideal in public debate and the public reaction which follows the identification of any new social plan with the word "bureaucracy," is therefore most significant to anyone interested in our ways of thinking about government.

Few words have been more effective in creating opposition to any form of institutional change among the intelligent and conservative people of America than the term "bureaucracy." The word seems to have a real content, and the dangers incident upon changes which may lead in this direction appear grave indeed. They are not, however, dangers which are supposed to be familiar to the man on the street. They are shrouded in the mystery which surrounds the judicial process and accompanied by so many formidable words, that only the scholar is supposed to be able to understand them.

It is interesting to note that the terrifying symbol of "bureaucracy" never needs to be invoked to attack a measure which on its face seems unwise or inhumane. Such measures are usually discussed on their "practical" merits without recourse to the mysterious language incident to the term "bureaucracy." The function of such purely symbolical arguments is, rather, to stop reform movements which on their face seem quite rational and desirable. Such schemes must be opposed on account of their "tendencies." Thus we see kindly and humanitarian men formed into an organization to oppose the Child Labor Amendment. These men are sincerely opposed to child labor. They do not deny that Federal control would be more effective in stopping it than a hit-or-miss system of state control handicapped because it is limited by arbitrary state lines. Yet they are afraid of the establishment of Federal bureaus, even for good purposes. In general, where this word has been effective in stopping change, we find the evils complained of admitted but the measures of regulation opposed—on the ground that the evils are less dangerous than the tendencies of the legislation.

It is worthwhile to analyze the argumentative use of the term "bureaucracy" in political debate today, because it is probably the most effective weapon of attack against the efficient use of centralized power which exists in the present climate of opinion. To attack measures as tending toward socialism, communism, or fascism is not nearly so potent, because no one is quite ready to believe that these schemes are real dangers. They are associated with certain distrusted individuals like the late Huey Long, or Upton Sinclair, and it is hard to call respectable people, like Secretary Wallace, communists. The analogy does not quite click. To say, however, that Wallace is a good sound American, but at the same time leading us into bureaucracy for laudable, but misguided, motives makes a plausible argument which carries weight. It permits us to attack the scheme without reading Mr. Wallace completely out of respectable society and associating him with organizations which would publicly deny him.

Another element of effectiveness of the symbol is that it can be used to attack plans, on the general aims of which there is no dispute. Thus the real-estate men of New York attack slum clearance on the ground that it tends to set up a bureaucracy. It would be difficult to call it communism, because there are too many people who think of themselves as capitalists who advocate it. It cannot be attacked on the ground that it interferes with the real-estate business because that puts realtors in too selfish a light. Only by calling it bureaucracy can one get the effective emotional response. The word also permits the real-estate men to believe sincerely that they are the champions of a greater cause than their own pocketbooks. This gives them the morale necessary to conduct a fight.

We have already analyzed positive symbols such as the

ideal of a fair trial, and law enforcement. The effect of negative symbols and their argumentative pattern is so different as to deserve a separate treatment. Bureaucracy is probably the most important of our negative symbols. It does not hold up an ideal. Instead, it pictures a vague terror. We will, therefore, dissect the institutional effects of the use of this term with some detail. They may be illustrated at the outset by posing the following question: Why is it that the real-estate men would have no valid objection if a great private corporation, organized for public purposes, had been clearing the slums and destroying their real-estate values? Why is it that the Government itself constantly resorts to the device of incorporating its activities to make itself look like a private individual, and thereby increases morale and efficiency? Why was it that the operation of the Panama Railroad was actually more successful when it acted as a private corporation, in which the Government owned all of the stock, than when it was a branch of the War Department?

The use of the argumentative technique which surrounds the word "bureaucracy" follows the same pattern, regardless of the practical situation about which the argument revolves. The ordinary sphere of this argument is found in cases where we are trying to explain why simple and humanitarian measures, which superficially seem to involve no disastrous consequences, are vicious in principle. Thus in speaking about the Child Labor Amendment, which would seem to the unlearned person harmless enough, scholarly or important persons are accustomed to talk like this:

The Child Labor Amendment would constitute a distinct menace to the family, to the home and to our local self-government. Under its language Congress could regulate the help children might give their parents in the home or on the farm, and it could "limit, regulate, and prohibit" any and all forms of labor throughout the entire United States by any person under eighteen years of age. Furthermore, its terms would authorize Congress practically to regulate and control the education of children under the guise of limiting or regulating their mental labor. . . .

It is not a Child Labor Amendment. It was not so intended. Although advocated by many well meaning people, it is a communistic effort to nationalize children, making them responsible primarily to the government, instead of to their parents. It strikes a blow at the home.[5]

Whereupon the American Bar Association rises, backed by a number of our sound educational leaders to protect the American Home by passing a resolution like this:

RESOLVED by the American Bar Association that the proposed Child Labor Amendment to the Constitution of the United States should be actively opposed as an unwarranted invasion by the Federal Government of a field in which the rights of the individual states and of the family are and should remain paramount.[6]

But it is not the home alone that is in danger. Everything is in danger and to prove this the late President Coolidge was cited as follows:

No plan of centralization has ever been adopted which did not result in bureaucracy, tyranny, inflexibility, reaction, and decline. The States should not be induced by coercion or favor to surrender the management of their affairs.[7]

A visitor from Mars might think from this utterance that President Coolidge had turned into a philosophic anarchist and was opposing all the present existing bureaus of the

5. Hon. William D. Guthrie, "The Child Labor Amendment," 20 *Journ. Am. Bar Assoc.* 404 (July, 1934).

6. 19 *Journ. Am. Bar Assoc.* 557 (Oct., 1933).

7. *Congressional Record,* July 3, 1926, p. 35, as cited 20 *Journ. Am. Bar Assoc.* 404 at 406 n. 7.

Federal Government. However, this was not so. If the discussion had been on some subject which was not so cluttered up with symbols, the visitor from Mars would have found the President talking quite practically and sensibly about it.

These arguments follow the general pattern of all "What are we coming to?" arguments. No symbolic logic, however, is complete without introducing another effective device with which all of us are familiar from childhood. For purposes of reference we may refer to it as the "It hurts me more than it does you" argument. Therefore, at the close of the article we find Al Smith quoted as follows:

After careful, and I may say prayerful, consideration of these arguments for and against the Child Labor Amendment, I wish to be recorded in the negative. No one can accuse me of being callous or indifferent to the needs of children. I won my service stripes in the war against exploitation of children many years ago when there were few enthusiasts, and many powerful opponents. I find it difficult and distressing to oppose now my loyal comrades of these early battles. I have, however, learned in recent years the bitter lessons of the Eighteenth Amendment. I devoutly hope that the people of this country will not permit themselves to be deluded by sentiment, tricked by false logic, coerced by minorities, or stampeded by rhetoric, into a repetition of their recent monumental folly in attempting to legislate morality into the United States Constitution. It does not seem possible that the same States which are relieving us of the curse of the Eighteenth Amendment will now impose another constitutional curse upon us under the guise of abolishing child labor.[8]

Few men in public have a greater sense of objective reality in the type of politics with which they are familiar than Al Smith. Therefore it is difficult to believe that he

8. Ex-Governor Al Smith, *The New Outlook*, October, 1933, as cited 20 *Journ. Am. Bar Assoc.* 404 at 406.

seriously thinks that only a few years ago "there were few enthusiasts and many powerful opponents" on the issue against the exploitation of children. One may search the literature of politics and government without finding any respectable persons who advocated the exploitation of children. All that they ever do is to confuse the issue with some important ideal, create a conflict between the issue and that ideal, and then show how sorry they are that the exploitation of children is necessary to the preservation of that ideal. This, of course, is exactly what Mr. Smith is doing here. There is no question about their sincerity while they are thinking in this way—nor any doubt about the reality of their sorrow for those who must suffer that the ideal may live. The symbolic argument lifts the speaker up into the clouds among vague, tearful, and sacred things, and once up there it is impossible to discuss practical matters.

In after years, forebodings about the calamitous effect of humanitarian action by governments usually look absurd. We read today with great amusement the genuine alarm once caused by the distribution of free medical supplies in England to the poor. The arguments, of course, follow exactly the same pattern as the above argument against child labor, since the possibility of argument with moral symbols is very limited. First we encounter the "What are we coming to?" argument. There follow citations of great men of the past and the discussion is concluded with the "It hurts me worse than it does you" argument. Note the dissenting opinion in the Nebbia Case where the learned justice showed that, even in an emergency where price-fixing was beneficial, we should not permit a state to exercise that power, since only by doing something which hurts us can we really exemplify principles.[9] Again, only a few years ago, the same logical pattern appeared in opposition

9. ". . . the adoption of any 'concept of jurisprudence, which permits facile disregard of the Constitution as long interpreted and respected will in-

to England's unemployment relief program. No one wanted to see the workmen starve, but better that than the joggling of the great symbol that every honest, hardworking man would always come out all right if he were unassisted. Hence the dole was ruining England. Today, of course, when England is spending over twice as much on the dole, she is pointed to by conservatives as the great example of the country which pulled itself out of a muddle by following sound principles.

We have chosen the opposition to the Child Labor Amendment for our principal illustration of the inevitable pattern of arguments which retreat into the realms of social symbolism only because we suspect that at this time most people will agree that this amendment would have had little effect upon the present increase in governmental power which followed the depression. We also suspect that most people would agree with its humanitarian purposes. We have not the space to argue these assumptions here; but if any reader is opposed to the amendment upon the practical ground that state control would be more effective, we will only call to his attention the fact that no practical grounds are discussed by those caught in fear of the bogeyman "bureaucracy."

There is scarcely a field of political thought where we do not find this symbolism operating today, though how the battle lines are drawn up seems almost accidental. For example, Al Smith is convinced that the regulation of child

---

evitably lead to its destruction. Then, all rights will be subject to the caprice of the hour; government by stable laws will pass.

". . . Grave concern for embarrassed farmers is everywhere; but this should neither obscure the rights of others nor obstruct judicial appraisement of measures proposed for relief. The ultimate welfare of the producer, like that of every other class, requires dominance of the Constitution. And zealously to uphold this in all its parts is the highest duty intrusted to the courts." Mr. Justice McReynolds dissenting in *Nebbia* vs. *New York,* 291 *U.S.* 502 at 558–559 (1934).

labor is bureaucracy. However, he insists that the more drastic regulation of public utilities is not bureaucracy. In his mind, the one is like the prohibition amendment, and the other is not. Equally respectable people will claim that public-utility regulation is bureaucracy and child labor is a practical reform. The problems which get tangled with these ideals seem the result of chance contacts, of friendships, or of dinner-table arguments. Entirely aside from those who are directly and financially affected by the Child Labor Amendment, we find a great mass of respectable, conservative persons, whose interests would not be affected by the regulation, opposing it simply because they confuse the practical problem with the verbal symbols which they revere.

The writer has, for example, seen many administrative schemes tremendously complicated, and even ruined, because someone happened to make a speech pointing out some principles which otherwise might have been ignored. The administration of the recent recovery legislation is full of such instances. For example, under the Agricultural Adjustment Act, great administrative power is given to the Secretary of Agriculture because the enforcement of regulations is too slow if done by the judicial organization. It is interesting to note that among the first cases in which the Secretary attempted to enforce a license under the act was an injunction proceeding before a court of equity, tried on the ground that the administrative remedy designed for the purpose of escaping the cumbersome legal process was inadequate.[10] The reason the administrative remedy was inadequate was because it had become so cluttered up with gestures toward the judicial process which the act itself attempted to avoid. This happened because those administering the act were trying to obey all legal principles at

10. *U.S.* vs. *Calistan Packers, Inc.*, 4 *Fed. Supp.* 660 (N.D. Cal. S.D. 1933).

once. Thus the administrative process, which started out to be simple, actually became more complicated than the judicial process. Such confusion is ordinarily referred to as an example of the evils of bureaucracy. Ironically enough, the annoying red tape of governmental bureaus is more often than not the result of the efforts of learned men to make them resemble judicial institutions. Thus government becomes "bureaucratic" because it is usually operated by men obsessed with the legal symbols which are supposedly designed to avoid bureaucracy. All this is puzzling to one who does not understand the effects of symbols upon learned and respectable people. A characteristic complaint is as follows:

If the angel Gabriel were to come down from heaven and head a successful rise against the most abominable and unrighteous vested interest which this poor old world groans under, he would most certainly lose his character for many years, probably for centuries, not only with upholders of said vested interest but with the respectable mass of people whom he had delivered.[11]

To the humanitarian reformer the observation seems eternally true. Yet, like most doleful utterances which condemn the human race as a whole, it fails to describe the situation. Respectable people, when not concerned with the preservation of the symbols which dramatize their ideals, are notoriously humane. They are apt to make all sorts of sacrifices for the good of humanity. The American Bar Association, though it appears to radicals to be the last stronghold of special interest, is in reality sincerely concerned with legal reforms, many of which directly attack the lawyers' means of livelihood. In fact, procedural reform designed to throw the lawyers out of lucrative business will often get the unselfish support of the American Bar. It is only when reform gets tangled up with the ideals which

11. From Hughes, *Tom Brown at Rugby.*

seem to give prestige to the judicial institution itself that we find an emotional resistance to the abolition of admitted abuses. Respectable people are not as bad as reformers would paint them. They are only caught in ideals which happen to have, at the time, no emotional relevance to the complaining reformer.

There are few ideals in America today, more important in their emotional effect, than that of "a government of laws and not of men." Any project which seems to interfere with this ideal encounters the greatest difficulty in obtaining public acceptance. No institution can gain permanent prestige without conforming to it. Violent collisions with the ideal are supposed to end in dictatorship. Lesser violations lead to bureaucracy. Everyone assumes that they know what is meant by the ideal, in general, and that legal scholars have a vast, intimate, and truly scientific knowledge of its details and mechanical structure. Any attempt to define it with precision leads us into a maze of metaphysical literature, perhaps larger than has ever surrounded any other symbol in the history of the world.

It is not important here to analyze what the legal scholar thinks the ideal means to him. The legal scholar exists only in answer to a demand that someone be entrusted with the task of making the phrase appear to have deep and complicated rational and scientific implications. In a society which preferred processions or rituals to libraries, the scholar would perform the same function in an entirely different way. The hackneyed phrase that the sources of law are found in the hearts of the common people, contains much more truth than most poetry. Therefore it is necessary to discover what the ordinary "thinking" man connects with the use of the phrase, and why he may be roused to hostile action by any word which goes contrary to it, such as bureaucracy.

The explanation that fear of bureaucracy and reverence

for a government of laws result from the unwillingness of free Americans to submit to complex regulation on the one hand or arbitrary power on the other, is generally accepted because it reflects the way Americans like to think of themselves. Nothing, however, could be further from the truth. So far as regulation is concerned, few people in the world pass so many laws which interfere with such intimate details of their lives. Prohibition was adopted with enthusiasm, and clung to long after it was shown to be an utter failure. An examination of the statutes of any of our states shows an amazing tendency to regulate all sorts of moral and individual conduct, such as the details of education, the size of bed sheets in hotels, the kind of speeches which may be made in public, etc. American civil and criminal codes are notoriously long and complicated.

In that control over our affairs by a governing force usually referred to as business, we permit great employers almost absolute power over the livelihood of perhaps the greater percentage of our population, and allow them to use this power without even giving reasons for their action. We do this through a slogan which clothes our great employers with a mystical sanction not differing in effect from the divine right of kings.

In October, 1934, the A & P Grocery Company, operating over three hundred stores in Cleveland, announced that it would withdraw from business in that city, throwing about two thousand employees out of work. The reason given was that there was a teamsters' strike which prevented the delivery of groceries to the stores. The announced withdrawal, however, was to be permanent. While it was not impossible for the A & P to continue business in Cleveland, it was no longer convenient. Subsequently, the A & P agreed to reopen after a settlement of many of the disputed questions. However, few questioned either their power or their right to permanently close the stores.

Obviously, here is an exercise of arbitrary power which would be difficult for an admitted tyrant to undertake. Yet we find the Cleveland Chamber of Commerce supporting the action of the A & P grocery chain. It is obviously against the interests of Cleveland to have twenty-two hundred men thrown out of work and on the relief rolls. However, the Chamber of Commerce preferred a violent dislocation in the economic structure of Cleveland to having its symbols of bureaucracy joggled. Had the Cleveland Chamber of Commerce thought of the A & P as a sort of "government" we would no doubt have found them bitter in their criticism of this arbitrary exercise of governmental power. Since the symbol is not attached and since the members of the Chamber of Commerce have emotionally put the A & P into another category, they are equally religious in their devotion to a principle which cannot do other than cause them financial inconvenience.

The argument of the Cleveland Chamber of Commerce, since it is a symbolical argument, proceeds along exactly the same lines as the argument against the Child Labor Amendment. It closes with the familiar "It hurts us worse than it does you" theory. We find a resolution of sympathy for the loyal employees who were thrown out of work because of the operation of a great fundamental principle.

One might have imagined that the occurrence would have been an object lesson of the folly in permitting industrial war to involve whole communities of nonparticipating people. No one would seriously contend for the right to create a public nuisance by fighting outside of court over an ordinary lawsuit. Why, therefore, should labor and employers inconvenience millions of others by publicly fighting over labor disputes? Compulsory arbitration, enforced by courts, might seem, from this point of view, to contain in it less danger of the unprincipled use of arbitrary power to the detriment of innocent bystanders than the present succession of wars to the finish. Therefore, while one might expect both labor and capital to oppose it, it would be reasonable to anticipate that disinterested persons at least would find it in accord with their interest. Such sensible reactions, however, do not occur when the play is cast as a battle over fundamental ideals of government. Compulsory arbitration does not represent government by law in a climate of opinion supporting industrial anarchy, guided by great principles of individual liberty, because in such a climate the fundamental principles of law point clearly to the necessity of industrial anarchy if a government of law is not to perish. A statute compelling compulsory arbitration is not a government of law, because it conflicts with the fundamental principles of a higher law above mere statutes. Such extension of governmental powers is similar to the Child Labor Amendment. It is not to be argued as a compulsory arbitration scheme. Instead, it should be exposed as an attempt to get misguided people to destroy their own government by offering them a temporary specious advantage.

So long as this battle of symbols goes on, even the passage of a compulsory arbitration law cannot be effective until the situation is swept clean of the symbols. On question of principle, great masses of people will always take sides. Which side they take depends not upon self-interest, or any practical appreciation of the problem, but on the chance of association or temperament which makes them emotionally responsible to one set of symbols or another.

Examples of this self-sacrificing devotion to anti-bureaucratic principles by intelligent people are found everywhere. We quote an editorial approval of the rejection by Williams College, of Federal government aid for needy students on the ground that, by refusing to permit assistance to its students, the college is in some mysterious way preventing "an impairment of our cherished liberties." The typical symbolic argument follows, in exactly the same pattern as the Child Labor Amendment argument cited above.

Dr. Dennett's Sound Position

(From *Springfield Union*.)

In declining the offer of FERA funds for students at Williams College and in a statement of his reasons for so doing, the new president, Dr. Tyler Dennett, reveals the high mental capacity to think things through. The offer of such Federal aid is, as he states, based on the assumption of an emergency and the presumption that at some unknown date it will be possible for the Federal Government to withdraw the aid offered. Dr. Dennett doubts this prospect, but rather expects that his college, as well as other colleges, would come to regard such aid as an essential part of income and so oppose the resumption by the Federal Government of its proper functions.

He believes that this would be a deplorable outcome and that it would be much better for the colleges to adjust themselves to changed economic conditions, reduce their budgets accordingly and, if necessary, reduce their enrollment.

That, in our opinion, is the proper attitude, not only for self-respecting and self-reliant colleges to take, but the proper one for people generally to take in their own future interests. The extension of Federal aid, even without a perilous extension of Federal authority, along such lines commonly means a weakening of the saving spirit of self-reliance, a restriction on the dynamic force of public and private initiative, and an impairment of cherished liberties.[12]

The writer of the editorial, of course, would not have a state university reject aid from the state. Nor would he at-

12. This editorial from the *Springfield Union* was thought to be sufficiently important to be repeated in the *New Haven Register* of November 10, 1934.

tack the Federal grants to agricultural work. Probably if the F.E.R.A. grant had been dressed up in these familiar clothes he might not have involved it with the symbolism of bureaucracy. However, instead of appearing as something familiar, it comes from one of the dreaded alphabetical subdivisions of the New Deal which is supposed to be heading us for bureaucracy. While the bold action of Williams College probably will have little or no effect upon the future extension of power of the Federal Government, at least, when we are all suffering under tyranny, its alumni can point with pride to the fact that their college saw the light and attempted to stem the tide.

As another example of the effective use of this symbolism we point to the fact that for years users of municipal public utilities have rejected with scorn municipal ownership, even under conditions where such ownership would be a distinct advantage to them. Of course we do not here contend that all municipal ownership is good. In some communities it may be advantageous. In others it is not. However, the campaigns against it have been most effectively conducted on the general principles that it was an invasion of the rights of the individual, and that its tendencies were dangerous, even where its practical results might be good, and this slogan has been effective against all practical arguments in countless instances. It was to preserve such things as the private operation of public utilities, that the American Bar Association fought against child labor, and Williams College declined the aid of the F.E.R.A.

It is depressing to note that collateral sacrifices before the altar of individual liberty, such as the gesture of Williams College, have had practically no effect in stemming the progress of governmental regulation. Today, the public utilities are threatened both by the Federal Government and by municipalities. We quote from the *New York Times*.

UTILITIES REVIEW LOSSES AT POLLS

Some Executives See Industry Facing Darkest Period of the Depression. Gird for Bitter Battle.

Companies Intend To Use All Legal Weapons To Prevent Municipal Extensions.

The position of the electric light and power industry is now regarded by some executives as having reached the darkest period of the depression, as a result of Tuesday's victory of municipal ownership proponents at the polls. This conclusion is drawn because the voters favored private operation a year ago when ample PWA funds appeared available under the easiest possible conditions, whereas the recent elections were conducted with little hope for Federal funds.[13]

Yet such is the faith of intelligent people in the traditional symbols of government, that it would be impossible to convince the editor who praised the sacrifice of Williams College that its action would not have some effect on stopping the Government at Washington in its mad career. Actually, the blind devotion to these symbols, instead of aiding us to combat change, prevents us from seeing and taking the necessary precautions to meet a change which is already upon us. Most of the sacrifices made in their honor by disinterested people are in vain.

Thus it is that the symbol of bureaucracy owes its emotional appeal neither to the dread of regulation nor to the fear of arbitrary power nor to a realistic appreciation of practical consequences. Though in the hands of some it may be used to cloak some selfish interest, its real effectiveness is with those who are willing to forsake all selfish interest because they are following a dream. What is that dream, and from whence comes its emotional appeal?

It has its roots in the necessity which Western peoples

13. *New York Times* (Nov. 11, 1934).

have for believing that somewhere in this world or in the next there exists a justice beyond human caprice. A policeman may treat us unjustly at a crossing. We pay our fine rather than go to the trouble of appealing through the courts to the Supreme Court, cynical about the virtues of policemen, but serene in the faith that if we only took the time and trouble we would achieve justice. A legislature threatens to pass inconvenient laws, but we remain calm, realizing that there is a constitution which makes us safe. When we test out our legal resources we are disappointed more often than not. But even then we take comfort that our defeat was the accident of an unskilful attorney, or of an unworthy court. The fundamental principles are there, beyond the court, only waiting for better judges to apply them. They are being restated by great scholars who are courageously fighting to eliminate the unreasonable from our law. Even when our decisions are imperfect or unjust, there is hope, because the law is getting closer and closer to its ideals as we study it. In any event, we take comfort in the thought that the ideal is all right even though its application is wrong. The essence of human dignity is to struggle to obtain impossible ideals.

Any sort of heaven, if it is to be successful, must be far away. If we bring it too close, we begin to see its imperfections and realize that it is not Heaven at all. A heritage of Protestant theology leads us to demand a logical heaven of carefully formulated principles. As courts approach the complicated affairs of life we see that our logical heaven is full of flaws. As they retreat from control over our affairs, deciding cases only after long struggles to get the case to them in proper form after delays of years during which the real cause of the litigation is forgotten—we see the outline of what they are doing more dimly and its imperfections are lost. It is easier to ignore the dross, and collect the pure gold.

If the American people were actually free from countless petty restrictions, it is not likely that they would build a mansion in the judicial heavens dedicated to the principle, before which we make such curious sacrifices, that there should be no such restrictions. If we were not so constantly subject to arbitrary and uncontrolled power over our very means of existence, we would not require the dramatization of the abstract ideal that no such power could exist in America, provided that the case could be properly presented to the Supreme Court of the United States. The only absolute essential of a heaven is that it be different from the everyday world. In our present plight we need the comforting belief of a legal paradise, where neither annoying governmental regulation nor arbitrary power unfettered by fundamental principle, is tolerated. Therefore, when the symbol of "government of law" is attacked, the gaunt specter of bureaucracy arises to haunt us. The arbitrary treatment which is accorded us in our daily lives threatens to be no longer tempered by the thought that somewhere above in some cool, calm judicial chamber is stored a great mass of counterprinciples which would rise to our aid if we only had time and money to get at them. We therefore rise as one man to defend our paradise, and to put down at any cost the reformer who appears with a scheme which our best thinkers inform us will destroy it. We rely on our priests to tell us just what endangers this paradise—and they in turn get their information on the real sinister purpose of a plan like the Child Labor Amendment by a process of mental magic which is never disclosed to us.

Those who control our judicial institutions feel this necessity of keeping judicial principles as far as possible from practical cases, even though they do not formulate this feeling into words. Persons who do not understand the nature of social symbols are constantly surprised at the slowness and "inefficiency" of the legal process. Reform after reform is launched designed to make it quick and sensible. Such reforms are useful in making the institution conform to another prevailing ideal, i.e., the ideal of efficiency. Yet the judicial institution, by an instinct which tells it that efficiency and practicality are judicial suicide, always succeeds in making of the procedural reforms something as complicated and cumbersome as the process which was abolished. Courts do not become "efficient" because they cannot become efficient and still remain courts. Legal procedure is faced with the inherent necessity of keeping the actual complicated facts of cases out of court. When there is added to this the task that it must also dramatize the ideal of business efficiency, which takes in all the facts and statistics, it does its best to reconcile the conflicting symbols, but the result is complicated beyond the imagination of those who proposed the reform.

Ideals of law arise from the hearts of the people, not from refinements of intellectuals. A judicial institution, founded on a culture which demands the dramatic presentation of impersonal justice, composed of fundamentals which can never stand the test of practical efficiency, will reject instinctively as bureaucratic all attempts to make the law practical. Intellectuals will curse the stupidity of judges who follow these ideals of the folkways in vain. So long as they fail to understand the comforting function of the symbol in representing justice in a world where there is little of fairness to the common man—in representing freedom from arbitrary action in a world where the arbitrary action of business anarchy reigns supreme; in representing a check on governmental power in an age of rapid and inevitable centralization—they will be futile as reformers. Their only function will be the necessary one of making the institution represent another conflicting ideal—that of efficiency.

The observer who understands the functioning of these symbols will also understand the contradictions which are so puzzling about the law—for example, the paradox that, while a trial is the fairest way of settling disputes, all good lawyers should keep their clients out of court; the paradox that arbitration is to be encouraged because it is a better way of settling disputes than the judicial process, and discouraged because contracts for arbitration oust the court of jurisdiction. They will understand the long fight against the declaratory judgment, and the fact that now that this simple device is adopted it takes a book to explain it which is longer than the former books upon the older and supposedly more complicated methods of pleading.[14] They will understand why the New York Code, by so desperately trying to make procedure simple, ended by making it the most complex procedure in the world. They will understand why the long struggle to talk the language of economics and sociology before courts meets only with lip service. They will understand why we must constantly attempt to restate the fundamental principles of the law, and why, though the effort is always worthwhile, the result is always useless.

On the basis of this discussion we may attempt to answer the questions which we posed at the outset. The attitude described by the term "bureaucracy" is so deep seated that it destroys the confidence of officials in their ability to take practical action unless they are able to escape into some other atmosphere. If they call themselves a corporation, or a political party, or any familiar symbol which permits freedom of action, their difficulties disappear.

Since the Roosevelt Administration, over twenty-five thousand administrative regulations, supposed to have the force of law, have been promulgated in Washington. This

14. The most authoritative and scholarly work on the subject is by Edwin M. Borchard, *Declaratory Judgments* (1934), containing 669 pages.

has caused great alarm. Articles and editorials have been written about it. Indexing and classification and all the elaborate techniques of scholarship are proposed as a cure. Of course there is no cure, so long as governmental officials, cowed by the symbol of bureaucracy, try to make themselves look as much like a rule of law as possible. In that atmosphere they are bound to trip over themselves, because what they are trying to do is not to appear arbitrary and bureaucratic by following a written formula for every practical judgment. When they form a private governmental corporation under the laws of the State of Delaware they can act differently, because we are not accustomed to think of the arbitrary action of corporations as bureaucratic.

To the same attitude may be traced the enormous importance of the *sub rosa* political machine. If it were proposed that New York should officially perform the necessary services done by Tammany, it would be condemned as advocacy of bureaucracy in its worst form. The opportunities for corruption, favoritism, etc., would be pointed out and the complete inability to curb and control them demonstrated. A man from Mars might think that while it might be difficult to control these evils in a public bureau, it would be infinitely more difficult to control them in a political machine which operated in the dark, and with responsibility to no one. The thinking man of today, however, would simply fail to see the relevance of the argument. He does not mind Tammany Hall because he does not expect much of it. And thus, because it escapes the hampering effects of the attitude we have called a fear of bureaucracy, the political machine constitutes our temporal, as opposed to our spiritual, government.

So long as the taboo against practical action by official government persists, we will find centralization of power difficult to accomplish. When stern necessity forces that centralization, we will find that as a result of the taboo all sorts of curious subterfuges will be resorted to. It may be that the government corporation is the way out; or it may be that the taboo is gradually disappearing with the necessities of a new day; or it may be that with a rising business recovery government will be able to turn back the reins to American businessmen. We are, however, not interested in prophecy, but only in the curious institutional effects of this negative symbol, which are particularly marked in times of change.

CHAPTER X

A Philosophy for Politicians

THE observations in the foregoing chapters present a troubling paradox. Social institutions require faiths and dreams to give them morale. They need to escape from these faiths and dreams in order to progress. The hierarchy of governing institutions must pretend to symmetry, moral beauty, and logic in order to maintain their prestige and power. To actually govern, they must constantly violate those principles in hidden and covert ways. Throughout this book there has been emphasized the need for a constructive philosophy of government. Yet the reader may well wonder whether such a philosophy can be woven out of such contradictory observations. Therefore the foregoing chapters may appear purely destructive. They seem to lack any formula which can inspire groups of people to support an effective social organization.

In answer to such an objection it must be admitted that dispassionate observation or dissection cannot lead or inspire. Accurate detailed photographs never bring out that blurred beauty which thrills us at twilight. To the artist, the human body is a far more poetic and beautiful symbol than it is to the physician, who is interested in it chiefly because of its diseases. When therefore a person needs cheer or decoration it is well to call in an artist. When he requires a diagnosis he needs a physician. And therefore the excuse for apparent destructiveness of the foregoing chapters is that the writer is attempting to dissect social institutions rather than to dramatize them.

Yet the diagnosis would not be complete if there were not some indication of the kind of formula which is capable of dramatizing our ideals, and at the same time of giving us freedom to progress along the road of experiment and discovery. It will therefore be the purpose of this chapter to speculate on possible constructive theories of government which might in the future lead us to discoveries in the art of human organization.

The present day is marked with a paralyzing lack of faith in both government institutions and their theories. The man on the street has lost confidence in the industrial feudalism which formerly gave him a job. This lack of faith is called radicalism. The businessman has lost faith that the National Government will serve as a buffer between him and the conflicting interests attacking his power. This is called a failure of business confidence. It is an undefined fear, and it fastens itself to whatever is new that appears over the horizon. Thus the Securities Act, the Holding Companies Act, and, indeed, every act of Congress which is out of the ordinary take their turns as the things which are blocking recovery. When diverse groups gather with interests so different that they cannot unite in opposition to any specific act, the general fear is attached to naïve personifications like "the brain" trust. "Professors" in government are attacked as if there were a body of such persons who were advocating a definite program in Washington. The Constitution is praised in general as the great bulwark, even though there could be no possible agreement in the group which was praising it as to how that Constitution should reconcile their conflicting interests. The Supreme Court hovers over the whole picture, and it is to it that prayers are addressed. However, they are fearful prayers, because the group knows that there is never any certainty as to what the next decision will be. Yet in times of confusion and fear, there is nothing that so comforts the heart of timid men as a combination of prayer and denunciation. For this purpose the Constitution becomes for most conservatives the symbol of security in which all conflicting hopes and fears are somehow resolved. The *New York Herald-Tribune,* as this is being written, is printing at the head of its editorial columns the President's oath to support the Constitution. And such is the peculiar complex of fear today that it is entirely probable that the editors think that somehow they are making the country safer by this gesture. They think it is a good thing, just as prayer is a good thing. Hopeful people today wave the flag of national power. Timid people wave the Constitution. Neither group is quite coherent as to specific objectives, but both feel better because of these respective ceremonies.

As a matter of fact the lack of faith in the future is not caused by specific legislation or the advocacy of specific objectives. It is the failure of practical institutions to function which has raised doubts in the hearts of conservatives. Twenty years ago no one worried about socialism, because it was thought to be impossible; just as water running up hill is impossible. Automatic economic laws prevented it. Today we see before us both fascism and communism in actual operation, with their governments growing in power. Economic law no longer prevents such types of control. The only bulwark against change is the Constitution. But with the disappearance of the economic certainties, the actual words of the Constitution no longer appear like a bulwark. There is no settled faith in our form of government as the only workable type. Therefore the unified drive which accompanies settled faith is lacking. When belief in current symbols wavers, social unrest grows.

Mr. Sherwood Anderson, in his recent book, *Puzzled America,* notes the evidences of that lack of confidence everywhere. He thus describes the feeling that he found in all the highways and byways which he traveled:

And so there it is—"If I could believe. I want belief." It is a cry going up out of the American people, I think it is about the absolute net of what I have been able to find out about Americans in these last few years of traveling about, in all of this looking at people and talking to them. "I want belief, some ground to stand on. I do not want government to go on being a meaningless thing."

There is no gainsaying the truth of that observation about government. The symbols of debt, credit, currency, thrift, are all turned upside down. Ancient virtues do not bring their supposed reward. Unsound principles do not seem to lead to inevitable destruction. No one can give a formula which reconciles the conflicting ideas of today. The dole, unemployment insurance, huge governmental spending, seem inevitable. However, the humanitarian values which they represent, and which prevent us from abandoning them, are not yet tied up with any theological structure which gives us peace and certainty for the future.

The writer does not pretend that he or anyone else can invent a formula to remove us from this sea of doubt. Such formulas are not constructed by individuals. They come from the place from which language and poetry come; they grow up with the institutions which they support. However, if they are to be successful, this much is required of them: they must permit practical institutions to function with security, and provide them with freedom to experiment; they must be supports and defenses; they cannot be guides. Nevertheless, for the purposes only of a platform from which to examine the present-day confusion, we will offer a theory which we will call a philosophy for humanitarian politicians. It runs as follows:

From a humanitarian point of view the best government is that which we find in an insane asylum. In such a government the physicians in charge do not separate the ideas of the insane into any separate sciences such as law, economics, and sociology; nor then instruct the insane in the intricacies of these three sciences. Nor do they argue with the insane as to the soundness or unsoundness of their ideas. Their aim is to make the inmates of the asylum as comfortable as possible, regardless of their respective moral deserts. In this they are limited only by the facilities of the institution. It is, of course, theoretically possible to treat the various ideas and taboos which affect modern society, just as the alienist treats the delusions of his patients as factors which condition their behavior. This precludes any classification into sound or unsound theories. No psychiatrist, today, attempts to differentiate the *content* of foolish ideas, and of insane ideas. It is equally possible to adopt a point of view toward government where ideas are considered only in the light of their effect on conduct. To a certain extent, the government which civilized nations impose on savage tribes does succeed in taking this attitude; and success in dealing with such tribes is largely determined by the ability of the governing group to utilize taboos, instead of trying to stamp them out as unsound.

The advantages of such a theory for purposes of thinking about government are that we escape the troublesome assumption that the human race is rational. We need not condemn policies which contradict each other solely on the ground that the action of government must be logically consistent. We need not constantly worry about permanent cures, and discard day-to-day policies because of their effects on the morale of the irrational people we are governing in the future. We need not delay such necessary undertakings as public relief because we are worried about their effect on the character of the recipients. We need not compel persons on relief to pauperize themselves and surrender the insurance policies which may afford future relief to their children because of a moral notion that no one is entitled to relief who is not a pauper. The theory eliminates from our thinking the moral ideals which hamper us wherever a governmental institution takes practical action—ideals which create the necessity of a *sub rosa* political machine. It frees us from the necessity of worrying about names, and arguing about the respective merits of communism, fascism, or capitalism—arguments which have the unfortunate effect of creating phobias against practical and humanitarian measures. Such phobias are constantly preventing the day-to-day practical appraisals of a situation which is the essence of practical government.

Such a theory allows us to realize that cultures do not change because of the imposition of forms of government, and that the real contribution of new theories can only be to provide a faith which permits men to do practical and humanitarian things in government with confidence that they are not leading to some undefined danger. The fear that a recognition of the great humanitarian ideals of Russian governmental philosophy would result in the substitution of Russian culture and habits for our present way of life, has been a very real one in the last few years. Yet the fact is that we could not think as Russians think even if we tried. Russia jumped from stagnation into modern industrial activity, carrying with it the idealogy of the Middle Ages. It never went through those ages of thinking of debts and credits as the only logical natural way of distributing the products of an industrial machine. Russian literature, with some noteworthy exceptions, was never influenced by the natural-law conception of the West. It was either pure fantasy, or stark realism. The political thought of the Russian masses was medieval. Hence Russians were able to distribute goods, unincumbered by those symbols of debt and credit which are so necessary for our own bookkeeping, because they had never learned them. They were able to look at the distribution of goods as a purely mechanical problem of production and transportation, without connecting with it the moral problem of the preservation of national character.

Centuries of background make it as impossible for us as a nation to use Russian symbols as to use the Russian language. We may catch the humanitarian ideal of the Russian, but not his queer logic. Our Government, even when it moves along the purely humanitarian lines of the distribution of food, power, or financial support of tottering institutions, must pretend that it is an individual buying and selling in a competitive world. It does this by incorporating itself in great government banking and credit institutions, keeping books like private enterprises, buying, selling, and loaning to each other. This symbolism seems necessary in order to get that freedom of action which is essential for the distribution of relief. The very existence of such great corporations as the Home Owners Loan Corporation (with 800,000 mortgages), the Reconstruction Finance Corporation (probably the soundest investment trust ever incorporated), the Commodity Credit Corporation, the Tennessee Valley Authority (with its affiliates), and the numerous others shows that the symbols of capitalism are just as adapted to humanitarian distribution of wealth as any others, provided we have the will so to use them.

From the political theory with which the alienist operates his insane asylum, we may observe these changes in the use of capitalistic ideals, not with alarm, but with satisfaction, as indications that perhaps a violent upheaval may be unnecessary to make an adjustment to new conditions.

The theory permits us to recognize that economic predictions can be nothing more than political guesses—no more accurate than predictions of the results of elections. What we can predict with a fair degree of assurance is that symbols do not lose their relevance by being violently overthrown, and therefore revolution creates its own antitoxin. When people in the mass realize the actual possibility of the distribution of more of the comforts of life, symbols which stand in the way of that possibility may either modify their meaning or use, or they may be violently overthrown. But even when they are overthrown they rise again in an altered form. Germany under Hitler has many striking resemblances to Germany under the Kaiser. Russia under Stalin is not so far from Russia under a benevolent despot as many imagine. It is true that the notion of equal distribution of goods to the proletariat as the chief justification for the exercise of governmental power, contains ideals which appear to be new; but if we examine them we find that they are at least as old as Christianity.

The concept of government as an insane asylum liberates us from the notion that wise men think up principles and schemes of government for their duller fellows to learn and follow, and that thus social change is accomplished. It frees us from the notion that "thinking men" decide between the relative merits of communism and capitalism, and choose the better form. Finally, the theory is based on a humanitarian ideal which seems to be indestructible in the march of society—the ideal that it is a good thing to make people comfortable if the means exist by which it can be done.

Thus the theory might work as a practical philosophy for politicians. Yet it will never work as a general political theory. Its realism is too apparent, as also is its implied scorn of the human race. The reasons for its failure are the reasons for the failure of all common-sense theories of government in a rational world. In the first place, it cannot be an effective social force among the masses who want to believe that government is moral, rational, and symmetrical. Nor can it be satisfactory to intellectuals who want to believe that governmental theory is the product of ages of careful scholarly thought. Any theory based on a pure humanitarian ideal that anyone can understand is too simple and emotional to support complicated ratiocination. The detailed understanding of mechanical and social organization to carry out humanitarian ideals therefore does not inspire the intellectual. It is seldom recognized how close the intellectual is to the folklore of the people who support him, and the fact that he expresses current folklore in words which the mass does not understand only makes him a heroic figure of that folklore. His verbiage is the shining cloud into which he is expected to disappear. Therefore, the philosophy which is here represented is not, and cannot be, a philosophy which will work pragmatically for intellectuals. If it be true that economic, legal, and political theory is only the folklore of modern society, the reverse side of the paradox must be kept in mind. Folklore which is frankly recognized by a people to be folklore is from that moment no longer folklore. Its magic is gone, and a new folklore, which is not so recognized, must arise.

What is needed today is the kind of a theory which will be effective both as a moral force and as an intellectual playground, yet which will permit politicians to come out of the disreputable cellars in which they have been forced to work. This kind of theory might make it possible for men with social values to coöperate with political organizations without the present disillusioning conflict between their ideals and necessary political practices. The reason that such a theory is needed is that political organization is the only tool which a government faced with practical problems can use. It therefore needs a respectable set of symbols.

But if we are to speculate on how politicians acquire symbols, we are faced with questions like the following: What made political organization in this country a surreptitious enterprise, lacking in respectability? What kind of a philosophy supports the openly acknowledged government by political parties in Russia, Germany, and Italy? What place does that great repository of conflicting ideals, the judicial system, occupy in such government?

In the past, when the amount of control by a central government required to keep wheels turning and men employed was negligible, we got along well enough with a group of independent businessmen in actual control of the distribution of food and lodging. The practical achievements of that undefined and unorganized group in America have been inspiring. It has constituted the group in our society with the highest morale, and also the least hampered by the political philosophy of the day. It is out of that group that our discoveries and achievements in human organization have come.

Yet there was a time, not so far distant, when business was hampered, just as political organization is now hampered, by the lack of a place in the sun. It was the politician in the early days who had for his support all the natural-law symbolism of the eighteenth century. He represented individualism, freedom, the dignity of the law, the scorn of restraint by a centralized power. Great lawyers were not the servants of business interests, but, like Webster, argued great principles arising out of small cases, such as, *Marbury* vs. *Madison,* the Dartmouth College Case, the Milligan Case, and others. The phrase "due process" was not originally intended to protect vast organizations under the pretense that government direction of corporations was taking property away from individuals. There was a certain undefined social handicap on those who engaged in "trade."

As business organizations grew after the Civil War, they gradually began to use for their support the ancient symbolism of freedom and liberty, until, in the quaint poetic fancy of our day, the United States Steel Company has become an individual whose powerful organization must be protected at all hazards from tyranny. The freedom of the press has come to mean the noninterference with great chains of newspapers, pouring out propaganda, even though under no stretch of the imagination can it be said to be the free opinion of those who actually write it. Liberty of individuals to live unmolested by the power of overlords has become confused with the liberty of great industrial overlords to hold in their uncontrolled discretion the livelihood of individuals. The very Declaration of Independence is now the symbol of great business organizations, who insist that every corporation is born free and equal, and that holding companies are entitled to life, liberty, and the pursuit of power. The ideal of free competition is used to stamp out competition. Thus great organizations became the actual government of the people in their practical affairs. The governments at Washington and at the state capitols became the spiritual government whose chief function was that of a repository of ideals and ceremony. These governments were held in constant check, and prevented from usurping the practical powers of business organization by that institution which always represents the ideals of Western civilization, the judicial system.

Hampered by this spiritual environment, when state and national governments were compelled to desert the incense-laden air of their temples and accomplish practical things in a real world, it became necessary to resort to undercover methods. The Supreme Court of the United States could stop practical government in the open. It could not affect it when it retreated into the subterranean channels of the political machine. Thus it was that the great public-works programs of cities like Chicago were accomplished by undercover machines. The rights of inarticulate groups in New York City were protected by Tammany Hall. The practical assistance by way of tariffs which the United States Government has given to business in the past twenty years was the result of a powerful political machine whose headquarters were in Pennsylvania. The political machine as an institution separate from recognized government thrived in the United States as in no other country in the world. It was called in whenever the Government, bound by its ideals to stay aloof from reality, was compelled to enter into the affairs of an everyday world. We were always just about to get rid of it, but we never did. The reason of course was that we refused to permit recognized government to become a practical force.

It was in this way that our great industrial feudalism obtained the freedom to develop to which we owe our industrial progress. It was a revolution in which centralized power succeeded scattered individual efforts; but no one recognized it as a revolution because the old symbols were retained. It was called by reformers both hypocritical and corrupt; yet in a world where men demanded symmetry and logic for their comfort, and experimentation for their progress, it was, by and large, the only type of organization which adapted itself to such needs. Its success is attested by the growth of the country, and by its enormous increase in productive capacity. It was impregnable from the attacks of reformers so long as it continued to keep order in the industrial world.

When, however, in the great depression, the industrial feudalism failed to produce and distribute goods, it left both the conservatives and the reformers in complete confusion and indecision. With the loss of prestige of the industrial baron, the liberals had their opportunity, and reform became possible for the first time. But the only kind of reform anyone could think of was to make the older system actually live up to its principles. And it soon became apparent that governmental principles were not made to be observed except on Sundays. This idea was hard to express, but it finally found a slogan in the words "Recovery before reform." This meant that it was all right to urge business institutions to live up to their principles so long as there was no possibility of such recommendations being carried into effect. But when business was so weak that legislative reforms actually could be carried out, it became dangerous to advocate them.

There was a profound paradoxical truth in the slogan "Recovery before reform." It represented the fundamental axiom that the theories of government are worthless as guides in practical affairs. It was founded on the truth that spiritual government and temporal government, at least in a world where reason is worshiped, must not be represented by the same institutions.

With the reasons why this industrial feudalism lost its power to solve the disorder which confronted us at the beginning of the great depression, we are not here concerned. Everyone has a different explanation of the depression. These explanations begin with the conventional search for a scapegoat, either in the form of a group or an event; and end with a sort of fatalistic explanation of society in terms of rhythms and ups and downs. Whatever the reasons, the phenomenon was clear. A method of control and distribution of goods gradually became not method but anarchy. There was no cohesion among those who were in power, even to unite and preserve their profits in terms of enlightened selfishness. It was similar in many ways to the collapse of the feudal system of an earlier day.

In countries where the breakdown of industrial government was complete, political machines publicly recognized as a centralizing force and backed by various ideal creeds suddenly appeared as the only source of power. The rise of the new political force was sudden and painful in proportion to the failure of former institutions. The creeds supporting these political machines were different, but the effects were astonishingly similar. In Russia, the political machine rode in on a humanitarian philosophy; in Germany and Italy, on a hard-boiled Machiavellian philosophy. Yet marvels of coöperation and order out of chaos followed the dictatorships in Russia, Germany, and Italy. This was accomplished by taking the political party—the only going concern by which government actually operates in practical affairs—and giving it a public creed and a place in the sun. Governments by political parties in these countries became logical and consistent, and devoted to what their peoples thought was a simple and understandable ideal, uncomplicated by the contradictory ideals which governments usually are compelled to represent. Since it is the basic ideal of a political party that its principles are the only sound ones, logically there could be only one recognized party.

Yet curious results appeared in countries with dictatorships, unpredicted by the more idealistic of those who supported these drastic changes. With the devotion of the people to a single ideal, and their consequent rejection of any competing values, intolerance and cruelty raised their ugly heads. Judicial systems, always the great storehouses of those contradictory notions which allow people to be different, found themselves reduced to a position of hollow pretense—a mere formal link with the past. And, curiously enough, the cruelty was as great in Russia, pursuing a humanitarian ideal, as it was in Germany with the Machiavellian philosophy of the Nazis. Both countries failed to achieve spiritual security. Both were compelled to operate on a pitch of emotional enthusiasm and fanaticism which masses of people cannot long sustain.

Such phenomena are described as revolutions, and observed with dread by everyone not caught in their high emotional drive. The explanation of their cruelties and excesses given by rational men is always that they are forced to pursue unsound theories. Thus the people who thought up the doctrines of communism were blamed for Russian intolerance, and those who thought up fascism were blamed for persecution in Germany.

There followed in America that rule of phobias which paralyzed practical action on many wide industrial fronts.

If we adopted humanitarian ideals about the distribution of goods, there was grave danger of communism. If we admitted the need for a central government to ally itself in practical objectives with large existing business concerns, there was grave danger of fascism. Radicals, used to humanitarian ways of thinking, feared fascism most. Conservatives, used to insulating themselves from humanitarian ideals, feared communism most because it seemed almost Christian in many of its implications. People in general could not realize that we could not adopt Russian economic symbolism, even if we chose, any more than we, as a nation, could adopt the Russian language. They could not understand that the German situation arose out of the mad psychology of a defeated people, a situation not likely to be duplicated in a less humiliated group. Therefore the phobias against common-sense methods in this country added to the spiritual confusion. This confusion impeded organization. While Russia increased its industrial production from 1929 to date by 139 per cent, our industrial income fell by almost one third in spite of a more efficient machine civilization. Yet it should be remembered that this same confusion prevented the intolerance and cruelty which follow when great people march in step to a single ideal.

In the confusion of present events we can observe that when societies become devoted to a single ideal—whatever it is—and pursue it with consistency and logic, marvels of human coöperation are accomplished. But there is a price to be paid in spiritual instability which sooner or later brings its reaction. From the past, we may note that nations in time of war, at least under the modern war of democracies, achieve unity to an extent which seems extraordinary to one viewing the wartime economy from the tangled confusion of peacetime values. Under the spell of a single value or illusion, people march in step. Here, at last, is planned economy. As the war progresses, we find all of our older cherished symbols swept away the moment they interfere with the prevailing illusion. Smaller moralities are lost in one great morality. Milder illusions are swallowed up in the great illusion. Free speech is the first to disappear. The ideal of a fair trial, so important in symbolizing the right of dissenters to live, merges into the court-martial. The whole judicial process becomes meaningless and metaphysical, because a greater and simpler illusion, which we take for the only reality—the illusion of the glory of the war—obsesses the nation. The fundamental principles of economics are violated without a thought. Ceremonies in honor of older conflicting values are still kept up, but everyone realizes they are only ceremonies. Universities are open, but education in ideas stops. Courts release criminals to fight in the army, and wink at the persecution of pacifists.

However, even in war, there are still those who cling to peacetime values, and who will not be silent. Their speeches and arguments frighten us because we dare not deny publicly that these peacetime ideals are gone. We are at a loss to answer them, and, therefore, we either imprison them or shoot them. But this does not stabilize the emotional situation, because nothing is more effective than martyrdom to dramatize the ideals of dissenters. That curious, complicated rhythmical dance which we call life goes on at an exaggerated tempo when men march in step to one ideal; but, as in a dance, no movement or idea can carry very far without falling back, just as, when a member of the ballet has moved gracefully and idealistically to one side of the stage, there is nothing else for him to do but move back, or be thrown back, or else to retire from the ballet—and the penalty for retiring from the dance of life is death.

Thus, in peacetimes, when the lack of coöperation between men is distressingly evident, and when the endless argument about the contradictions involved in our symbols seems to have no hope of ending, we look back to the unity of the time when nations were drawn up in battle lines and we demand a moral substitute for war. Then, it is the war ideal which assumes only a ceremonial robe. We become madly excited about athletic contests where groups of men work in perfect coördination, with all of the values of life subordinated to the winning of the game. These games symbolize for us the values of educational institutions, in spite of the fact that they are diametrically opposed to everything that the institution is theoretically striving to do. Great educators intellectually know that football games are nonsense, yet emotionally they are unable to face the gap which the absence of such games would leave in the college world. Thus, on a small scale, on the football fields, and in the accompanying arguments in academic halls on the value of and the danger of overemphasis of football, are reënacted the arguments for and against the logical simplicity of war, as opposed to the ideological tangle which we call peace.

Perhaps there is one nation which has actually discovered a moral substitute for war in time of peace. Certainly Russia, with an international policy which is now the most opposed to war of any nation in the world, is marching in step, and offers a spectacle of internal coöperation which would have been thought impossible ten years ago except when men were fighting. Yet in achieving this moral substitute for war through an ideal of the maximum production and distribution of goods, it has also acquired the disagreeable incidents of a unified striving after one ideal, which requires the repression of all conflicting values. Its army has become the most respected and desirable profession. Its judicial process, though representing as all judicial systems do the ideal of a fair trial, and the dramatization of all the other conflicting ideals of a people, becomes in practice a mere perfunctory gesture. Dissenters are taken out and shot without an adequate hearing. A drab uniformity prevails in the land. The ideals of art and literature are encouraged; but, without the possibility of expressing a conflicting ideal, they become commonplace and mediocre.

Unquestionably, Russia has accomplished great things; nor has the price paid for the wartime spirit devoted to peaceful industrial development been too high. Yet it should not be forgotten that the unwavering devotion to one set of values, to the exclusion of others, always has its consequences in blood and terror. It is maintained through an understanding of how crowds respond to the simple and understandable ideal of Christian soldiers marching toward a humanitarian goal. For example, Walter Duranty writes of Russia:

The Bolsheviki must be right psychologically. A crowd in movement is a dynamic force, thrilling and terrific. A crowd standing, in whatever numbers, has potential power, but it is static—a reservoir, not a mighty river flowing. In the Bolshevist system of marching crowds there are two sound psychological factors. First, when you march, when you advance in solid ranks, stepping disciplined to music, you cannot fail to feel that you are part of something moving; that you yourself are an instrument of progress, however, humble; that you and the millions like you that form your nation are going somewhere, moving forward, all together.[1]

The same phenomenon is apparent in Germany:

The most spectacular symbols of the new regime are the vast mass demonstrations staged at periodic intervals and on an unprecedented scale. In Germany, these demonstrations are, perhaps, more mighty than elsewhere for the reason that Germany has adopted the idea of the corporal's guard, translated into "coordination," more thoroughly than any other country. There are no civilians left in Germany, only soldiers of the Third

1. *New York Times Magazine* (Feb. 3, 1935).

Reich, although the emphasis on uniformity has not interfered with the variety of organizational uniforms.[2]

In Germany there was discovered a moral substitute for the simplicity of war by imagining a war against the Jews. This was at least one of the penalties paid for the feeling of unity and coöperation which was achieved under Hitler. The judicial process, representing in Germany as elsewhere a great storehouse of competing ideals, suffered under this new unity. Yet the excesses of Hitler might have been avoided, had the more conservative government which preceded him recognized the necessity of representing to the German people a bold, aggressive, national personality which had the courage to make gestures of defiance, rather than appeals for mercy, to the rest of the world.

Thus, though marching people are able to accomplish astonishing things because of their devotion to one ideal to the exclusion of all competing ideals, they have not reached the stability of spiritual peace until they are able to stop marching. And they cannot keep on marching forever. Revolutions cannot change, or destroy a culture. The old symbols imbedded in the popular mind, after centuries of thinking in their terms, cannot be destroyed. Therefore, when the marching stops, they flare up again with a vitality which is the stronger because men have been executed for them without a trial. Thus it appears that the more illogical the process of social change is, the less disorder and repression accompany it. By proceeding in different directions at the same time, the ancient habits of thought are preserved while molding them to new needs.

And herein lies the greatness of the law. It preserves the appearance of unity while tolerating and enforcing ideals which run in all sorts of opposing directions. The judicial

2. Otto D. Tolischus, *New York Times Magazine* (Feb. 3, 1935).

system loses in prestige and influence wherever great, popular, and single-minded ideals sweep a people off its feet. It rises in power and prestige when society again becomes able to tolerate contradictory ideals. It provides a way of talking about all the unsolved and unsolvable problems of society; and it offers an elaborate set of institutions, so that we may talk in different ways about the same problems without appearing to contradict ourselves.

Therefore the law is a barometer of the spiritual contentment of a people; and we can observe the rise and fall of that type of stability by observing the rise and fall of the courts.

In Russia, when the enthusiasm of a new hope was high, but the fear of old ideas was disturbing to the confidence of those in power, the judicial system became a mere gesture toward the past. When the Russian Government took a breathing spell, and felt it could tolerate a few conflicting ideas, a vast system of courts arose to fill in the spiritual gap caused by a too practical administration of justice. When fear again raised its head, and renewed emphasis on the single ideal was thought necessary, the Russian Government proceeded to execute offenders outside of its growing judicial system.

In the same way, in Germany, we find the Hitler Government attacking the independence of the judiciary, and making political reliability a qualification for judicial office. Yet the persistence, in Germany, of the older symbols represented by the judiciary is evidenced by the fact that in the reformed code passed by the Hitler Government, only forty sections out of thousands in the code were changed. In a like manner, courts disappear before courts-martial in times of war, only to reappear again when we are able to endure the existence of ideas which contradict the main, simple ideal of absolute loyalty to a government at war. The charge, therefore, so often made by realists, that law is inconsistent with its own notions is not an indictment but a commendation. The law fulfils its functions best when it represents the maximum of competing symbols.

IN a world of such dreams a curious dilemma confronts the social and economic sciences. These sciences must act as a kind of folklore, and to perform this function must be believed as truths. They must support a spiritual government, and to give this support must depart from a real and enter into an ideal world. They must give practical institutions a logical place in that ideal world, without interfering with their freedom in practical affairs. These functions cannot be fulfilled by a mere theory that the world should be governed like an insane asylum. Therefore the illustration with which we began this chapter will never appear in the future as the guiding star of any human organization. Though it permits us to escape from the confusing consequences of calling men rational, it is defective as a working philosophy because of its contemptuous attitude toward the human race.

Creeds which do not hold a preachable ideal of society are denounced as cynical. Machiavelli counseled his prince to keep in mind that government was necessarily run by knaves and thieves. Machiavellism, because it refuses to let mankind play a dignified rôle, has been denounced for centuries as an improper attitude for a governing class to assume. It has never been a source of group morale. It has, instead, been principally a justification for intrigue. To use an insane asylum, rather than a jail, as an analogy, is perhaps a more tolerant and a less moral judgment; but, nevertheless, such a judgment does not endow mankind with the dignity or the hope or the tragedy which most persons with qualities of leadership feel that it actually possesses. Disillusioned men do not make effective leaders.

So it is that when leaders seize power by virtue of a philosophy of disillusionment, they become lost in that greatest of all illusions, the beauty and sanctity of the bold exercise of power, unhampered by humanitarian or other contradictory ideals. Few writers of his time had the insight into the function of ideals which is evidenced in the writings of Pareto. Yet when he wrote, he was unnoticed. He is today translated and sold in Italy and in the United States just as the notion of the necessity of unhampered power is gradually gaining ground. And the net practical result of Pareto's writing, as a governmental philosophy, is to make everything appear cynical and unsentimental except the ideal of power itself. Thus he becomes to many only the justification for a Mussolini. This would no doubt have been far from his own intention. In many respects, Pareto is a thinker of the same sort as Rabelais. Yet Rabelais softened his observations with a laugh. He did not appear to be preaching constructive truth. Pareto laboriously analyzes what Rabelais takes for granted; and hence becomes thought of as a leader of thought, rather than a satirist. And therefore, many of those who think that Pareto, with pitiless logic, has discovered that there is no reality behind political and economic theories, jump to the conclusion that the symbols themselves are useless, insincere, and hypocritical. I do not mean that this is a fair interpretation of Pareto. It is only the inevitable result of realism as a political philosophy.

In this way, philosophers like Pareto become, without intending it, the prophets of the hard-boiled use of power. Under their penetrating logic, slogans disappear. But, unfortunately, the humanitarian ideals, which those slogans called up in the minds of masses of people, also disappear. Cruel and inhumanitarian governments are spiritually unstable. It is even harder to make society cruel and hard-boiled over a long period of time than it is to make it continuously humanitarian. Thus hard-boiled dictatorships are compelled constantly to whip the masses into enthusiasm for their single narrow ideal of the stern exercise of power. The dramatic examples which they must use to do this become more and more extreme, until a countermovement brings some sort of spiritual balance. In Germany it takes the form of renewed persecution of the Jews; in Italy, an Ethiopian war.

It would seem, therefore, that those who realistically regard ideals and principles as escapes from reality are pursuing a half truth which leads to disillusionment. It is true that at times we eat and sleep and at other times we engage in parade and ceremony. Yet neither type of conduct is an escape from the other. Both must be served by governmental institutions, if they are to be successful.

The distribution of the comforts of life in accordance with accepted ideals of efficiency and social justice presents two separate problems; the one mechanical, and the other psychological. The mechanical problems of distribution began to be solved when we ceased to regard nature as a great moral force and sought to control our physical environment. We have not as yet recognized the psychological problems of government as anything other than logical and moral forces controllable by the proper application of sound principles of law and economics. Therefore, though everyone today would agree that it is desirable that the great productive machine of this country produce and distribute goods as rapidly as possible, they regard the observance of sound traditional principles as of even more importance. Only in time of war, when we are pursuing a traditional ideal of combat, is it permissible for the Government to take control.

If by some magic we could convince the American people that the distribution of the equivalent of $200 in goods each month to every person was as important an ideal as winning a war, we would immediately turn every wheel in the country—not fearfully and reluctantly but with enthusiasm. Everyone would be busy because instead of a surplus we would be confronted with a scarcity in terms of the new requirements. The effort to make up the deficiency would break down tariff walls, let in cheap goods, stimulate labor-saving devices, and throw the country into that fever of activity and enthusiasm which in the past has been part of the glory of war. In war no one worries about balancing the budget, but only about producing munitions and feeding troops, and hence these objects are accomplished with a minimum of spiritual trouble. No one believes any longer that nations cannot afford to fight wars. They can fight so long as their goods last. In the same way they could distribute goods in peacetime so long as these goods lasted, if only the military spirit could be transferred to something constructive.

The question is whether the science of government, by understanding the function of symbols and ideals, can make men as enthusiastic about sensible things as they have been in the past about mad and destructive enterprises. There is no doubt about the desire of that great class of intelligent and conservative persons that production and distribution of comforts should be carried on at maximum efficiency and capacity. The chief problem is to rid ourselves of the paralyzing fears that if this be attempted in a direct and sensible way, by the type of organization which would work in a military emergency, it would lead to all sorts of indescribable dangers. It is better, we feel, to starve in the midst of plenty than to desert the traditions of the past. Since our great industrial feudalism grew up uncontrolled, it must continue uncontrolled or liberty will perish from the earth. It is the same argument which has always been made to justify the disorder and lack of unity of feudalistic systems. It is similar to the arguments which justified the church in stopping the scientific experiments of Galileo. Its effectiveness never fails so long as the principles which we formulate are more important to our thinking than the facts which we observe.

The inhibiting effects of traditional ideals are not felt by everyone. However, it is always that great, conservative, orderly class of people who have been running the small affairs and giving support to the large affairs of the nation who are most affected by the social disease of slavery to symbols. This is the class from which one might expect common sense and efficiency. It is the only class from which orderly change without violent social dislocation can be hoped. Yet they are the very ones who are most readily prevented from reacting in a common-sense or humanitarian way, because they are the group which has been doing the reading and thinking, i.e., worshiping in connection with existing organizations.

It is for this reason that sensible and humanitarian schemes become the exclusive property of persons who are regarded as cranks and demagogues and are received with enthusiasm by those elements of society considered by the best people as unstable. This aggravates the social disease in times when change is desperately needed. Respectable conservative people confuse the sensible and necessary reforms with the fanatical and nonrespectable people who advocate them. No good, they insist, can come from such a source, and therefore they are forced to invent and believe in absurd arguments to attack reasonable proposals. In this way we find, throughout history, the finest and most humanitarian people lined up solidly in defense of indefensible social abuses. A few of them, no doubt, are the beneficiaries of such abuses, but most of the defenders are engaged in a battle for the defense of pure symbols which they have confused in their minds with the safety of the nation and their own class. They are compelled to take and cling to a weak position in the social conflict, and one entirely against their own interest, because their way of thinking prevents them from seeing where that interest lies.

There was a time when physicians marched around the palace of Versailles in protest against the adoption of surgical techniques. That time has gone forever in medicine, simply because of a change in attitude. That time is still with us in government. Phenomena similar to the medical parade of protest may be found in every newspaper and in every conversation among men of character and respectability, today, whenever they talk about social problems.

This familiar group fear may be illustrated by a conversation which took place among a group of learned and good men of the writer's acquaintance, consisting of a prominent professor, a financier, and a great lawyer. Someone mentioned the fact that the United States Government was sending unemployed actors about the country to give free plays. One of the members of the group, the great lawyer, and essentially a kindly man, became speechless with indignation at the idea. He was willing to recognize that actors out of a job had to be fed, but to care for them in such a way that both actors and public got amusement out of the situation filled him with horror. If government distribution of food and lodging ever became pleasant, and permitted the beneficiaries to hold up their heads with dignity, people might like it so much as to make it permanent, and this would be bad because it would be a change in governmental function. The fact that he suspected that there might be enough goods produced to make a permanent dole entirely practical increased rather than diminished his fear of the future until he was incapable of intelligent thought on the subject.

If it had been a question of hospital treatment for sick actors, he would have recognized the obligation, and his fears for the moral character of the actors and the public would not have unbalanced his judgment. He would not have insisted that it is impossible to run an efficient hospital except for profit. But to put food (beyond a mere subsistence) and amusement on the same plane as the distribution of medical supplies filled him with uneasiness about the disappearance of freedom from the earth, once people were fed. The same attitude induced a United States District Court and a Circuit Court of Appeals to hold that housing for the poor is not a public purpose for which the Government can condemn land. Had it been a hospital for disabled veterans, there would have been no worry or even any discussion.

These people were kindly, intelligent, competent, and powerful in their communities. Yet all their talents and good will were useless in the solution of a real problem because they were caught in the handcuffs of a traditional ideal. And yet it needed such a slight shift in attitude to free them and make of their talents an effective social force. The inhibiting effects of traditional attitudes may be found to the same degree among the people of stability and character who have been ruined by the economic process as among those who have prospered. The writer, traveling through the West, was discussing the political and economic situation with a prominent sheep owner. Years ago he had been wealthy, but the drop in agricultural prices had ruined him. He still retained control of a vast acreage, but the bank which was his principal creditor had compelled him to sell his ewe lambs until his herd was far below that required for economic use of the property. (Had the *Government* compelled him to run an understocked ranch, it would have been denounced as bureaucratic inefficiency.) His mortgage had mounted until there was little hope of his ever achieving solvency. Yet, as happens in most such cases, the bank found it more profitable to let him stay on the land and work for nothing, rather than to move him off and manage the property with expensive labor which was difficult to obtain. His own ancient loyalty held him there, a loyalty to the ideal that men must pay their debts. He was being supported by the bank advancing expense money. In getting this money he was compelled to undergo the supervision of bank officials down to the minutest details of his monthly grocery bills, in a way that was not only peculiarly irritating but also inefficient.

This man had recently attended a woolgrowers' convention and heard a stirring speech on the Constitution and the evils of bureaucracy. The speech struck home and his chief worry was that the Government was tending to interfere with the liberty of individuals. "Why," he explained, "they will be regulating the kind of bed sheets that farmers buy next." When the writer called to his attention that his last month's bills had been audited by the bank in a way which would have been impossible for the most bureaucratic government imaginable, he replied, "Oh, that's different." He was opposed to every plan that was suggested which would have relieved him of peonage to a banking system which had set its institutional force to preserve an interest rate of 8 per cent under which the business enterprises of his whole community would be nothing but a succession of failures.

There are thousands of men like these occupying positions of influence and prestige in every community in the land, afraid to advocate practical measures even to help themselves for fear of ultimate consequences in terms of old ideals. On such people—lawyers, industrialists, agriculturists—of character and standing, orderly change must necessarily depend. Is there no hope that they can combine with their sterling qualities, character, and integrity a little of the elasticity which enables them to help themselves? Is there no prospect that they can continue to regard their traditional symbols with reverence, obtaining the spiritual advantage and comfort of those symbols without misusing them as weapons to attack practical and humanitarian action?

It is not in their failure to comprehend actual situations that these people are deficient. Shake off their more solemn masks and in the privacy of intimate conversation great lawyers will talk about the law in operation with common sense and candor, and even economists will show signs of understanding the social system. Put them back on the platform, however, and they immediately recast themselves into devoted preachers reciting a creed.

The fact that such people are quite capable of actual understanding of things as they are is again illustrated by the power which satire and humor has over them. The keenest objective observations about government in the past has been spoken by satirists and humorists and instantly recognized by the mass of people who laughed with them. Certainly there are no new ideas about government in this book which were not familiar to Rabelais, or to Swift, or to the countless others that have startled the respectable people into sudden flashes of understanding of the kind of a world they were actually living in, only the ideas disappear as the laugh dies away.

In a logical and moral world, serious literature dramatizes the symbols of a people. Flippant literature contains their accurate observations. Search the pages of the humorists of the past, and, excluding that type of humor which may be loosely termed buffoonery, you will find the observations of the modern psychiatrists about love, the observations of the anthropologists about group morals, and the observations of the political and legal realists about law more shortly and accurately stated than in the most learned treatises. Yet there is a curious lack of social effectiveness about truth stated as comedy. It carries no permanent conviction. It creates no enthusiasm for action. It is apparent from the flippant form in which these observations are put that the observer does not completely believe what he sees in front of him. This lack of faith of the humorist, who is really only a doubting observer, is of varying kinds. He may recognize the existence of the world which he sees, but deny its right to exist with the bitterness of Swift. He may be untroubled by any philosophy, and therefore consider his best and most accurate work as something of a trivial character, as Mark Twain considered Huckleberry Finn. Or he may recognize that the topsy-turvy world which he sees is inevitable, and take refuge in a futilitarian and cynical position, as did Anatole France. None of these intellectual positions permits the use of his best powers of observation as a tool for the government of mankind. None of them frees the readers of the humor of the day from the inhibiting effects of their taboos. Man can act as a leader only in his more solemn moments. He cannot command respect and authority with a smile on his face.

Thus it is that satire, while enormously effective in social change, operates only as a destructive force. Good-natured humor does not change the ideals of a people. But when the smile is wiped out and the bitterness of a Voltaire is substituted, the truth as a purely destructive force is let loose like a scourge or a lash. Progress there may be in such violent purges. Yet it is accidental and not scientific progress. It sweeps away the good with the bad. One does not have to use ridicule today to get rid of some theory of physics or medicine which has been proved unworkable by experiment. Scientific progress is accomplished in more effective ways than by attacking error with satire.

The question which confronts the student of government is what kind of a social philosophy is required to make men free to experiment—to give them an understanding of the world, undistorted by the thick prismatic lenses of principles and ideals, and at the same time undamaged by

the disillusionment which comes from the abandonment
of ideals. How may we make the truths of which men are
dimly aware only in humorous or satirical moods into constructive forces to avoid senseless panic when old principles meet new conditions? How may we affect the attitude of that great mass of substantial, intelligent, idealistic,
and kindly people whose opinions and actions count most
in times of stability, so that they will cease to see impending moral chaos in practical and humanitarian action?

WE began this chapter with the idea of speculating on the
social philosophy which may take the place of those curious
sciences of law and economics which have provided us
with the certainties of the past. Such a speculation is haz-
ardous. The only sound lesson that history teaches is that
one cannot in one era predict the ideals of the next. No one
whose life had been conditioned by those quaint but powerful symbols of chivalry could have predicted that an ideali-
zation of human greed would one day make the despised
activities of medieval moneylenders the most admired of
human activities. If one should be so fortunate as to predict the class which was rising to power in times of change,
he might dimly outline the legal and economic conceptions
of the future. The writer, however, frankly admits that in
the speculation on the creed of the future which is to follow he has deserted the objective position from which most
of this book is written and become a preacher and an advocate, rather than an anthropologist.

That old certainties are losing their force may be seen
everywhere, not only in the hopefulness of radicals, but in
the pessimism of conservatives. Power comes from optimism, not from timidity and fear. Today, our ancient certainties are supported only by fear of the unknown. They
are not entertained with hope. Those who rule our great
industrial feudalism still believe inalterably the old axioms

that man works efficiently only for personal profit; that humanitarian ideals are unworkable as the principal aim of government or business organization; that control of national resources, elimination of waste, and a planned distribution of goods would destroy both freedom and efficiency. Yet these ideals, which once were sources of energy and hope, which once permitted industrial technicians the freedom to experiment and develop constructive techniques, are today used to obstruct great governmental projects and to sabotage industrial production. The financial class which was sustained in power by these ideals is gradually resigning from the business of government as the functions of that government require greater control over the distribution of goods.

There was a time when the profit creed was held with hope and not with pessimism; when it was thought capable of solving all problems, even those of human justice. The solution of the conflict between labor and capital was just around the corner. The problem of distribution of goods was to solve itself through the automatic operation of enlightened selfishness. Even that greatest of all problems, war, was thought to be disappearing, because in an atmosphere where men worked only for profits nations could not afford to fight the expensive wars of modern times. When the World War rudely destroyed that illusion, hope and enthusiasm still remained. Was it not a war to end war? Were we not fighting to establish once for all that great pacifying principle that competing nations composed of competing individuals achieve both industrial and international peace through the pursuit of their own personal gain?

In such an atmosphere there was unifying force in the profit creed, born of optimism and faith. It gave the great mass of people their certainties and loyalties; it left their industrial overlords free to develop without the hampering effect of preconceived principles. The very inconsistencies of the creed aided the development of a great productive machine. War itself stimulated new industrial enterprise and left the world with a greater productive capacity than before.

Yet each new achievement in efficient organization, under the creed that men worked only for profits, diminished the number of those who were permitted to work for profits. Managers of factories were no longer the owners. Those who operated the industrial machine and actually distributed its goods did not have the symbols of power. Those who were in general control were too absorbed by the symbols of finance to give their personal attention to production and distribution. In reorganizing railroads, underlying bonds were more important than problems of transportation. Distribution of the product of an industry was never an end in itself, but an incident to enable someone to make a profit.

Sustained by these ideals men worked for the great industrial bureaucracy with a loyalty and devotion which had nothing to do with their personal interest but was founded on a great faith. But the time came when these devoted followers were not even permitted to work. Men who had the ability and skill to produce goods were not permitted to use that skill. Farmers ruined themselves producing food, not for profit, but only on account of habit, and millions of industrial workers were not allowed to work at all. The reason given why industry had to stand still was lack of business confidence. In other words business leaders were afraid to act for themselves. They were even more afraid of the Government acting for them. Therefore suffering and insecurity in a time of surplus goods is thought to be the only road to future prosperity.

And thus the profit creed changed from one of hope to one of fear. Conservatives clung to it as a drowning man to a straw, rather than following it like a flag. We recognized that this creed could not keep us out of a depression, and looked gloomily at the future as one long series of the ups and downs which we had known in the past. We saw no way of creating employment in the future except by throwing men out of work in the present by balancing the budget. War was generally regarded as inevitable under our economic system, without the cheering illusion that the next war would be the war to end war. Economic life was a choice between two evils: acceptance of present suffering even though it is avoidable because of the existence of available goods, or plunging the country into future economic or moral ruin by inflation. Even social abuses could not be reformed because reform frightened those wise and conservative leaders whose courage had been slowly leading us out of the depression, just before they got so scared.

There is no constructive force in such pessimism. It is the last struggle of a dying philosophy of government. Industrial empires no more than military empires can be built by men obsessed with great fears. Social institutions, caught in the futility of combined fatalism and realism, may endure for centuries as they have in China; but they are never sources of achievement. Belief in any philosophy, however fantastic, molds a people in the image of that philosophy; and so it is that ancient symbols which are no longer sources of hope become forces which stifle human energy. It is for this reason that in a country as bursting with energy as is America, we can predict the general acceptance of a new and more hopeful philosophy of government to replace the confusion of our present ideals of law and economics. Other depressions have come and gone without altering faith in the economic principles of the past. Yet never before has there existed the present public awareness that the application of those principles is causing a great industrial machine to operate far below its productive capacity.

The fundamental social axiom of the past was that man, by working only for his personal profit, in the long run produced the most ideal social results. Of course this profit motive had to be checked and balanced against its own excesses by law, by ethics, and by religion. But thus curbed it was part of nature's great plan. Attempts to interfere with it led to disaster. Great institutions like the law and the church, representing contradictory ideals, had to be carefully insulated from control of practical affairs by devices like trial by combat. And thus arose a spiritual government scattered between Washington and the various state capitols, and a temporal government scattered between New York and the various state financial centers, the one representing the great ideals and the other the fundamental axioms of social control.

We suggest that the formula of the new social philosophy which is appearing may be the fundamental axiom that man works only for his fellow man; that it is *this* tendency which must be curbed by law, ethics, and common sense, so that there may be incidental room in the system for the man who works only for personal gain, just as there was incidental room in the old economic creed for the humanitarian. Under the profit creed the chief danger was from well-meaning but impractical humanitarians. Under the new creed the chief danger will be from well-meaning but impractical profit takers.

Sometimes in clear outline, sometimes in strange and distorted and destructive forms, the new conception of man as a creature who does not work for himself is appearing all over the world. In Germany and in Italy the normal man is supposed only to work for his fellow countrymen, and the difference between social organization in peace and war has faded. In Russia the normal man is thought of as one who works for the toiling masses of the world. In all of these countries the axiom that the normal man in the long run works only for his own profit is put down as dangerous radicalism. Fanatical devotion to this single ideal is such that it makes human liberty an unimportant value, and even kindness is stifled for purely humanitarian motives. There are explosive dangers to world peace and security in such fanaticism. Nevertheless out of this creed has come a certain morale and order, to take the place of former discouragement and anarchy. For better or for worse, a new abstract economic man who does not work for his own selfish interest, but only for others, has appeared on the mental horizon of the world.

In America this new abstract man is arising out of confusion instead of revolution. He therefore has no fanatical adherents nor any defined logical outlines. He is appearing in institutions not organized for profit and increasing in importance as those institutions expand. A few years ago hospitals and educational institutions were growing into vast and efficient organizations. Their success in violation of the profit creed was explained by the fact that the abstract doctor or professor is a curious freak of such rarefied qualities that he is not motivated as a normal man would be. No inference was permitted that doctors who ran complicated hospitals without possibility of profit could run anything else. Thus distribution of goods to those in want, care of the old or the unemployed, were supposed to be entirely different from distribution of medical supplies to the same people. Charity was a beautiful human quality, which might even be a vocation for those abnormal people not interested in business. It might be an avocation of a great industrial leader who could become interested in unemployed, not as an obligation, but to prove to the people that even such a giant of power and efficiency had his tender moments. But the idea that such activities could be an obligation of business or government, rather than a sentimental interlude, was considered dangerous to those great principles which kept Americans from growing beards and drinking vodka like the Russians.

Today, with amazing speed, what used to be called charity is becoming a recognized obligation of government, and, through it, powers of control over the industrial structure are evolving which is bringing a new class of technicians into power. The movement began with the substitution of community chests for pure largesse in order to get organized efficiency. With the depression, the support of such work was taken over by the Government amid the fear and trembling of all right-thinking people. And now we are startled to observe that the greatest employer of labor in the country is not an industrial baron, but Harry Hopkins, a social worker, operating a growing organization in violation of all the axioms of our former economics. He is constantly confused in his objectives by those who insist that his work is dangerous as an aim in itself, and therefore must be primarily used as a method of priming the economic pump, of stimulating producers' goods, of aiding consumers' goods. He must employ men on useful things to avoid waste, but he must not have them engaged in needed activities because that would be governmental interference with business. Yet in spite of this confusion the work goes on, and a Social Security Bill recognizes the obligation in permanent form.

It is natural that right-thinking men should maintain that what they see going on before their eyes is impossible. Adam Smith, on the basis of the axiom that men work only for profit, predicted that the modern industrial corporation could not develop because no man would work as efficiently for a great organization as he would for himself. In the same way, conservatives today prove with equal conclusiveness that men will never work as efficiently for a government as for a great corporate entity created under the laws of Delaware. Yet it is beginning to be doubtful if such taboos will be strong enough to keep that great class of technicians and experts, interested more in the direct objects of their work than in the symbols of finance, from using their skill to preserve the resources of the nation and distribute its goods. As yet the economic philosophy and social bookkeeping necessary to convince the popular mind that a nation can afford the expense of having all its people hard at work producing and distributing wealth have not been formulated. Sensible and practical plans are still confused with violence, revolution, and the overthrow of an entire class. Yet people are gradually becoming accustomed to the idea, and, as their fear dies, new forms of social bookkeeping gradually appear.

Is it true, as an economic principle, that man works only for his fellow man? The answer is, that it is neither more nor less true than the axiom which gave prestige to a commercial class, that man works only for himself; or the axiom supporting the institution of chivalry, that men work only for the love of pure ladies; or the belief of a medieval priesthood, that men work only for a future life; or the axiom of the law, that men desire only logical justice. Society is composed of all sorts of people and each individual is a whole cast of characters in himself, appearing on the stage of his consciousness in rapid succession. Young men do not think as old men, and even old men do not react alike. "Truth" is irrelevant as a test of an economic philosophy. The value of such a philosophy can only be judged by the value of the governing class whose power it supports. The hope for this new humanitarian economic creed in America must be based on the belief that there exists a huge reservoir of technical skill, capable of running a great productive machine with new energy and efficiency, provided that social ideals can be accepted which permit this reservoir to be tapped.

Will such a philosophy make the world a satisfactory place, and will the radicals cease from troubling and be at rest? Of course not. There can be no conception of social justice without social injustice, since the one idea cannot exist without the other. We must expect the old struggle for prestige and power to go on as strenuously in a world where comforts are adequately distributed as in a world where they are not. There will be radicals under any type of social organization, forming parties of dissent and demanding a new order, so long as men struggle to improve their lot in this world. Such changes in fundamental attitudes and values are a function of life. The world will never see a permanently valid philosophy until science discovers a method of making Time stand still.

Yet, granted that such changes in social ideals and values are a part of social life, there is no reason in the nature of things why they should be accompanied by such violent and painful dislocations. There is no reason why the members of an entire governing class, both good and bad, should be thrown out of power simply because popular ideals have undergone a change. There was a time in the medical profession when new theories had to be denounced because they interfered with the prestige of established physicians. Later, and within the memory of the reader, doctors belonged to the medical party of the homeopaths or the party of the allopaths, and the public had to choose between them. It is no longer true that whole classes of physicians must defeat a new technique or lose face before the public. Without knowing the details of medical theory, the public nevertheless understands the nature of those theories, and the constant search among competent physicians for new hypotheses.

Today, in government, if theories of the class in power

are damaged, it reflects on the entire class; and both competent and incompetent members suffer equally. Thus, efficient bankers are compelled to oppose checks on inefficient bankers because of the principle of the change. This is only because the prestige of the entire group is tied up with a set of usages whose continuance is regarded as a matter of fundamental principle which must override all temporary considerations of convenience and common sense. In this way incompetents are maintained in secure positions, and honest men are compelled to come to the defense of the corrupt practices of their fellows. We stand or fall by classes, each with its separate brand of oratorical literature, such as capitalism, socialism, fascism, or communism. Each class is compelled to defend the indefensible practice of its members as necessary incidents to their more ideal aims.

Is it hopeless to attempt to induce the same atmosphere in the conduct of social organizations that we have obtained in medical organizations? Must men always be compelled to line up on different sides and fight for one or the other of two conflicting principles, both of which need representation among the ideals of government? Must the believers in the Constitution combat sensible plans, and the advocates of sensible plans attempt to destroy the Constitution by their bitter realism, to the perpetuation of senseless oratory and high-sounding prejudices and to the end that all change be made as violent as possible? If so, the expert will always be at a disadvantage before the orator who by his fanaticism is able to make ignorance led by prejudice appear as truth led by courage.

There is no reason to believe that the public is not as capable of orienting itself toward governmental theories as toward medical theories. It is not necessarily true that the only choice is between naïve faith in principles and cynical denial of the validity of principle. A crowd at a baseball game gets the full emotional value of the game as a symbol of pride in the home town, without making themselves suffer for it in practical affairs. When the same sort of understanding becomes part of our thinking about governmental symbols, we can use the Constitution as a great unifying force without foregoing sensible and practical advantages on its account.

Society shows an uncanny skill in selecting the best technicians once it understands just what those technicians are doing. Efficient ballplayers have an advantage over theatrical ones. Competent physicians have a greater advantage over personalities like Lydia Pinkham as belief in broad general principles and great remedies fades. In the same way we can imagine a condition of public understanding of the function of government as a practical affair which will put orators at a disadvantage before technicians.

There are signs of a new popular orientation about the theories and symbols of government which is arising from a new conception of the function of reason and ideals in the personality of the individual. A new creed called psychiatry is dimly understood by millions of people. Popular magazines are appearing, discussing from an objective point of view problems which used to be considered the exclusive property of the moralist. A conception of an adult personality is bringing a new sense of tolerance and common sense to replace the notion of the great man who lived and died for moral and rational purposes. Under these new attitudes men are becoming free to observe the effects of changing beliefs, without the discomfort of an older generation which swung from complete certainty to utter disillusionment.

Such a conception, once accepted, will in the long run spread to government and social institutions. Governments can act in no other way than in accordance with the popular ideals of what great abstract personalities should do. In medieval times nations were holy and kings led crusades to dramatize that ideal. In modern times governments act in the image of great businessmen. The codes to which national conduct attempts to conform are only enlargements of popular ideals of individual codes. When individuals must be logical, consistent, courageous, thrifty, generous, forgiving, implacable, and morally upright, governments dramatize all these values. National policies can only be a confused representation of popular ideals. As the notion of a tolerant adult personality grows in popular comprehension, the opportunity for a scientific attitude toward government will necessarily broaden. Once that conception becomes an unquestioned assumption, the day of the high-class psychopath and fanatic in social control will be over.

It is true that there is little in the present conduct of the governments of the world which can by any stretch of the imagination be called adult. Everywhere we see unnecessary cruelty used to dramatize even humanitarian creeds. Fanatical devotion to principle on the part of the public still compels intelligent leaders to commit themselves, for political reasons, to all sorts of disorderly nonsense. So long as the public hold preconceived faiths about the fundamental principles of government, they will persecute and denounce new ideas in that science, and orators will prevail over technicians. So long as preconceived principles are considered more important than practical results, the practical alleviation of human distress and the distribution of available comforts will be paralyzed. Nevertheless one who desires to be effective in society must be permitted to hope and to work for that hope. The wages of pessimism are futility. The writer has faith that a new public attitude toward the ideals of law and economics is slowly appearing to create an atmosphere where the fanatical alignments between opposing political principles may disappear and a competent, practical, opportunistic governing class may rise to power. Whether such a hope is well founded or not it is impossible to say, but to that hope this book is dedicated.

INDEX

Abstract men behind law and economics, 77–86
Acheson, Dean, 53
Administrative investigation vs. trial by combat, 188, 189
—— jurisdiction, 189, 190
—— law, 64, 190–194
—— regulations, 226, 227
—— tribunals, 182, 204–206
Adultism, 269
Advisory opinions, 185
Agricultural Adjustment Act, 114, 117, 182
Alienist in criminal trial, 163
American Bar Association, 210
—— Law Institute, 25, 51, 190
Analogy, Joseph Butler, 60, 65
Anatomy, analogy, 23, 24, 26, 27, 29
Anderson, Sherwood, 231
A & P stores, 217, 218
Appeals, 15
Appellate courts, 85
Arbitration, 128, 187
Argumentative technique law, 45
Aristotle, 4
Artificial price fixing, 93
Atonement, doctrine of, 62
Austin, 57

Baker, Newton D., 143
Barber surgeon analogy, 27
Bargaining in criminal cases, 153, 154, 155, 162
Benevolence vs. governmental principle, 61–63
Bituminous coal, care of, 74, 75
Blackstone, 50, 56
Blame as solution of social problems, 76, 96–98
Borchard, E. M., 226
Brain trust, 82, 230
Budget balancing, 94, 110, 262

Bureaucracy, 199–228; in Heaven, 189
Business administration, science of, 89, 90
—— and philanthropy, 87, 88
—— schools, 89, 90
—— symbols, 238
Butler, Joseph, 60, 61, 65

Capone, Al, 154, 155
Cardozo, Mr. Justice, 197
Centralized power, philosophy of, 100
Ceremony as jurisprudence, 70
—— vs. rational literature, 60
Charity, 120, 264
Chase, Stuart, 4
Child Labor Amendment as bureaucracy, 209–212
Chivalry, 259
Citrus fruit case, 182
Citrus Fruit Marketing Agreement, 18, 19
Civil trial, the symbol of individualism, 174
Clarification as judicial function, 183
Coke, 59
Collective bargaining, 115, 116
Commerce Clause, 117
Commonwealth vs. De Lacey, 136
Communism, 105, 110, 118, 231, 234
Compromising in criminal cases, 153, 154, 155, 162
Compulsory arbitration of labor disputes, 218, 219
Conflicts, in ideas, utility of, 124, 125, 268; in ideals of penology, 11; in ideals of jurisprudence, 69; in legal ideals, 31–44
Constitution, 117, 118, 123, 124, 230, 231
—— in theology, 67

Constitutionality of the New Deal, 172, 173
Coolidge, Calvin, 210
Corporate reorganizations, 187
Corporations, governmental, 16, 228, 266
Court martial, 130
Courts, 127
Criminal insanity, 11
Criminal law and popular ideals, 132; as a control, 147, 153; as a moral drama, 154, 155; in primitive tribes, 131
—— penalties, logic of, 11
—— responsibility, 11, 12
—— sentences, 11, 12, 165–168
—— trial, 128

Darrow, Clarence, 3, 6, 26, 118
Dartmouth College Case, the, 238
Debs, Eugene, 137, 140
Declaratory judgment, 176, 185, 186, 226
Delays in constitutional decisions, 172–177
Delegation of powers, 20
Demagogues, 253
Dennett, Tyler, 220
Depression, the, 106
Devil, 8, 28
Dictatorship and law, 43
—— danger of, 82, 83
Discretionary review of administrative bodies, 191, 192
Dissection, analogy, 23, 24, 26, 29
Distribution of goods, 108, 109, 110, 122, 252
—— problem of, 251, 252
Dole, 61, 111, 120, 254
Dramatization of principles, 9, 10
Dred Scott Case, 197
Due process, 20
Duranty, Walter, 246
Dyer, Gus W., 81, 82

Economic interpretation of history, 91

—— man as an automaton, 77, 86
—— theories must be false, 98–100
Economics above morality, 72
—— and law, 72
—— as folklore, 237, 238; as philosophy of temporal government, 73; as preaching, 21
—— vs. humanitarianism, 76; vs. politics, 21; vs. reform, 75, 76
Economy of Abundance, The, by Stuart Chase, 4
Education of the legal man, 22–24
—— public, 86
Efficiency vs. law, 194, 225
Emergency and the Constitution, 175
Emerson, Ralph Waldo, 38
Epic Plan, 110
Equity, 28; vs. law, 62, 63, 64
Ethics, 54
Exhaustion of administrative remedy, 190
Experimentation in government, 21, 98, 195; in constitutional law, 193
Expert vs. orator, 268, 269
Experts in constitutional law, 173

Fair trial, 132–143
Farm strike, 93
Fascism, 105, 118, 231, 234
Fear of regulation, 255, 256
Federal Emergency Relief Administration, 221
Ferguson, "Ma," Governor of Texas, 24
Folklore, cf. law, 237
Ford, Henry, 195
France, Anatole, 258
Frank, Jerome, 32
Frankfurter, Felix, 180
Free trade vs. protection, 72
Free will, social, 96, 98

Galen, 23–25, 71
Galileo, 253
Germany, 236, 241, 243, 246, 247

Gitlow vs. *People of New York,* 136, 140

Go-Bart Importing Co. vs. *U.S.,* 154

Gold Clause Cases, 176, 197
—— purchase plan, 93

Government corporations, 16, 228, 266; housing, 96; spending, 11, 72, 116

Governmental interference with business, 94, 174; regulation of business, 194

Graft, 5

Group free will, 96, 97
—— sin, 97, 98

Guffey Coal bill, 177

Hamilton, Walton, 74, 75

Hard cases make bad law, 61

Hearsay, 15

Hearst, William Randolph, 118

Hegel, 189

Herndon vs. *Georgia,* 197

Hippocrates, 70

History, economic interpretation of, 91

Hitler, 247, 248

Holy Ghost in jurisprudence, 66

Home Building and Loan Assn. vs. *Blaisdell,* 175

Homeopath, 267

Hopkins, Harry, 265

Hospitalization as government ideal, 254, 255, 268

Hot Oil Case, 117, 176

Housing by government, 255

Huckleberry Finn, 258

Human nature, 4–8, 92

Humanitarian attitude toward society, 47–48; economics, 263, 264; man, 86, 87; plans, 253

Humor as accurate observation, 257, 258

Hutchins, 54

Ideals as behavior, 7

Imperialism, 112

Independence of judiciary, 186

Industrial anarchy justified by law, 75
—— feudalism, 122, 240, 241

Inflation, 72, 105, 116

Injunctions, 192

Insane asylum as a model for government, 232, 233, 239

Insanity as a defense, 163; criminal, 11

Insurance as a symbol, 121, 122

Insull trial, 133

I.R.T. receivership, 180

Issues in litigation, 178–184

Italy, 250, 251

Jeanne d'Arc, trial of, 135, 140

Jhering, 57

Johnson vs. *Manhattan Ry.,* 180

Judicial control of administrative bodies, 189, 190
—— government, 173
—— parables as social training, 77
—— review of legislation, 192, 193
—— system, 127

Judiciary as symbol of unity, 188

Jurisdictional facts, 189, 190

Jurisprudence as symbol of government, 46, 71; definition of, 56–57; practical function of, 49–52

Jury, 13, 14
—— trial, 144, 145

King compared to Supreme Court, 123

Kurzer vs. *N.Y. Chicago St. Louis Ry. Co.,* 13

Labor legislation, 176
—— regulation, 115

Lag, cultural, 92, 93

Laissez faire, 85, 116, 124

Lake Cargo Rate Case, 179

Law, and economics as advocacy, 104; as a justification for disobedience, 156; as a parable, 129; as a paradise on earth, 224; as argumentative technique, 45; as folklore, 237; as repository of ideals, 247; as series of ideal dramas, 42, 127, 187; definition of, 33, 34, 35; economics and sociology, 18; enforcement, 149–171; in action vs. law in books, 32–34; Institute, American, 25; reviews compared with religious tracts, 66; rule of, 216; schools, 44–51, 54–56; scientific approach to, 33–37; vs. efficiency, 194, 225; vs. equity, 62, 63, 64, 190; vs. preaching, 77, 78.

Laws, multiplicity of, 159, 160
Legal vs. economic man, 80
—— man as sinner, 78, 86
—— mind, 101
—— scholar, 129
—— scholarship vs. practice, 31, 32
Legalisms in prayer, 68
Legislative intent, 37
LoGiudiece, Paul, case of, 11
Long, Huey, 24, 118

Machiavelli, 249
McCooey, John, political leader, 26
McReynolds, Mr. Justice, 212, 213
Magistrates' courts, 41
Malpighi, 55
Mann Act, 133
Man on the street as jurist, 65
Mansfield, Harvey, 180
Manton, Judge, 181, 182
Marbury vs. *Madison,* 238
Mark Twain, 258
Marx, Karl, 72
Massie trial, 149, 150, 158, 163
Medical analogies, 267; attitudes, 55; theology, 71
Medieval banking contrasted to modern machine politics, 73
—— church, 126
Melanesian criminal law, 131
Merchant class compared to politicians, 73
Milligan Case, 238

Mitigating circumstances as a criminal defense, 162
Monetary legislation, 116
Mooney Case, 135, 139
Moot case, 180, 181, 182, 186
Moral attitude toward society, 47, 48; government, 60–61
Morgan and Maguire, *Cases on Evidence,* 80
Mortgage moratorium case, 175
"Muddling through," 123
Mussolini, 250

N.R.A., 4, 81, 112, 113, 117, 118, 194, 195
Nebbia Case, 175–179
Nebbia vs. *New York,* 117, 212
New Deal, 81, 107, 112
Newton, Isaac, 50
New York Code, 64
—— Milk Case, 179
—— Post Office, motto of, 95
—— procedure, 226
Nix vs. *Heddon,* 78
Nortz vs. *United States,* 176

Obsolete laws, 154, 160
Omissions from court record, 179
Orator vs. expert, 268
Original sin, 97, 126

Paradoxes in legal institutions, 226
Pareto, 250
Partisan presentation of trials, 184, 185
Patterson vs. *Alabama,* 141
Penology, ideals of, 11
Pessimism about principles, 259, 260
Philanthropy, 87
Philippines, 111, 112
Physical sciences vs. social, 2–4
Pinkham, Lydia, 269
Planning, social, 21
Pleading problems in theology, 68
—— reform, 226
Police and law enforcement, 153
Political corruption in Chicago, 5

Political machine, 26, 239; vs. bureaucracy, 227
Politicians, 28; vs. economists, 21; vs. scholars, 19
Pound, 58
Powell, Thomas Reed, 101
Powell vs. *Alabama,* 141
Power as an ideal, 250
Preaching analogy, 25
Price fixing, 93
Primitive societies, 4
Principles as guides, 105, 125
Prison reform, 146, 147
Private prosecution of crime, 164
Procedural reform, 129
Procession of progress, 91, 93
Professors in government, 230; in Washington, 53
Profit motive, 73, 74, 259
Prohibition, 132, 152, 157
Prosecuting attorneys, 151, 153, 154, 169
Prosecution in England, 164
Protection vs. free trade, 72
Psychiatrist in criminal law, 163
Psychiatry, 77, 269, 270
Public attitudes, 16, 17; education, 22–24; health, 2; works, 94, 111
Puzzled America, 231

Quasi-judicial powers, 191

Rabelais, 250, 257
Rational conflicts, 11–18; explanation of society, 3; moral attitude, 47, 48, 59; principles as tools, 10; thinking, 5, 29, 30
Realism as a method of attack, 6
—— vs. reality, 6, 7
Realist attitudes, 15, 37, 38, 51, 125
—— definition of, 6
Record, judicial, 178
Recovery before reform, 240, 241
Redeemer, 62–63
Reed, Senator James A., 36
Reform, 110, 225; of criminal law, 161, 162

Regulation as judicial function, 182
Relief, governmental, 111, 120, 254
Religious tracts, 67
Remus Case, 163
Respect for law, 149, 151, 152, 156
Responsibility, criminal, 11, 12
—— in tort, 13, 14
Revolution, 107, 108
Robber barons, 5
Robinson, Edward S., 144
Robinson, Victor, 55, 71
Rousseau, 113
Rugged individualism, 188
Russia, 19, 234, 235, 241, 243, 245, 246
Russian Cheka, 42
—— judicial system, 39–42
—— N.E.P., 40
—— revolutionary conscience vs. due process, 39, 40, 42
Ryan vs. *Panama Refining Company,* 117

Sacco-Vanzetti Case, 138
Satire as accurate observation, 257, 258
Scarcity, economics of, 4
Schechter Poultry Corporation vs. *U.S.,* 118, 195, 177
Science of business administration, 89, 90; of practical politics, 70
Scientific approach to law, 33–37
Scottsboro Case, 141, 142
Searches and seizures, 147, 155
Security Act, 113, 114
Self-liquidating public works, 94
Sentences, criminal, 11, 12, 165–168
Share croppers, 112
Share-the-wealth, 110
Sickness, attitude toward, 12
Sin, 8
Slum clearance, 208
Smith, Adam, 72, 265
Smith, Alfred E., 97, 211
Socialism, 231, 234
Social bookkeeping, 16, 121, 196
—— justice conception, 267

Social vs. physical sciences, 2
—— planning, 21, 115
—— sciences, function of, 249
—— Security bill, 120–122, 177
—— sin, 86
—— training by judicial parables, 178
Society, ideal picture of, 89, 95
Sociological man, 86, 87
Sociology as separate science, 88
Soviet law administration, 39–42
Spiritual instability in government, 250
Spiritual vs. temporal government, 124–126, 241
Steffens, Lincoln, 124
Steuer, Max, 6
Strategic position of courts, 174, 178, 188–192
Supreme Court, 117, 118, 195–198, 230; and economic theory, 196
Swift, 257, 258
Symbol slavery, 253
Symbolic conduct, 17

Taboos, 11, 22, 95, 233
Tammany Hall, 27, 239
Tannenbaum, Frank, 146
Taxation, 116, 122
Technicalities, legal, 184
Technocracy, 110
Temporal vs. spiritual government, 99, 100, 105–127
T.V.A., 16, 17, 82, 177
Theology, 59–67
Theories as guides, 259–270
Tort, responsibility, 13, 14, 15, 16

Townsend Plan, 110
Tracts, religious, compared with law reviews, 66, 67
Trial, criminal, 128–148; civil, 172–198; by combat and the Constitution, 194; by combat, method of avoiding, 185; fairness in, 134–143; of Jeanne d'Arc, 135–140; record, 178, 182
Trials, examples of, 13–15, 44
Tugwell, Rexford G., 4

Unemployment, 106, 107
—— relief, 61, 111, 120, 254
Union of law and economics, 76, 77; of legal and social sciences, 100–102
U.S. vs. *Wierton Steel Co.,* 176

Villard, Oswald Garrison, 118
Voltaire, 258

Wage fixing vs. tyranny, 83
Wagner Labor bill, 177
Wallace, Secretary of Agriculture, 115
War, moral substitute for, 245; psychology, 243, 244
Washington's farewell address, 1
"What are we coming to?" argument, 211
Wickersham Commission, 151
Williston, Samuel, 53
World War, 260

Zelitch, Judah, 39